D0247561

Talking
with
Serial Killers

Christopher Berry-Dee

Talking
with
Serial Killers

—

A chilling study of the
world's most evil people

JOHN BLAKE

Published by John Blake Publishing,
2.25, The Plaza,
535 Kings Road,
Chelsea Harbour
London, SW10 0SZ

www.johnblakebooks.com

www.facebook.com/johnblakebooks
twitter.com/jblakebooks

First published in paperback in 2003

ISBN: 978 1 78606 974 0

All rights reserved. No part of this publication may be reproduced, stored in a
retrieval system, or transmitted in any form or by any means, without the prior
permission in writing of the publisher, nor be otherwise circulated in any form
of binding or cover other than that in which it is published and without a similar
condition including this condition being imposed on the subsequent purchaser.

British Library Cataloguing-in-Publication Data:

A catalogue record for this book is available from the British Library.

Design by www.envydesign.co.uk

Printed and bound in Great Britain by Clays Ltd, Elcograf S.p.A.

7 9 10 8

© Text copyright Christopher Berry-Dee, 2003

The right of Christopher Berry-Dee to be identified as the author of this
work has been asserted by him in accordance with the Copyright, Designs
and Patents Act 1988.

Papers used by John Blake Publishing are natural, recyclable products made
from wood grown in sustainable forests. The manufacturing processes conform
to the environmental regulations of the country of origin.

Pictures reproduced by kind permission of: Popperfoto; *The Democrat and
Chronicle*, Rochester, NY; *Daytona Beach News Journal*.

Every reasonable effort has been made to trace copyright-holders of material
reproduced in this book, but if any have been inadvertently overlooked the
publishers would be glad to hear from them.

John Blake Publishing is an imprint of Bonnier Books UK
www.bonnierbooks.co.uk

CONTENTS

Talking with Serial Killers

CHRISTOPHER BERRY-DEE

Lest we not forget the suffering these beasts of humanity cause, this book is dedicated In Memoriam to:

Leanna Williams (died 23 August 1994)

Now on Death Row, Ellis Unit, Texas, Santiago Margarito Rangel Varelas (#999159) is a revolting human monster even when viewed alongside the rebarbative exploits of other killers of our children. His victim was Leanna Williams, his two-year-old stepdaughter. Varelas had been married to Leanna's mother for less than four months when the child died. But during that short time he had carried out an unrelenting barrage of violence and sexual abuse on the infant; the violence alone would have been enough to kill a healthy adult, and this started almost immediately after the wedding.

Leanna died of multiple brain haemorrhages after repeated kicks to the head. Most of her ribs were broken and she had been sodomised. Varelas told police that the child had fallen inside their home at 4415 2nd Street in Bacliff, Texas. However, it is even almost as repugnant and difficult to believe that Leanna's mother told sickened investigators that she was unaware of what was going on, especially since Varelas was also indicted on charges of indecency involving Leanna's sisters aged five and nine.

Acknowledgements

As Professor Elliott Leyton, the world's most widely consulted expert on serial killing, and former FBI Special Agent, Robert Ressler, the world's most renowned offender profiler, both agree, that unless you are a police officer or a psychiatrist, both of whom have unique access to the penal system, it is almost impossible to gain access to interview a single serial murderer, let alone two such creatures. I have interviewed, at length, over thirty.

Apart from the financial outlay, which may cost many thousands of dollars, only for the offender to change his or her mind at the last minute as you arrive at the prison gate, one has to build up a relationship with a killer over many years of correspondence before they begin to trust you. But, this is only a fraction of the work involved.

Even to begin to understand the subject under study, one has to research their history back to birth. Meet with their parents, relations, friends, schoolteachers, work colleagues, the victim's next-of-kin, the police, attorneys, judges, psychiatrists and psychologists, even the correctional staff who are charged with their welfare while in custody, often on Death Row. Then, like the razor wire that forms an impenetrable barrier around the prisons, one has to negotiate a way through the red tape that wraps up our killers. Without the permission of the Department of Corrections, you go nowhere. Only when each of the above has been 'tick-boxed' do you get to meet them – the most dangerous human predators on Earth.

As Sondra London says in her excellent book *Knockin' on Joe*, 'Getting involved with these people is a dangerous matter, because when you concentrate deeply on any personality for an extended time, you find yourself drawn into their world ... And while you are in their cages studying them, they are studying you.'

I have often had cause to contemplate the words of Friedrich Nietzsche: 'Whoever fights monsters should see to it that in the process he does not become a monster. And when you look into the abyss, the abyss also looks into you.'

Non-fiction is not possible without a collective effort by many people, and the study of violent crime on a first-hand basis can be, at once, rewarding, exciting and distressing. But at the end of the road, the time comes to reflect on that journey and to remember all those individuals and organisations who, in their various capacities, helped to make this book possible and, hopefully, worthwhile.

Many of their names already appear in the main text. Others do not, but they were equally important in the development, research and writing of *Talking with Serial Killers*.

I would particularly like to thank, where appropriate, the victims' next-of-kin. The killers featured in this book have taken their revenge on society and there is no adequate measure for the agony they have wrought. Death is tangible, grief less so. Yet, despite the tragic losses of loved ones, those left behind have shown compassion for the killers of their children. Without their help, without their anguish, without their indelible pain, this book could not have struck the emotional balance it is hoped it has achieved.

I also thank the many Departments of Corrections for allowing unrestricted access to their penal systems and the offenders who were interviewed. Numerous law enforcement officers, attorneys and judges who have honourably discharged their professional duties, not only in bringing the offenders to justice, but in assisting, where they could, in the detailed research for this book. And, strange as this may seem, thanks are also due to the serial killers and mass murderers who allowed me into their dark worlds, for if society is to learn anything about how these beasts tick, we must, however abhorrent it may seem, listen to their words, their truths and lies.

As always, I am indebted to my close friend, Robin Odell. A superb writer and editor in any event, Robin knows this subject better than most. He has taken much of my raw manuscript, and polished it into the completed work sitting before you now.

For their personal support, perhaps now is the moment to thank a few of those who were patient enough to listen to my thoughts on serial homicide for months on end. Therefore, I extend much gratitude to my father and mother, Patrick and May. Great friends, Jackie Clay, Graham Williams, David 'Elvis' Murphy, Ace Francis, Bob Noyce, Phil Simpson, Barbara Pearman, and Tony Brown, who kept my spirits up when they were low. My television producer, Frazer Ashford, and my staff at *The New Criminologist*. Colleagues, Elliott Leyton (Professor of Anthropology, Memorial University of Newfoundland, who will be as critical as always and is bound to argue the toss about XYY chromosome disorder; and David Canter (Professor of Applied Psychology). Also thanks to Adam Parfitt and John Blake of Blake Publishing, who were brave enough to publish this book.

Finally, a very special thanks with much love to my special PJ, because it did work out all right for you in the end, and I will always miss your company, and Alyona Minenok from Novosibirsk, Russia. The late night talks with you helped me immensely.

Christopher Berry-Dee
Director "Criminology Research Centre"
Southsea 2001

HARVEY LOUIS CARIGNAN
USA

'The guy's the fuckin' Devil. They should have fried him years ago, period, an' they would have queued up to pull the switch. When he was dead, they should have driven a stake through his heart and buried him, digging him up a week later to ram another stake in, just to make sure he was fuckin' dead.'

RUSSELL J KRUGER
CHIEF INVESTIGATOR, MINNEAPOLIS PD

It was 24 September 1974 and early morning in Minneapolis. The sun was up and patrolmen Robert Nelson and Robert Thompson were cruising along 1841 E 38th Street when they spotted the 1968 black-over-pea-green Chevrolet Caprice. It was parked across the road from a diner. Thompson made a slow circuit of the block, while his partner checked the police bulletin details issued the day before.

'That's it,' said Nelson. 'That looks like the car. All we gotta do is find the driver. He's a big guy and, according to this, he's built like a gorilla.'

The two officers peered through the Caprice's window and scrutinised the interior. Sure enough, there was the red plaid car rug, pornographic magazines, and a bible. By the gearshift, they noticed several packs of Marlborough cigarettes; all items that had been detailed by a previous rape victim of the man the police were searching for.

While Nelson telephoned his precinct, requesting assistance, Thompson wandered into the diner, asking the owner if he knew who had been driving the car.

'Yeah, sure,' came the suspicious reply. 'He just saw you guys and high-tailed it out back.'

Minutes later, Harvey Louis Carignan was stopped, briefly questioned then arrested. He was taken downtown, read his Miranda Rights, and booked on charges of homicide and rape.

With up to 50 kills, one of America's most vicious serial murderers would never use his hammer again.

* * *

'Even now, it sometimes seems my childhood was short, only a few days long. There is nothing about it I cling to and nothing to look fondly backwards toward. From where I sat then, and sit now, it was, and is, truly a pit of despair.'

CARIGNAN, IN A LETTER TO THE AUTHOR, 14 APRIL 1993

Born on the wrong side of the tracks at Fargo, North Dakota, on 18 May 1927, like so many serial killers, Harvey was an illegitimate child who never knew his genetic father. His 20-year-old mother, Mary, was ill-equipped to care for her sickly boy who failed to thrive and, in 1930, during the lowest point of the Great Depression, she started farming him out to anyone who would look after him. Thereafter, the youngster was moved from pillar to post, and school to school, unable to form family roots or enjoy a solid education.

Very early in his formative years, Harvey developed a facial twitch and suffered from bed-wetting until he was 13 years old. He also suffered Saint Vitus' Dance – or childhood chorea – a disease which manifests itself with uncontrollable spasmodic jerking movements.

At the age of 12, he was sent to a reform school at Mandan, North Dakota, where, according to his FBI 'Rap Sheet', he remained for seven years. During this time, he alleges that he was constantly bullied and sexually abused by a female teacher. In a letter dated 12 June 1993, he writes:

'… I had a teacher who used to sit at my desk and we would write dirty notes back and forth. I was either 13 or 14 at the time – and just show me a 14-year-old boy anywhere who wouldn't willingly and happily sit in a schoolroom and exchange porno notes with his teacher. I never got to lay a hand on her without getting slapped, but she would keep me after school and make me stand before her while she masturbated and called me names and told me what she was going to make me do – none of her threats she ever kept, damn it! The bitch wouldn't even let me masturbate with her! I took my penis out and she beat the living shit out of me! She had enormously large breasts. She was truly a cruel woman …'

Harvey Carignan stayed at the Mandan reform school throughout his teenage years, then in 1948, at the age of 21, he joined the US Army, who welcomed him with open arms. Harvey was no longer the weedy little runt who, allegedly, had suffered mental and sexual abuse since the age of four. The high-carbohydrate and well-balanced diet at Mandan had helped him grow into a strapping, well-nourished and immensely powerful young man.

Carignan began his murderous career in 1949 when, during the early evening of Sunday 31 July, he killed 57-year-old Laura Showalter following an attempted rape in a small park at Anchorage, Alaska. Death came swiftly after he smashed her head, causing terrible brain injuries. The victim's face had been virtually destroyed from chin to forehead, bone and tissue crushed to a pulp under a battering from his massive fists.

'This killer was so strong,' said a police officer, 'with one punch he blasted a hole through her skull like a rocket slamming into a tank.'

On Friday, 16 September 1949, Carignan attempted to rape a young woman called Dorcas Callen who managed to escape his assault. The soldier, who was clearly drunk, although it was only 11.00 am, had confronted her near a tavern in Anchorage Street. When the man asked Dorcas to take a ride with him, she refused and turned away.

'Hey,' he shouted, 'I think I know you … maybe.'

'Please go away,' Dorcas pleaded. 'You don't know me.'

She was now very scared. She knew that a woman had been bludgeoned to death in the neighbourhood only weeks before. But the big soldier confronting her was angered by her refusal, and she could not get away from him. Before she could move, the man grabbed her and began to drag her away from the street. They fell into a ditch beside the road, and he was all over her, tearing at her clothes, his hands touching her breasts, and between her legs. In moments he could rape her.

Dorcas fought frantically to find a handhold in the soft dirt walls of the ditch. He was very strong, almost inhumanly strong. Screaming, she managed to clamber out of the ditch and ran across the street to the tavern where she phoned the police.

In hospital, she relived the terror of the attack in detail through a bloody mask of bruised and bloodied facial skin. 'He turned into something from Hell. His fury came out of nowhere, like he was suddenly switched on with evil,' she said through swollen lips.

It was her description of her attacker that led to the arrest of Carignan later the same day. He stood trial for the first-degree murder of Laura Showalter in 1950 in the District Court for the Territory of Alaska, Third Division, Justice George W Folta presiding. The prosecution held as their ace card, a confession to murder given to Marshal Herring. Harvey Carignan was found guilty and sentenced to hang. At the subsequent appeal in the Supreme Court of the United States, Justices Reed, Douglas, Black and Frankfurter agreed that Harvey Carignan's conviction had come about because of a breach of the McNabb Rule. This held that confessions should be excluded if obtained during an illegal detention due to failure to carry a prisoner promptly before a committing magistrate. Because this rule had been violated, the Justices ruled Carignan's confession as inadmissible. Thus Harvey escaped the hangman's noose but forfeited his freedom with a 15-year sentence. Prisoner #22072 was transferred from the Seward Jail in Alaska to the US Penitentiary at McNeil Island, Washington State.

During his interview with the author, Carignan stated, 'Laura Showalter … Dorcas Callen? Those names mean nothin' to me.'

* * *

Carignan was transferred to US Prison Alcatraz, California, on 13 September 1951, where he spent the next nine years. On 2

April 1960, at the age of 32, he was paroled. Except for his few years in the Army, he had not been at liberty since he was a child of 11.

After landing at San Francisco's waterfront jetty wearing a cheap prison-issue suit, with his bag of belongings at his feet, he watched as the small prison launch chugged its way back across the bay to 'The Rock', as Alacatraz is universally known, then he boarded a train for Duluth, Minnesota. There he moved in with one of his three half-brothers but, on 4 August 1960, just four months after his release, he was arrested for third-degree burglary and assault with intent to commit rape.

Fortunately for Carignan, the rape charge was dropped through lack of evidence. If the rape charge had been proven, he would have returned to prison, never to be released again. However, as a parole violator, he was sentenced to 2,086 days in the Federal Prison at Leavenworth, Kansas.

Carignan was back in the community in 1964, and moved swiftly to Seattle, where, on 2 March, he registered as a parole convict C-5073. On 22 November that year, he was arrested by the Sheriff of King County for traffic vagrancy and second-degree burglary.

20 April 1965 saw him in the dock once again when he was sentenced to 15 years in the Washington State Penitentiary at Walla Walla, one of the tri-state cities comprising of Richland and Kennewick, on the south-east border of Washington and Oregon.

Now locked up in one of the oldest and most notorious prisons in the United States, Carignan applied his mind to making up for his earlier lack of education. He obtained a high school diploma, took many college courses in sociology and psychology, and submitted papers on sexual psychopathy, the paranoid personality, and the well-adjusted individual. He read constantly, gained top marks, and studied journalism

– all of which impressed his tutors. But there was a darker side that surfaced when he was alone. When talking with his fellow inmates, Harvey fantasised about nubile, young girls and he had a fixation about young flesh. He has often stated, and maintains even today, that young girls have to be his ultimate choice, which for a man now aged 74, is a very unhealthy desire indeed.

* * *

Middle-aged, and an ex-convict with unappealing physical characteristics, Harvey's chances of dating a teenager following his release from prison were remote, so he met and married Sheila Moran, a divorcee with three children. She had her own house in Ballard, the Scandinavian district of Seattle, where they made a home together. Coming from a decent upbringing, Sheila was soon left under no illusions about the personality of her new husband who hung around with a bunch of villains. He was always out until the late hours, tearing around in his car at breakneck speeds. Then, following Carignan's vicious assault on her aged uncle, she decided to pack up her things and take her children. She would simply run away. For his part, Harvey decided to kill her, and waited in vain for an entire night with a hammer clutched in his hand, but, fortunately, Sheila did not return home.

Harvey married again on 14 April 1972. Alice Johnson, a somewhat dim-witted, plain woman in her 30s fell for him, and this naïve and gullible cleaning woman with few friends thought she'd met a hard-working, decent man. Alice had been married before and had a son, Billy, aged 11, and a pretty daughter, Georgia, aged 14, whom Harvey was soon lusting after.

By this time, Carignan had managed to lease a Sav-Mor gas station from the Time Oil Company, and it came to Alice's attention that he always had a string of young girls working the pumps. But no sooner had one started, she left, to be replaced by another girl just as young and pretty. While this behaviour aroused her suspicions, gossip led her to the confirmation that her husband was totally obsessed by teenage girls. He would approach any girl he saw, with obscene suggestions and remarks, and when Alice confronted him with reprimands, he screamed and shouted at her, beat her son, and skulked away throwing lurid glances at Georgia, which made his stepdaughter feel decidedly uncomfortable. Not surprisingly, the marriage collapsed soon afterwards.

On 15 October 1972, Carignan raped and killed a teenager called Laura Brock, near Mount Vernon, Washington State.

* * *

A 'wanted' ad placed in the *Seattle Times* on 1 May 1973 provided the first link in a chain of gruesome events. Help was required at a local gas station and the notice caught the eye of 15-year-old Kathy Sue Miller. She wasn't looking for a job for herself, but for her boyfriend, Mark Walker. Next morning, however, when she rang the contact number advertised, Kathy was intrigued when the man who answered said he was looking for girls. She gave him her address and telephone number and agreed to meet him after school. They arranged that he would pick her up in his car outside the Sears Building in Seattle, then drive her over to the gas station to fill out a job application form.

Kathy's mother was worried. She did not like the fact that her daughter had given her number to a stranger and she felt uneasy about the way the interview had been arranged. In particular, she disliked the thought of Kathy getting into a car with someone she had never met before. Running through her mind was a recent news article about Laura Brock, who had been raped and murdered while hitchhiking.

'I mean it, Kathy,' Mary warned her daughter. 'Don't even think about meeting him.'

Impatiently, Kathy promised not to and left for her classes, a stack of schoolbooks under her arm.

Mother and daughter shared the same bus that morning and Kathy got off first near Roosevelt High School. Mary watched through the grimy window as her beautiful daughter hurried away, turning once with a smile to wave back.

That afternoon, Kathy disobeyed her mother's orders, and met Carignan as arranged. He had been waiting with growing impatience and his heart skipped a beat when he saw a tall, strong, athletic girl walking in his direction. Her blonde hair was darkened to a burnished butterscotch colour and fell to the middle of her back in thick waves. Kathy had green eyes, and just the faintest suggestion of freckles sprinkling over her fair skin. She stopped opposite Carignan's car to cross the road, and he watched as the young woman, wearing a blue-and-white jumper, a navy-blue blouse and blue-tinged nylons waved in his direction.

Carignan leant across the front passenger seat and pushed the door open. However, Kathy walked to his side of the car and spoke to him through the window. Her first sight of Carignan was somewhat unedifying. He was an unattractive man with a peculiarly domed forehead. He had a receding chin and a deep scar over one eye. In fact, Carignan looked years older than his true age of 46, with his skin deeply lined, and bags and wrinkles beneath his eyes. His usual expression was a glowering frown, and to smile, he had to make a concentrated effort. But, this time, he turned on all the charm at his disposal.

'Hi! You must be Kathy,' he asked, with a broad smile beaming across his face.

Kathy noticed the dimple on his chin, then smiled back. 'Sure, that's me.'

Motioning her to get into the car, he said, 'We need to fill in the application forms and they are back at my office, just hop in. I'll drop you off home when we've finished.'

Kathy felt uncomfortable. 'My mom isn't too happy about this,' she explained, and Harvey moved up a gear.

'Can't say that I blame her. I've got children of my own. Married, too. Nice house, lovely woman. Yep, we can't blame your mom for being careful.'

Kathy was almost convinced by the man's reassurance. 'You sure this is OK?' she asked.

'Absolutely. Tell ya what, I'll even introduce myself to your mom when I drop you off. Everything will be fine then.'

Kathy Sue Miller was never seen alive again. Carignan, whose violent record was known to the police, was questioned at length and his movements watched for 24 hours a day, but there was insufficient evidence to charge him with abduction, let alone murder. Then, on Sunday, 3 June, two 16-year-old boys driving their motorbikes through Tulalip Reservation, just north of Everett, found Kathy's body. It was wrapped in black plastic and was naked. It had decayed so badly it was initially impossible even to tell its gender. When the autopsy was carried out, it was found that the teeth matched Kathy's dental records. From the damage to the skull, it was clear that death had resulted from a severe battering.

Even with the discovery of the body, 'Harv' the Hammer' still managed to escape the clutches of the police. He moved first to Colorado and later to Minneapolis, Minnesota, where he murdered Eileen Hunley on 4 August 1974. Her body was found on 18 September in Sherburne County. In response to the murder, Carignan commented, 'She was my common-law wife an' I thought she was seeing a black man so I stopped her in the street … I ran her head into a lamp pole, and stamped her face on to a drain cover until she was dead. Then I tried to feed her to some pigs.'

* * *

A string of sexual assaults on hitch-hikers in the states of Colorado and Minnesota in the latter part of 1974 bore Carignan's stamp. They were mostly carried out by a large man broadly matching his description wielding a hammer as his assault weapon. At least seven died and the remainder were scarred mentally and physically for life.

On 8 September 1974, a female hitch-hiker was picked up by Carignan, driven to a rural area near Mora, and was sexually assaulted. She was then beaten about the head with a hammer and sexually assaulted with the hammer handle. The victim was left in a field to die, but survived. She was subsequently able to give a description of the assailant and the vehicle he was driving.

On 14 September 1974, Carignan picked up a woman called Roxanne Wesley, who was having car problems in a south Minneapolis parking lot. On the pretext that he was going to drive her to get help, he took her instead to a rural area in Carver County, sexually assaulted her several times, including forcing a hammer handle into her vagina, and also beat her about the head with the hammer and left her in a field to die. This victim also survived and was able to crawl to a road for help. She was also able to give a description of her assailant and his vehicle, including other distinguishing features of the car's contents.

Two teenage female hitch-hikers reported on 19 September 1974 that they had been picked up by a man and driven into the country where he threatened to rape and kill them. One of the girls was struck in the mouth by Carignan, breaking a front tooth. Both were eventually able to escape by jumping out of his car when he stopped at a road junction. Again, their descriptions of the man and the vehicle, matched the descriptions given by the previous victims.

The next day, Minneapolis Police received a complaint from two other teenagers who said they had been approached by a man who offered them $25 each to assist him in picking up a car in northern Minnesota and driving it back to Minneapolis for him. The two girls said that they were driven to a rural wooded area where the man asked one of them to follow him into the woods, presumably to get the other vehicle he had talked about. He took a petrol can and a screwdriver with him. A short time later, the girl who remained in the car heard screams so she ran to a nearby house to call the Sheriff. Subsequently, the other girl was found unconscious with severe head wounds as a result of hammer blows to the head. Their description of the attacker matched Carignan in every respect.

On 21 September, another report of a similar assault in which the victim survived was received and, a few days later, Carignan was arrested.

* * *

What follows is part of a charge relating to five counts regarding offences committed on a 13-year-old girl. The name has been deleted to protect the victim's identity, and the document has been supplied courtesy of the Minneapolis and Hennepin County Prosecutors. It has not been published before.

Aggravated Assault. Aggravated Sodomy. Indecent Liberties.

Sodomy upon or with a child. Aggravated Sodomy.

'The said ——————, was hitch-hiking in Minneapolis when the defendant, driving a truck-camper, stopped, picked her up, engaged her in conversation as to where she was going, stated that he would take her to her destination directly, forced her to commit oral sodomy upon him with the threat of hitting her with a hammer which he picked up from a

compartment between the seats of his truck, compelled her to remove her clothing by threatening to "put a hammer through your head", attempted to shove the handle of the hammer up into her vagina, struck her several times in the area of her buttocks with the hammer when she resisted the advances of the defendant, again compelled her to commit oral sodomy on him, drove to a corn field where he compelled her to lie on her stomach where he attempted to have intercourse with her through the rectum, then, for the third time, again compelled her to commit oral sodomy on him. That the defendant then permitted the victim to dress and drove her to home of a friend situated at 5644 Lakeland Avenue, Crystal, Hennepin County, [Minnesota], where he allowed the victim to get out of the truck-camper; that in addition to the foregoing, the defendant told the victim that his first name was "Paul" and that his last name was "Harvey".

In separate trials conducted in 1975 and 1976, Carignan was convicted of just two of the murders and a number of other offences. He was given prison sentences amounting to 100 years plus life. In truth, he may serve only 40 years.

* * *

'I know where your house is. I know you have a young, pretty, dark-haired wife and two kids.
You have a silver Mercedes car. But I will make sure nothing an' no one hurts you or your family as I have friends in your country who look after me.'
HARVEY CARIGNAN'S CHILLING WELCOME WHEN THE AUTHOR, CHRISTOPHER BERRY-DEE, VISITED HIM IN PRISON.

Harvey Louis Carignan, known variously as 'Harv the Hammer', or 'The Want-ad Killer', currently resides behind the grim walls of the Minnesota Correctional Facility, Stillwater, which is on the Minnesota–Wisconsin border. An industrial prison, it is now the state's largest, close-security, level five institution for adult felons, and the population is currently around 1,320.

For five years, I corresponded with Harvey, and finally interviewed him during a 'full-contact visit' in March 1995. This was the first and only interview granted by 'The Hammer' since he was arrested for multiple rape and homicide on 24 September 1974.

Because individuals like Harvey have traversed such extremes, their souls have become liked locked rooms hiding mysterious secrets. It therefore takes a certain sensibility to draw them out. For each case, I take an in-depth approach, spending an enormous amount of time getting to know the unique qualities of each individual, rather than depersonalising them with generalities based on their crimes. While I develop an empathy for my subject, I always take care not actually to sympathise to the extent that their dramas start playing in the theatre of my own mind. It is a constant balancing act between identification and analysis.

To learn from a person, you must put yourself in their place, follow their train of thought and feel their emotions; however, while you follow the often dysfunctional thinking of your subject to some extent, you never become like them. You remain yourself. You may draw close for a while, close enough to get a sense of these often foreign ideas and emotions, but you must always pull back to restore the integrity of your own moral and mental boundaries.

And what was it that Carignan's psychiatrist had told me? Yes, that was it: 'You'll get to interview Harvey, or something living inside his head. You'll get to interview him, and Evil will get to interview you.'

Harvey was called to the interview by his personal pager, and one's first impression of this homicidal maniac is of a lumbering hulk of a man, standing well over 6ft tall. He weighs 18st and has an ape-like appearance. He has massive frame, a Neanderthal-like balding dome, and huge hands attached to over-long, gangly arms which hang from immensely powerful, sloping shoulders. Carignan has piercing blue eyes, and talks in a low, husky voice. At face value, his overall persona portrays a gentle, even understanding, giant of a man; however, we all know that such appearances can be deceptive. 'The Hammer' is, in fact, one of America's most evil and notorious serial murderers, who even today, aged 74, can still do one-arm pull-ups for 15 minutes at a stretch without so much as a grimace.

Five minutes dragged past agonisingly without either of us saying a word, while all the time his dangerous eyes stared into my face. It was as if some alien creature, an insidious force even, was gently probing into my mind using long, squirming tentacles of enquiring thought, exploring, touching, sensing with taste and smell. Then, a secret but twisted smile started to play around Harvey's mouth. His lips, moistened by saliva, were slightly open, but otherwise his face was without expression.

This stone-cold serial killer was insidiously fascinating to observe at such close quarters, for he is the wolf in sheep's clothing, part-human, part-Antichrist and the stuff of our children's worst nightmares. Then he spoke for the first time.

'Ya, know, Chris, never did I commit a crime then commit another to keep it quiet. I committed murders to ensure that false accusations of rape would not occur.'

The ice was broken, and my previous belief, that Harvey lives in a continual state of denial – a world where he admits some guilt, but not total responsibility for his brutal and heinous crimes – was confirmed.

As the interview continued, when he did admit he raped and

killed a young woman, it was, so he claimed, as the result of their provocation. He said that it was always the victim who brought up the subject of sex when he offered them a ride in his car.

Nowhere can this better be illustrated than in his account of a lift he gave to a woman, a perfectly respectable 20-year-old nurse, whose car had broken down.

The truth is that he offered to fix her car, but beforehand he explained that he needed to fetch his tools. He forced her into his car and drove her into the country where he brutally raped and attempted to kill her by smashing into her head with a wheel wrench.

Carignan's account is of course something different, for he argues that she got into his car of her own free will. His story contains a smattering of the truth and a bucketful of lies. It is at once disturbing and disgusting, yet offers a fascinating account from the mind of a homicidal sexual psychopath and fully-emerged serial killer who, it is believed, may have slaughtered up to 50 women. What follows is not for the faint-hearted:

She got in and may have been somewhat nervous, but she did not seem afraid. During the ride we talked about another girl I used to see, one who had left because I had not given her $30 I had been giving her each and every week. It was not payment for anything, but a gift. The girl riding with me said she would never exchange sex for $30 – making it seem she believed the other woman had and that herself despised her for what the first woman had done. I tried to enlighten her thinking, but she was adamant in her statement that she would not have sex for $30 because those were in her words and not that she would not have sex for money, which was my thought at the time.

It was then that I got the drift; that she thought I was offering her the same amount for sex and she was turning down the offer – but I am not saying she wanted money to *have sex at all. The way the conversation went it could have been either, that she would not have sex for $30 or she would not have sex for any amount of money. It was no big deal to me at the time, so the conversation had no special meaning to me until much later when I tried to remember everything that was talked about and how it was said.*

When we got to my friend's place where the tools were supposed to be, I stopped the car, turned around, and immediately drove away. My friend had told me if his pick-up, a 1973 3/4 ton Chevrolet, was not in the yard, to not hang around because his sons did not like me. This was a surprise because I did not know his boys. I had never met any of them. [Carignan did not have any so-called friends.] Anyway, I drove away and stopped the car just before driving on to the main road. I put my arm around her and, although she hesitated, she did move over closer to me when I indicated with arm pressure that is what I wanted. It was not a pressure that forced her to move, not a hold that would have moved her had she declined. Instead, it was an indication of what I would like her to do, and she complied. I can remember my thoughts as plain as if it was yesterday: 'She wants it!' This is in spite of the fact that I wondered why she had been so adamant in denying she would have sex for $30, which in my mind could have been any amount at the time. I slid my arm behind her head, put a slight, almost gentle pressure on her neck, and she bent down – not because of the pressure but with her own strength – unbuttoned my pants, took out my penis, and stroked it while we kissed, until I indicated with the same kind of pressure that I wanted her to suck it. She did.

When she finished, I told her, 'Spit that damned stuff out', when I saw her sitting there holding the semen in her mouth. She did – but I did hold on to her in case she wanted to jump out and run away. I was not satisfied that she was not going to say I had forced her to do what she had done. She looked at me, giving me a strange smile – like I was a fool for thinking she would run – closed the door, and I drove on.

While we were starting out I told her, 'I want to fuck you. I know a place we can go!'

She asked, 'How long will we be gone? I must be back by one o'clock.' It was then about 10.30.

I did have a place in mind but it was miles away. So I drove along and pulled in next to a lake. When I stopped I saw a house in the midst of some trees and a man walking our way from another direction. I turned around and drove away. During this, the girl did not make any attempt to open the car door or get out.

Directly across the road from the lake a road led into a glen. It was about 500–622ft from the main road. When we got there, I went to the trunk and took out a blue blanket [subsequently recovered by the police] and threw it on to the ground, and I told her, 'Get ready!' I was not happy with her for some reason, but she was a very sexy woman, about 20 years old, and I wanted to have sex with her, especially since we already had after a manner of speaking. She took off my jeans and her panties and laid down on her back with her feet in my direction. The whole of her pudendum was pointing towards me – and it was beautiful, as was herself, a very pretty woman. Now, I do not know what other men look for or how they act, but I generally always look at the vulva, play with it. The prettier she looks in her genital area, the more I want sex.

Now, I only stopped to help the girl get her car started. When she climbed in, I only had it in mind to get the tools to fix it. Sex was not on my mind, and I did not kidnap her. Everyone assumes these women and girls as innocents. They generally are not. Each and everyone of them wanted something from me, either money, to drive one of my cars, or something they would not divulge. I never kidnapped them, or forced them to come with me. She is no different from the others. I am not a rapist, and the word itself is so revolting it turns my stomach.

Despite what anyone says, we had a delightful time in that clearing until she accused me of taking money from her purse, and then I thought, 'Here we go again.' I became much more angry than the moment called for and acted out within the content of that anger rather than against the accusation which called for no more than an explanation that I had not taken her money. The right rear tyre on my car had gone flat and I was changing it when she screamed out at me. She kept screaming the money was not hers and almost insanely demanding I return it. Then, in a wink, her tone changed and she told me how she wanted to trade her car for another. That I should give her $200 for the trade or she was going to say I had raped her. Until that instant, I had gone on with the business of replacing the lug bolts on the hub; but in that instant when she made that threat, I became what I see as being uncontrollably angry and I hit her with the lug wrench – and not with the hammer as she later testified, and what is generally believed. She was fully dressed and I can see it now as plain as it was happening even now. She fell to the ground as if she had been pole-axed and she slid slowly down a 12–14ft incline into a ditch, feet first, with her brown sweater rolling up until was under her armpits. I did not panic, but put the lug wrench in the trunk and the remaining lug bolt in my pocket, got into my car, and drove away. At about 15–20 minutes down the road, maybe 15–20 miles, I realised I could not leave the woman there to die if she was only wounded, and I had to know, so I turned around and went back. As I drove by, there were several cars and a tractor with a wagon

behind it stopped beside the road, and all of the people were
bending over someone that I knew was her, so I kept on
driving.

When Harvey had finished talking, I confronted him about the reality of the attack. I reminded this man that in fact he had left the young nurse for dead in that ditch but she regained consciousness several hours later lying in a pool of her own blood and suffering from almost lethal head injuries. It was practically nightfall and, in dreadful pain, she crawled over a mile through ploughed fields to a road where the farmer found her, and summoned help in the morning.

Carignan later passed the ambulance as he was returning to the scene of the attack, not to save his victim's life, but concerned that she might survive and be able to describe him and his vehicle. He returned intending to finish her off but, by then, she had crawled to safety. The only thing that kept the young woman alive was the news that her sister had given her the previous day, that she was expecting a child and she was determined to see the baby.

Harvey claims he had been sexually abused by just about every female he came across, including his relations, babysitters, and his teacher at the reform school. And, while we are all too aware that, during the last three decades, child abuse has become exposed as a social blight, there is absolutely not a shred of solid evidence to confirm that Harvey was abused on the scale he continually asserts.

What we can say with a degree of certainty is that he grew up with a grudge against women in general, perhaps directed toward his negligent mother and her family and friends. But, maybe this is all the evidence we need, for in a literal way, people don't grow up to hate women, or men, for no reason, so perhaps Carignan is telling the truth after all.

Recently, Carignan has said, 'I hate women with a passion …

They always played mind games with my head.' Nevertheless, his account of sexual abuse may offer something else of value to us, as we look into his past. Those few lines in his letters are full of contradictions and without any doubt, this may be fantasy-fuelled. It is an account tailored to suit him, being abused by a domineering 'truly cruel woman', while he, the poor young lad was helpless, yet at the same moment, apparently enjoying a situation in which he revelled.

As with so many killers, when Harvey Carignan came into this world he was immediately burdened by childhood problems. He carried the social stigma of being a bastard; a weak, nervous child; a bed-wetter who suffered from Saint Vitus's dance; and, like the British serial killer, Peter Sutcliffe, was bullied throughout his formative years.

He claims that women sexually abused him as a child, although these allegations are unsupported by fact. There is little doubt, though, that his mother and other female relations, including his aunts and grandmother, treated him with contempt. The psychological damage this caused may explain in large measure the passionate hatred that Harvey holds for women. He believes they all 'played mind-games' with his head, which perhaps accounts for his use of blunt instruments to mutilate and destroy the heads of his victims. His fury was such that he didn't just hit them once or twice. More often than not he smashed their skulls to an unrecognisable pulp using demoniacal and inhuman force.

Revenge – more particularly, revenge against women – played an important part in his motivation, and his *modus operandi* was always the same. But there is another side to this killer's motive, which is, on the face of it, bizarre. While he slaughtered older women, perhaps in the image maybe of his mother, aunts and grandmother (with a few exceptions) he often allowed his teenage victims to live, despite the horrific attacks committed upon them. In a few cases, he even drove them home or patched up their cuts and bruises. The reason for this contradictory behaviour might be explained by his clearly-stated sexual attraction to younger girls. In this respect, there can be no doubt that Carignan was, and still is, fantasy driven. Those fantasies of sex with young girls always give him immense pleasure, while thoughts of older women generated intense hatred for Carignan.

Throughout my extensive period of correspondence with Harvey, he made much of what he calls his 'string of pearls'. In effect, he implies that these 'pearls of wisdom' are priceless details which he releases only when he judges the time is appropriate for him.

'The truth is in my pearls of wisdom,' he bluntly stated. 'I am not going to reveal the pearls of this part of the truth at least for years,' he added before clamming up and refusing to answer any more questions about the nature of his crimes.

Harvey 'The Hammer' Carignan devoted the remainder of the interview to claiming that he is a man with much feeling. A man of great knowledge and, as he studies philosophy, he is worthy of having his words and thoughts considered by others. But within 'The Hammer', there is still a fatal flaw.

Despite having spent the better part of his worthless life behind bars, this monster, in every sense of the word, is totally unable to come to terms with his guilt. This is a trait he shares with many other serial murderers. Even with the evidence being consistent and overwhelming in every case of sexual assault, rape or murder, Carignan is psychologically compelled to transfer most of the blame for his crimes on to his luckless victims.

When he is exposed, and all of his excuses stare him straight back in the face as complete untruths, he has a fallback position. He retreats to the trench used by so many offenders, namely the refuge which blames the entire law-enforcement and justice system for fitting him up.

If the gravity and number of offences were not so serious, one might be forgiven for thinking that his excuses are laughable. Some may even argue that his letters are the ramblings of a madman and, as such, should be dismissed or, at best, ignored. However, Harvey is not mad by any definition. What he refuses to say, or hides between the lines, or chooses to forget to say, can ultimately be of greater interest, for in his pathological self-denial sits the true nature of The Beast.

At the present time, Carignan is eligible for parole, for no matter how many murders he has committed, no one in the State of Minnesota can serve more than 45 years in prison.

Harvey has a current pen-friend. Thirty-year-old Gloria Pearson was convicted of murdering her young son after a period of child abuse. They write to each other frequently and, in this respect, they are well suited.

This chapter is based on exclusive audiotape interviews between Christopher Berry-Dee and Harvey Louis Carignan within the Minnesota Correctional Facility, Minnesota in, 1996, and many years correspondence.

ARTHUR JOHN SHAWCROSS
USA

For a moment, his eyes zeroed in. Just a moment before, a rare smile had masked Shawcross's simmering fury; now that mask of sanity had slipped for the first time, and the fire of homicidal insanity flared in his eyes as he struggled to overcome the murderous emotions boiling within. The interview room went quiet, deadly quiet.

SHAWCROSS'S REACTION TO BEING QUESTIONED BY CHRISTOPHER BERRY-DEE ABOUT THE MURDER OF TEN-YEAR-OLD JACK BLAKE.

Deep within the Sullivan Correctional Facility, Fallsburg, New York, breathes the state's most notorious serial murderer, and his name is Arthur John Shawcross. Dubbed 'The Monster of the Rivers' by the media, I asked him how he had acquired the title.

'Because,' he replied, 'that's where I killed 'em. That's where the monster inside of me came out, an' he came out down by the river pretty often.'

The name 'Shawcross' is derived from the Old English *crede cruci;* which loosely translates as 'belief in the cross'. Early variations of the spelling were 'Shawcruce' and 'Shawcrosse'. Currently, there are about 5,000 Shawcrosses in the United States, even more in the UK and, by all accounts, Sir Hartley Shawcross, the former Attorney General of Great Britain, and Chief British prosecutor at the Nuremberg Trials, was a distant cousin of our serial killer in question.

'Art' was a small baby, weighing just 5lb. The infant was born at 4.14am on Wednesday, 6 June 1945, at the US Naval Hospital, Kittery, just across the Piscataqua River from Portsmouth, Maine.

The birth certificate records the father's name as Corporal Arthur Roy Shawcross, aged 21, and the baby's mother as Bessie Yerakes Shawcross, aged 18. His parents lived at Apartment 5, 28 Chapel Street, Portsmouth, Maine.

His father was no stranger to the police himself, being a bigamist who had served with the US Marine Corps during World War II. He landed on Guadalcanal with an artillery regiment of the 1st Marine Division, and in doing so earned a number of battle star commendations and medals. In February 1943, after mopping up the action, he and his fellow marines were sent for rest and recuperation to Australia, where he met Thelma June at a dance. They were married Monday, 14 June that year at Melby, Australia, and Thelma later gave birth to a son whom they named Hartley after their illustrious British namesake.

Arthur Roy Shawcross was granted a furlough in July 1944 and returned to the USA where he bigamously married his now pregnant childhood sweetheart, Bessie Yerakes, on Thursday, 23 November. Bessie, popularly referred to as 'Betty', was the daughter of factory workers who lived in Somersworth, New Hampshire. Her father, James Yerakes, was born in Greece, and her mother, Violet Libby, is of unknown Mediterranean descent. A week after Bessie was discharged from hospital with baby Arthur; her husband sent them to Watertown, upstate New York, where they lived with his sister while he completed his tour of duty in the Marines. Shortly after he was demobbed, the couple found a small place of their own in the picture postcard town of Brownville; the home of 1,200, lower-middle-class citizens, just a stone's throw from the Canadian border and Lake Ontario.

Young Arthur became the oldest of four children. His siblings were Jean, Donna and James and it would be fair to say that Arthur turned out to be the only rotten apple in a basket of otherwise good fruit. His education started normally enough at the Brownville-Glen Park Central School but personality problems soon surfaced. He resented his brother and sisters, with the exception of Jean, with whom he imagined having sex.

By the age of five, Art had created two imaginary friends. One was called 'Paul', apparently a lad of Arthur's own age; the other 'friend' was slightly younger, a blond-haired girl with no name. During the months to follow, he carried on long conversations in baby talk with these imaginary friends, which gave fellow pupils and teachers the impression that he was talking to himself.

'I had to have these friends,' he told the author, 'because I wanted someone to play with. No one else liked me.'

Now called 'Oddie' by his classmates, young Arthur became the subject of ridicule and bullying. He retreated into a twilight world of his own, often wandering from class to class in a dream.

He was easy meat for the stronger children who tormented him at every opportunity, and when they did so, he screamed and shook his fists, or went home in a sulk to torment his younger brother and sisters by way of revenge.

Realising that they had a problem child on their hands, the school welfare officers made enquiries, soon finding out that his parents spoilt Arthur. When he misbehaved, his mother would spank him lightly, or put him in his room. The school also reasoned that Arthur's father was excessively lenient to his boy.

Events took a more serious turn when Arthur ran away from home. Of course, he was quickly brought back, but then he took to travelling to school on a bus carrying a tyre iron with which to hit the other children if they bothered him. The young Shawcross had learned that what he couldn't achieve with his fists, he could make up for using a weapon. Just before his eighth birthday, the school called for a mental health evaluation on Arthur. Psychologists from the Jefferson County Mental Health Clinic felt that Mrs Shawcross was giving her 'attractive, well-dressed, neat child', mixed emotional messages. It seemed that the mother–son relationship was very complex, for while she treated her son like a little doll on the one hand, she also punished him at the drop of a hat for no apparent reason, which left the lad feeling very confused indeed.

Mrs Shawcross had taught her son to be neat and tidy, and she and her former marine husband imposed what might be called old-fashioned values with echoes of military discipline. Arthur had to keep his room spotless, his clothes had to be neatly folded at all times and, for the slightest infraction, he was spanked or sent to his room. In return, and in attempts to curry favour, Arthur showered his parents with gifts, never forgetting a birthday or anniversary, yet still appeared to be confused. He developed a fear of unusual noises but, slowly, confusion gave way to resentment. He stole money from his mother to pay off the bullies at school. He had no friends, was mean to his younger brother, and it was very difficult to get the truth out of him because he always seemed afraid. Added to this, the psychiatrists thought that Arthur perceived his father as favouring the other children, and that his mother was rejecting him.

Arthur's interest in school now fell apart, his progress slipped and he began to regress, sliding to the bottom of his class. The teachers put this down to a bad attitude rather than lack of intelligence, but the larger boys still bullied and hounded him. About this time he developed a characteristic blink, which he still has today. He also started to make a noise like a bleating lamb, and often lapsed into baby talk. He began suffering from nightmares and wetting the bed, which he continued to do until his early teens. Then he ran away from home again, only to be dragged back, screaming and protesting. Although the date is uncertain, a pivotal event occurred in the Shawcross household which turned it upside-down with lasting consequences.

Arthur was aged nine when his grandmother, on his mother's side, received a letter from Thelma June in Australia. In it, Thelma claimed, quite correctly, that in fact Arthur Roy Shawcross was her husband, and that they had a son now aged ten. Understandably, when Bessie Shawcross saw the note she took a serious view of her husband's secret, and from that day on, she hated every moment she spent in his company. Indeed, she decided to make his life a misery. Already an oversensitive and confused boy, Arthur now kept away from home as much as possible. He was ashamed of his father and he could not stand the constant feuding that had become part-and-parcel of his parents' lives.

He ran away again to spend hours on end with his grandmother whom he adored and, although basically a very thoughtful and kind lad, he had now developed a much darker side. In effect, his mind was splitting in two, and he was mirroring the behaviour of his mother who exhibited two sets of opposing attitudes and emotion.

By 1960, real behavioural problems began to emerge when young Arthur was in the seventh grade at the General Brown High School. In his spare time he started to torture small animals, skinning fish alive and toying with their bodies. He watched them suffer and saw how long it took them to die. He snared rabbits, taking his time to break their necks. He caught bats, putting them inside parked cars and watching as the drivers panicked. He tied cats together, pounded squirrels and chipmunks flat, shot darts at frogs nailed to his dartboard, and scraped the feathers from live chicks. On one occasion, he carried a sack to a nearby lake, and tossed it in the water. 'Who says cats can't swim?' he said to another schoolboy. When the terrified animal escaped and swam to shore, he picked it up and threw it even further. After four attempts to reach safety, the kitten drowned.

During this period of juvenile sadism, Shawcross learned that killing animals had one drawback; they made a noise and the excrement and urine leaking from their bodies soiled his clothing. To prevent this, he resorted to stuffing leaves and other debris into their body apertures, a bizarre practice which he later included in his *modus operandi*, when he took to murdering women and children. By the age of 15 the worm had really turned and Arthur became the scourge of his neighbourhood, especially where other children were concerned. He knew no fear, was very strong, and often discharged his .22 calibre air rifle at anyone he came across. If another teenager upset him, he would mercilessly pound them with a baseball bat, or beat them unconscious with his fists.

Arthur was now uncontrollable and any attempts by his tutors to discipline him resulted in him storming out of class, shouting, 'Shove this room up your fuckin' arse,' and similar obscenities.

Aged 17, and much to the relief of his teachers, he dropped out of school. Now, with time on his hands, he took to petty thieving, stealing anything that wasn't nailed down. He burgled the locality, looted summer cottages, and stole money from the cash register of a gas station, where he worked for a short time. He broke into local stores, taking food and cash, and shoplifted on an almost daily basis.

One Sunday night in December 1963, he broke into the basement of a Sears Roebuck store, and was arrested by the police after he triggered an alarm. The judge, however, was lenient, sentencing Arthur to 18 months' probation as a youthful offender. His mitigation, which appeared to find favour with the judge, was that he was stealing in order to buy Christmas presents, which was true.

By now, the teenage sadist, thug and burglar was exhibiting stranger behavioural characteristics, which included speaking in a childish, duck-like, high-pitched voice. Arthur also developed a weird habit of walking 'cross-lots', covering long distances at a fast pace, over-swinging his arms, holding his body erect and rigid like a one-man band, and walking in the straightest line over any obstacle that blocked his path. A cousin recalled Arthur doing this, and said, 'He'd tear his pants on a wire fence rather than use a gate several feet away. He'd walk into a swamp and have a hell of a time getting out. He really was nuts in those days.'

Aged 20 and already known to the police, Shawcross was charged with attacking a 13-year-old boy following a snowball fight. It seemed that he preferred the company of children much younger than himself, and he was often spotted secretively playing with children's' toys. The budding killer was also accident-prone. Apart from occasional blackouts, he knocked himself unconscious while pole-vaulting, suffered a hairline fracture of the skull when he was hit by a discus, took an electric shock from a faulty electrical switch, was hit by a sledgehammer, fell from the top of a 40ft ladder, and was hospitalised for the fifth time when he was struck down by a passing truck.

Around this time, although the date is not known, Arthur met Sarah Louise Chatteron. They were married in September 1964 at the Sandy Creek Baptist Chapel, and they had a son whom they named Michael. But blissful wedlock soon ended in acrimony. Sarah would later go on the record as saying, 'Arthur was very immature, and always faking illness or injury to miss out on work. Sex with him was lousy. He just couldn't keep it up.' The couple separated in August 1966, with Shawcross blaming Sarah for the break-up. He complained that she refused to give him oral sex, which was his favourite, but neither of them mentioned his constant acts of adultery.

Single once again, Shawcross hit the fast-food joints and dance halls. He wrecked his souped-up Pontiac, and then he met Linda Ruth Neary whom he started to date, but on Friday 7 April 1967, he was drafted into the Army. If anything could sort out Arthur's psychological problems, surely the Army could, and so 22-year-old Private 52967041 Arthur John Shawcross started his training at Fort Lee, Virginia.

The rookie soldier's first taste of military justice occurred when a sergeant criticised him for 'goofing off'. Official army records show that Shawcross responded, 'What do you think I'm doing, pulling my pud?' He was fined $27 for his insolence. He completed his basic training at Fort Benning, Georgia, and was designated a supply and parts specialist. When he failed to show up for a work detail, he was fined $11 and restricted to the post for 14 days. After that, he accepted army discipline, and his service record shows no subsequent charges. On various intelligence tests, he scored from subnormal to slightly above. His efficiency ratings ranged through 'fair' and 'good', but were mostly 'excellent'. This was an early example of his improved behaviour in structured settings.

While on leave, he married Linda Neary in October 1967, after which he was flown in a c-130 transport to South Vietnam where he served a somewhat indifferent 12-month tour of duty with the Supply and Transport Company of the 4th Infantry Division based at the South Vietnamese city of Pleiku. At this time, South Vietnam was suffering the Tet Offensive when the VC/NVA launched co-ordinated attacks on virtually all the major cities and towns. With seemingly no end to the war in sight, US forces were stretched to the limit, needing every serviceman they could muster for duty.

An examination of Arthur's service record reveals that he saw no action apart from dodging the occasional incoming shell. But he tells us an entirely different story, claiming that he was based in the Central Highlands, and was a 'Rambo-type', one-man, first-strike weapon, fighting in the heat of the action. In one of his letters to the author, he wrote enthusiastically:

Another time I went on patrol and shot a kid chained up into a tree. He killed one GI, with an M1 our own weapon, too. That made three. Again on petrol [sic] I killed two women in a river, after they had killed two GI's. They had a map of base camp, plus AK47 rifles and ammo, food and $280,000 in money belts. I split the money with some guys, smashed the AK's and ammo, took everything else back to camp. We let the bodies drift in the current downstream.

In another handwritten account, this erstwhile 'Rambo' described how he allegedly committed other atrocities. These are disgusting accounts which must be taken with a pinch of salt:

I shot one woman who was hiding some ammo in a tree. She didn't die right off. I tied her up, gaged her [sic], then search the area [sic]. Found the hut with another girl inside of the age

*about 16. Knocked her out with the butt of the gun and carried
her to where the other girl was. There was a lot of rice, ammo
and other stuff in the hut. I tied the young girl to a tree, still
gaged, tied her legs too. They didn't say anything to me at all.
I had a machete that was very sharp. I cut the girl's throat.
Then took off her head and placed it on the pole in front of
that hut.*

*That girl at the tree peed then fainted. I stripped her then
… First I gave her oral sex. She couldn't understand what I
was doing but her body did! I untied her, then retied her to
two other small trees … She fainted several times. I cut her
slightly from the neck to crotch. She screamed and shit herself.
I took my M16, pulled on a nipple then put the gun to her
forehead and pulled the trigger. Cut off her head and placed
it on a pole where they got water.*

On reassignment furlough in Oklahoma, Specialist Fourth Class
Shawcross, repaired weapons and made reluctant visits to the
camp psychiatrist. He was honourably discharged in the spring of
1969, and moved with his wife to Clayton, on the St Lawrence
River. He promptly put in a disability claim for war injuries and
although a Veterans Administration examiner found no
substance to Arthur's claim, the former soldier's constant
badgering won him a $73-a-month disability pension for leaving
the examiner in peace.

Seven months after leaving the Army, Arthur Shawcross was
divorced again and soon in trouble with the police. He had
found employment at a paper factory, the city's largest
employer, and he repaid the firm for giving him a job by setting
fire to the place, causing $28,000 worth of damage. Within three
months a hay barn mysteriously caught fire, and it was Arthur
who raised the alarm. Three days later, he set fire to a milk
bottling plant. This was the city's second-largest employer and,

this time our community-minded Arthur was at least considerate enough to telephone the fire brigade, then stand back admiring the red vehicles as his handiwork reduced the building to ashes.

Shortly after melting the milk depot, he bungled a robbery at a gas station. The proprietor, who knew Shawcross by sight, called the Sheriff and he was arrested, confessing to all of his crimes, which included the arson attacks. Hauled before the Court, Jefferson County Judge Milton Wiltse, who was an irate old judge from the 'whip 'em and hang 'em school', sentenced Arthur to five years imprisonment in Attica.

* * *

At the start of his prison sentence, Shawcross was subjected to a psychological evaluation. He was assessed as 'an immature adolescent with a schizoid personality who decompensated [disintegrated or broke down] in ego functioning under the influence of unemployment stress, employment stress, rejection by wife. He should be viewed as a schizoid arsonist who requires supervision, emotional support and immediate referral to a mental clinic on parole later projected homicidal attempt of at least two of his arsons should not be underestimated. He is a fair parole risk … will require psychiatric treatment plus close supervision.'

Shawcross was paroled on Monday, 18 October 1971, after serving just 22 months in prison. At first, he worked with Frink Sno-Plows in Clayton but he was laid off four days later when it was learned that he was a thief and arsonist with a criminal record. Just after Christmas, the Watertown Public Works Department hired him under the Federal Emergency Employment Programme. A supervisor assigned him to a far corner of the 60-acre landfill at the end of Water Street. As it transpired, his first murder victim lived a mile away.

Early in 1972, Shawcross attacked and raped a 16-year-old girl in an underground room of Watertown's old railroad station but, luckily for him, the victim failed to report the incident to the police. Then he met an old school friend called Penny Nichol Sherbino. She was a short woman with a good figure, lively brown eyes, tawny hair and a rural vivacity that took the form of a ready laugh and a giggle. They dated for a short while before taking their wedding vows on Wednesday, 22 April 1972, and setting up home in a neat, two-storey apartment at 233 Cloverdale Apartments in Clover Street.

On Sunday, 7 May, 15 days after the wedding, Arthur was shuffling along Clover Street with the intention of fishing Kelsey Creek. Set into a triangle of woods and marshland bordered by Interstate Highway 81 and State Routes 37 and 12E, the creek was just a mile from his home. It was about mid-morning when 10-year-old Jack Blake rushed up to him asking if he wanted any worms as bait. Jack went out fishing that day with Shawcross and was never seen alive again.

The Blakes were a rough family, but they loved their children, and Mary Blake had warned her impressionable son not to associate with Arthur Shawcross. She didn't like the cut of the man who was always boasting about his service in Vietnam, and showing the boy photographs of naked women.

'He was a weird sort of guy,' she said. 'He rode around on a white, woman's cycle.'

When Jack didn't return home later that day, Mary reported to the police that her son was missing, explaining that Jack had wanted to go fishing with Shawcross and, despite her warning, had probably gone against her wishes.

Suspicion, therefore, fell upon Shawcross from the outset. He denied being with Jack that day, and with no other evidence to suggest otherwise, Shawcross was released following two interviews with police who now thought that Jack was a runaway from home.

On Friday, 26 May, Shawcross was again in trouble with the police. This time he was caught stuffing grass cuttings down the shirt and shorts of a six-year-old boy, and spanking him. For this offence, Shawcross received a $10 fine and a reprimand from the Court.

Tragedy struck Watertown again on Wednesday 2 September 1972, when Shawcross raped and strangled eight-year-old Karen Hill. The blonde-haired child had been staying with family friends in Pearl Street because her parent's home, had, ironically, been destroyed by fire.

The chances against any American citizen falling into the clutches of a predatory homicidal sexual psychopath are about 350 million:1. However, Karen's chances increased considerably when such a monster came on the scene as she played on her front lawn during this beautifully clear Sunday.

At about 3.30pm, a man answering Shawcross's description was spotted by children leading Karen across the iron Pearl Street Bridge over the Black River, just a short downhill walk from where Karen had been staying. Although the children didn't know the man by name, they, and specifically a teenage girl, recognised his distinctive white cycle with its brown mudguards and a basket, which he had leaned against the south parapet wall. From a distance, the curious children watched as the man lifted Karen over the railings and gingerly led her down the precipitous bank ostensibly to show her the fish.

When the alarm was raised that Karen was missing, the children came forward to tell the cops what they had seen. At 10.00pm, search officers equipped with flashlights discovered a crumpled body. It was covered by a slab of concrete and laying face down, crammed into a sewerage outfall pipe on the south bank of the bridge.

Police dogs were called for. They tracked a scent up Pearl Street to Starbuck Avenue, and eagerly tugged their handlers left into Clover Street, straight to the stoop of Arthur's front door. He was arrested immediately. At the autopsy, the medical examiner discovered that Karen had been raped vaginally and anally. She had died as a result of suffocation under a mound of silt. Apart from those particularly disturbing aspects of this homicide, Shawcross had also stuffed weed and debris into the child's nose, mouth, vagina and rectum.

But what about Jack Blake? During his interrogation for the murder of Karen Hill, Shawcross hinted at the disappearance of the young boy, although he made no admissions. Nevertheless, this hint was enough to prompt the police into renewing their searches. Their efforts were rewarded on Wednesday, 6 September, following their first sweep of Kelsey Creek which took four hours. Detective Gordon Spinner, along with Under-Sheriff John Griffith, noticed that long strips of bark had been peeled from a tree and neatly laid over a mound of spongy earth. Easing the bark away with his boot, Spinner recoiled in disgust as bluebottles rose from a lump of rotting flesh. The almost skeletal corpse was unclothed and a scrap of blonde hair was attached to the skull. Several of the bones were out of position, which indicated that animals had been feasting on the gruesome remains. Police also found a broken tooth, and Jack's clothing in the woods. His blue dungarees, black sneakers, green jacket with its arms tied together in a knot, and a T-shirt marked 'Blake' with a pen, with the slogan 'I act different because I am different', were all neatly folded some 30ft from the shallow grave.

Shawcross had never admitted this murder until he was interviewed in prison by the author. Piecing together what information is now available, the following scenario emerges of what happened on that fateful date.

Jack accompanied his killer to Kelsey Creek to go fishing. They walked across a railway track and into the marsh and trees nearby. Suddenly, the monster in Shawcross surfaced and he ordered Jack to strip naked. Reluctantly, and in fear of his life, Jack did as he was told, but then the terrified lad made a run for it. What happened next must have amounted to a cat and mouse chase through this remote marshy area.

Jack proved to be no match for the agile ex-soldier. Barefoot, the boy made it to the railway line – cinders were found embedded in the soles of his feet – and in a frantic attempt to climb over a four-strand barbed wire fence, he fell back into Shawcross's grabbing hands. Now, the lad was doomed. He was punched in the face and beaten unconscious. Shawcross says he raped Jack, cut off his penis and testicles, then ate them. He has since told psychiatrist, Dr Richard Theordore Kraus, that he had cut out the heart and eaten part of that, too. There is no evidence to confirm that he was being truthful or otherwise.

On Tuesday, 17 October 1972, Shawcross pleaded guilty to the lesser charge of first-degree manslaughter and, after proceedings, which lasted 20 minutes, he was sentenced to the maximum term of 2–25 years for the murder of Karen Hill by a disgusted Judge Wiltse, who had had the misfortune of having had Shawcross in front of him before.

* * *

Shawcross served $14\frac{1}{2}$ years in prison where he experienced a rough time from the other inmates whose brotherly admiration for each other's crimes did not extend to the rape and murder of children. The beatings and abuse started for Shawcross on his admission to Attica, and this treatment followed him through the penal system until he arrived at the notoriously tough Greenhaven Correctional Facility, at Stormville, New York.

Set into rugged hill country between the Hudson River and the Connecticut border, some 40 miles north of New York

City, this prison houses many of the State's most evil criminals where 742 prisoners (33 per cent of population) are rapists and murderers. For Shawcross, a convicted paedophile murderer, this was simply not the safest place to be. The prison psychiatrists diagnosed him as, 'a dangerous schizophrenic paedophile, suffering from an intermittent explosive personality', and it was noted that 'he heard voices when he was depressed, and engaged in fantasy as a source of satisfaction. He also has an oral-erotic fixation for the need of maternal protection.'

Placed in the A-1 protective segregation unit for his own good, Shawcross was a troublesome inmate in a unit of 41 men. For the greater part of his sentence, he continually faked illness or psychiatric problems to gain attention. However, Shawcross was no one's fool and, like thousands of convicted felons, he soon learned that the probable key to early parole lay in sucking up to the welfare officers, the prison shrink and the Church. Consequently, Shawcross started to behave himself and he became a model prisoner. He earned his high school equivalency certificate, and qualified in carpentry.

Now, well into his sentence, Arthur was found exhibiting all the welcome behavioural traits of a 'reformed' man. He figured that it was better to accept responsibility for the murder of Karen Hill, if only for the benefit of the psychiatrists and, apart from attending the religious services, he wheedled his way into a counsellor's job in the jail's mental health unit. While there, he learned the language of psychiatry and psychology and, in doing so, he eventually conned the support of a three-man State Parole Panel, who granted his freedom.

Arthur Shawcross walked out of the gates of Greenhaven on Tuesday, 28 April 1987. Although, he had been receiving excellent evaluations from one group of experts, their high opinion of his progress was not shared by everyone. A report from senior parole officer, Robert T Kent, noted, 'At the risk of sounding dramatic, this man could be possibly the most dangerous individual to have been released to this community in years.' Dr Kent's assessment was much nearer the mark, but what was the real reason for the release of such a dangerous man as Shawcross? The probable answer lies in politics, and the overcrowding of the entire US penal system. Apart from the federal prison population of approximately 89,000 men and women, New York has the third-highest confinement of inmates in the United States, with around 65,000 being incarcerated at any one time. New York is only beaten by Texas (approx 99,500), and California (approx 123,000). It is, therefore, not surprising to learn that the entire penal system is bursting at the seams.

Overcrowding is a serious problem, and so are the fiscal issues. New York's capital expenditure for its system is hammering on the door of $1.2 billion a year, with each inmate costing the taxpayer an average of $53 a day to keep. With these considerations in mind, it is also not surprising to learn that policy dictates that if there is the slightest chance that an inmate is 'reformed', then the authorities want him out of prison as soon as possible. With his ranking in the criminal pecking order as a mere first-degree manslaughter felon, Shawcross was simply an innocuous number in the system and, like scores of his murderous ilk, he was released merely to make room for another of the 18,000 new arrivals each year.

Arthur must have been counting his blessings because he had narrowly escaped a life sentence purely on the basis of economics, costing Jefferson County a potential small fortune if a full-blown murder trial ensued. He had plea-bargained his way into a far lesser sentence and to cap it all, and again for financial reasons, he had engineered an early, and ill-advised, release. These were mistakes that would cost New York State millions of dollars in the years to come but, more seriously, the lives of at least 12 women were sacrificed to bureaucracy.

* * *

Shawcross, now 42 years old, grey-haired and bulky, was a dramatic transformation from the strapping ex-serviceman who had entered the penal system $14^{1}/_{2}$ years previously. Divorced for the third time, he walked straight out of the gates into the arms of a pen-friend, Rose Marie Walley.

His attempts to settle down in a number of communities were thwarted because his murderous reputation dogged his every step. Local law enforcement agencies and the press were not slow to advise their citizens that a murderous paedophile was walking the streets. Eventually, Rose and Arthur settled in Rochester, a cautious, conservative city, sometimes dubbed 'Smugtown, USA'. Rochester owes its existence to the fast-flowing Genesee River, which Nathaniel Rochester harnessed to power his flour mills in the early nineteenth century. The river tumbles over a cataract that is a smaller version of the Niagara Falls, 80 miles to the west. Then it bores its way through a deep gorge on its way back to Lake Ontario. Despite being affected by industrial pollution, the gorge still provides a leafy sanctuary for anglers and lovers. Arthur Shawcross was one of those attracted by its charms and chose it as an ideal place to fish.

After staying in a hostel for a short while, Shawcross and Rose Walley set themselves up at 241 Alexander Street, a brown-stone and brick, bubble-fronted apartment just two blocks from Monroe Avenue, one of the city's busiest thoroughfares. To pay the rent, Rose enrolled as a nurse at the local hospital, while Arthur found work with Fred and Tony Brognia Produce, a vegetable and fruit wholesaler based in the public market, to the south of the city.

Despite the fact that Arthur was a 'bullshitter', he proved to be a good employee. Always on time, or even early for work, he would cycle an hour each way on a ladies-style, blue Schwinn Suburban bike, which had a shallow basket, the Stars and Stripes flag on the handlebars, and two deep baskets straddling the rear wheel, in which to stow his fishing gear. His weekday working hours were between 7.00am and 3.30pm, which left him the evenings to pursue his hobbies and recreation.

Around this time, Shawcross resumed his old philandering ways. He was enjoying an affair with Clara Neal, a 58-year-old woman who had 10 children and 17 grandchildren. On occasions, he would borrow her cars, either a small, metallic-blue Dodge Omni saloon, or a grey Chevrolet, using them for day outings, or to go fishing; yet he still found time to marry Rose.

The Brognia brothers soon learned from Arthur that he was a former convict, for he had told Tony that he had served time for murdering a man who had allegedly killed his wife in a hit-and-run accident. Meanwhile, he told Fred that he had been a Mafia hit-man in New York. When the brothers conferred, they quickly realised that their employee's stories just did not add up. After speaking with a local police officer, who informed them of Arthur's real criminal past, the Brognia brothers engineered Arthur's release from their employment.

He next turned to selling hot dogs on Main Street before landing a permanent job as a salad maker for G & G Food Services which provided catering services to hospitals and schools. Arthur worked nights, being paid $6.25 an hour, and this nocturnal employment regime seemed to be the cue for the onset of Rochester's reign of terror.

* * *

Dorothy 'Dotise' Blackburn was the 27-year-old mother of a six-month-old boy and two older children. She was a small-boned woman, with a slender figure, brown eyes and long brown hair. Petite and dainty, she was streetwise, with two convictions for loitering in 1985. She was last seen alive on Tuesday, 15 March 1988, after lunching with her sister at Runcone's Grill on Lyell Avenue.

Dotsie's body was found during the morning of Tuesday, 24 March, floating face-down in Salmon Creek, a stream that meanders through farmland and woods on Rochester's eastern fringe. A crew of labourers clearing debris and garbage that had clogged a culvert thought they had found a mannequin covered with a layer of silt. They soon realised, however, that they were looking at a woman's frozen body.

Her face had distinctive heavy eyebrows, full lips, slightly irregular teeth, and her left eye was shut. She had long, dark hair and wore jeans, a hooded sweatshirt and a single white 'Soda Pops' brand sneaker. Her navy top was pulled up from the belt line showing a bare midriff. At the autopsy, the medical examiner determined that she had died as the result of manual strangulation and noted that she had been bitten several times around the clitoris and on the vagina.

During his interview with me, Shawcross claimed that he had been driving Clara Neal's Omni, and he admitted that he had killed Dotise at Northampton Park because she had bitten his penis during fellatio.

'She was laughing at me,' he said, ' 'cos I couldn't get my pecker up … I slapped her around the head, an' she bit me. I got madder than Hell. That's what made me kill her. Then I dumped her clothes in a trash can, cleaned the blood from the seat, and drove home.'

* * *

Anna Marie Steffen, aged 27, was an emaciated prostitute who took to the streets to support a drug habit after her paralysed sister died. She was last seen alive walking along Lyell Avenue on Saturday, 9 July. Shawcross met her by the Princess Restaurant in Lake Avenue, and he walked with her to the back of the YMCA. Afterwards, he drove her down to the Driving Park and, during oral sex, he grabbed her throat and strangled her before rolling her body over the edge of the Genesee River gorge.

Her body was found on Sunday, 11 September 1988, by Hector Maldonado, while he was searching for returnable bottles so that he could buy cigarettes. The victim was lying on her left side curled in a semi-foetal position. A pair of Calvin Klein jeans were pulled down around the ankles and turned inside out. A white tank top with red shoulder straps was wrapped around the right wrist. Police found a pair of blue flip-flops nearby. A hank of hair had been ripped from the skull, and the eyes were missing from their sockets.

* * *

Dorothy Keeler was a drifter with an alcohol problem. Despite her distrust of strangers and dislike of men, Dorothy allowed herself to be befriended by Shawcross. She visited his apartment where he employed her as a cleaner and, on Friday, 29 July 1989, with the lie that he wanted to take her fishing, he lured her down to the brushy, five-acre Seth Green Island, where they stripped naked for sex. Afterwards, he accused her of stealing from his home. When she protested and threatened to tell Rose Walley about their affair, Shawcross beat her to death with a piece of wood.

Three salmon fishermen discovered the body on Saturday, 21 October, describing it as 'a bunch'a bones in clothes'. The corpse lay in the foetal position. The jeans were unzipped and pulled down. Three pullovers covered an assortment of upper body bones and a rib was fractured. The head was missing because Shawcross had returned to the murder scene to masturbate over the corpse. He had hacked the head from the body and had thrown it into the Genesee River. 'It floated for a bit,' he said, 'sort of swirled around in the current, then it disappeared. Just as I was walking away, it come up again. It sort of looked at me and smiled. Then it was gone.'

* * *

Patricia Ives, also known as 'Crazy Patty' was a 25-year-old drug-dependent school dropout with a baby boy who had been placed into foster care. The once-attractive woman, who used to bear more that a resemblance to film star Julia Roberts, was now a walking skeleton. A known prostitute with a ragged and unkempt demeanour, she had long, dirty hair, a sliced-bread complexion, and ragged needle marks from her elbows to the backs of her fingers. It was thought that she had AIDS and perhaps herpes.

A witness who was driving past the corner of Lake and Driving Park at about 7.30pm. on Friday, 29 September 1989, was the last person to see her alive. Later, he told police that he knew her, and that she had been in the company of a white male who was riding a bike with balloon tyres. There were fishing rods protruding from the cycle's rear baskets. The witness also added that he had watched as the couple climbed through a hole in the fence behind the tennis court of the YMCA.

Patty was reported missing the following day by her pimp and local burglar boyfriend who delighted in the name 'Ratface Billy'. Patty's body was found by children who were hunting for a lost baseball on Friday 27 October. They saw a foot sticking out from a pile of flattened cardboard lying under a large maple tree near the lip of the gorge. The corpse, clothed in black pants and a heavy sweatshirt, lay face up. A wedding ring was missing from her finger, there were no shoes or socks, and maggots had devoured most of her flesh.

Shawcross said that he had killed her because she went through his wallet. 'There were children playing nearby,' he said.

'I put my hand over her mouth and held her nose. She didn't struggle, didn't holler, and didn't fight.'

* * *

June Stott was the youngest of eight children and had learning difficulties. She was a shy, homeless woman who heard mysterious voices in her head and had taken to sleeping rough on Lyell Avenue. Aged 30, June wasn't a hooker or a drug addict, she was just a lost and lonely soul who thought that evil sprits were always chasing her. Shawcross knew her because she had visited his home for dinner a number of times. On Monday, 23 October 1989, he saw her sitting on a bench between Dewey Avenue and Saratosa. He suggested that they went fishing together on the banks of the Genesee River and she accepted.

Down by the water's edge, he tried to have sex with her and, when she refused, telling him that she was going to report him to the police, he strangled her. After removing her clothes and dropping them into the river, he drove Clara's dodge Omni back to her house where he picked up his cycle to ride home. Two days later, he returned to the body and dragged it down into the swaying cattails, where, using a knife he had found in her pocket, he cut open her body from the neck to the anus. Then he gutted her like a large fish, throwing the entrails into the swirling waters.

On Thursday, 23 November, Mark Stetzel was walking his dog in the northern Rochester suburb of Charlotte and, among the beached, rusting river barges, he noticed an ice-covered object that had been dragged into the reeds. It was a piece of frozen carpet, under which was the badly decomposed body of June Stott. A few feet away was a bloodstained Handi-Wipe cloth. The corpse was face down, but lividity staining showed that she had been rolled over long after death had supervened. The right leg was bent inward at the knee, elevating the buttocks, and thus suggested the possibility of anal intercourse, probably after death. The body was slashed from breastbone to crotch, the vagina was clotted with blood, and the genital lips were missing.

Shawcross said, 'I cut the vagina out and ate it. Then I covered her up with the rug, picked up all the excess stuff that was there and threw it in the river, and left.'

When I asked him why he hadn't disposed of the body in the river as well, he replied, 'Well, I kinda liked her.'

* * *

Maria Welch had a five-month-old son called Brad, and the 22-year-old woman was described as 5ft 2in in height, weighing about 100lb, with a light complexion, brown eyes and brown hair which she often dyed blonde. She was last seen alive by another hooker near Lyell Avenue, at midnight on Sunday, 5 November 1989. She was reported as missing by her 60-year-old boyfriend, Jim Miller, the following day. He told police that she had been wearing white sneakers, a thigh-length blue jacket, jeans, a purple T-shirt, and she would have had a gold chain around her neck. Her body was tattooed with a unicorn on her forearm, a marijuana leaf and a rose on her left ankle to cover up the name 'Leo'; a leaf on her right leg near the ankle; and 'L-O-V-E' over the knuckles of her left hand.

Maria's body was not found until Shawcross was arrested. He told the author that he had picked up Maria at the Marques Restaurant in Lake Avenue.

'We went down that area and parked,' he said. 'We sat and talked, for she was cold. Had the heater on high. Gave her $30. She took off her shoes, socks and jeans. Then took off the rest of her clothes. I only unzipped. I asked her if she was on the rag, and she said "No." But when I put my hand in her, I felt a Cotex and blood. I've never done it that way. I asked for my money back, and she told me to go fuck myself. I choked her until she passed out. Had some rope in the car and tied her hands behind her, plus her feet to her hands. I had to take out that Cotex and pushed in a bar towel. She came to, and asked me what I did to her. Then she wanted me to untie her. I was sweating like crazy. Kept wiping my head and face off. I pulled out that bar towel and it was almost clean. Then I mounted her. My sweat dripping into her face. That was when she said "I love you." I kissed her, then I killed her.'

* * *

Francis 'Franny' Brown was a 22-year-old drug addict. A mother at 18 with a baby girl, she had been talking with a neighbour shortly before she disappeared on Saturday, 11 November 1989 from the red-light district of Lyell Avenue.

A fisherman walking down Seth Green Drive found her body at 3.00am, on Wednesday, 15 November. In the early morning light, he thought he had found a tailor's mannequin. The corpse was naked, except for a pair of white 'Go-Go' boots. Shoulder-length hair framed her once-attractive face and her buttocks bore the home-made tattoo 'KISS OFF'. Her body was decorated with other tattoos including a cross on the right ankle, a wing on the left shoulder, and a butterfly around one wrist. She was in a slightly off-centre kneeling position, and she appeared to be clutching a cement block. The police thought that she may have been thrown over the top of the gorge and had come to rest against a small tree on the ledge.

Shawcross explained that they '… had sex, 69 oral. She asked me to deep-throat her so I did, but she got carried away. I didn't pull out so she could breath. She peed in my mouth and I kept pushing. Uncontrolled reaction to doing it that way. She suffocated. I used her also then while she was still warm. Even to kissing her and sucking her tongue and breast. Didn't have an orgasm. I put my on my clothes and got out of the car. Opened her door and rolled her over the cliff.'

* * *

Kimberley Logan, a 30-year-old black mute with learning difficulties, was last seen talking to a man answering Arthur's description near her home on Friday, 15 November. Later in the day, a man called Jimmie James literally stepped on her naked, battered and bruised body, which was partially pushed under his parked RV trailer in a yard in Megis Street. Kim had been strangled to death. Leaves and other matter had been forced into her nose and mouth. Her clothes were neatly folded nearby.

Shawcross has always denied this murder. However, following my interview with Shawcross, this case has now been closed to the satisfaction of the Rochester Police Department.

* * *

During the period of the Rochester murders, it must have seemed like a crime profiler's dream come true, for clues ran through the homicidal matrix like steel wire. Most of the victims were prostitutes who worked the red-light district of Lake and Lyell Avenues. The women were either strangled or beaten to death, and each was disposed of naked, or partially clothed, around the city, and close to, or immersed in icy cold water. The majority of the victims had vegetation debris stuffed into their ears, nose, anus and vagina. Their clothes were often found neatly folded and close to the corpses, which ranged in decomposition from skeletal to well preserved. In several instances, the body exhibited signs of having been partially eaten by wild animals, or cannibalised by the killer himself.

Recognising these patterns, and the obvious fact that a serial murderer was at large in the community, the Rochester police doubled the size of its Physical Crimes Unit. Round-the-clock surveillance by the entire Rochester PD Tactical Unit focused attention on the red-light district where many of the victims had last been seen alive. Hundreds of hookers were questioned by the police. Indeed, later in the investigation, June Cicero who had been warned to be extra careful, sadly ignored the advice and was killed by Shawcross within minutes of speaking with Vice Squad detectives. Investigators were reminded of the paramount importance of keeping crime scenes intact and of not jeopardising the search for trace evidence by over-zealousness. Thousands of dollars worth of new equipment was purchased for use by the police evidence technicians. NYSP/HALT, and FBI/VICAP forms were completed, and the services of both FBI and NYSP profilers were called upon to complete a psychological profile of the serial killer. But all this proved of little use, for the killings continued unabated.

* * *

Elizabeth Gibson, a one-time beauty queen, married the day she left school. A bright young woman, she turned to cocaine and she started passing bad cheques to feed her habit. She ended up a common prostitute who was last seen plying for trade on Lyell Avenue on Saturday, 25 November. Her body was found two days later by a deer hunter walking through woods ten miles to the east of Rochester. She had been suffocated. Police discovered tyre impressions in the muddy ground, and blue paint chips where a vehicle had scraped a tree. This paint was later matched to Clara's blue Dodge Omni, the car Shawcross often borrowed.

Down by the Genesee River, a familiar encounter had taken place. Shawcross had accused Elizabeth of stealing money from his wallet. She put up a fight, grabbing at his eyes and digging her fingernails into his face. During the struggle, she kicked out and snapped the gearshift of the car. Shawcross said, 'I tried to revive her. I wept a little.' Then, after dumping her body in the woods, he drove back to the city, dropping her clothes off en route.

* * *

Darlene Trippi, aged 32, was a petite brunette who knew Shawcross well enough for them to exchange gifts at Christmas. In fact, just a few days before she went missing, Shawcross had visited her home carrying a joint of venison; indeed, over coffee, they even discussed the murders that were plaguing Rochester at the time.

Much loved by her family, who chose not to dwell on their daughter's career as a prostitute, she was last seen alive by her married sister on Friday, 15 December, when she was touting for business on a street corner. Shawcross came on the scene and took the unwitting woman down to the Genesee River, where, he says she accused him of being hopeless after an aborted sex session. 'I got mad, then I choked her,' he said. After his arrest, Shawcross directed police to Darlene's frozen body. It was lying in a culvert, five miles beyond Salmon Creek.

* * *

Shawcross's penultimate victim was June Cicero, aged 34, a strong character with a drug habit. She had arrived in Rochester from Brooklyn, New York, in 1973, and she had been well known on the streets of Rochester for 16 years where she was regarded as something of a mother figure to many of the younger hookers who operated in the red-light district. Streetwise, and considered something of a wildcat by vice officers, June suddenly vanished without trace from the 'City Mattress', the local name for the red-light area, during the late evening of Sunday, 17 December 1989.

A police helicopter crew spotted her frozen corpse lying in the icy Salmon Creek on Wednesday, 3 January 1990. The body was naked except for a white sweater, white socks, and a single small earring with a distinctive pink stone.

Shawcross was seen standing on the nearby bridge parapet by the helicopter observer, and he was seen to drop something into the creek before driving off. It was this incident which led to his arrest. During a search of the scene, evidence technicians deployed a Luma-lite 2000A. This specially designed lamp casts a phosphorescent beam which illuminates trace evidence that would otherwise go undetected using normal procedures. Bathed in an eerie glow, small flecks in the snow proved to be human tissue. 'It was like human sawdust,' said a Scenes of Crime Officer.

Shawcross explained that he had taken June down to the river, where she called him a 'wimp'.

'I smacked her in the mouth', he said. 'I strangled her because she was going to call the cops.'

With the dead body in the trunk of Clara's car, he drove along Route 31 to Northampton Park. He then stopped and heaved the mutilated corpse into the frozen Salmon Creek which runs directly through a viaduct under the road. En route, he stopped at a Dunkin' Donut stall where he had a cup of coffee while passing the time with local cops who were discussing the string of murders.

* * *

Felicia Stephens was described as a small woman, five-five, about 115 lbs, with black hair, brown skin, and brown eyes. She worked as a prostitute and had the misfortune to climb into Shawcross's car, in Lyell Avenue, during the late evening of Thursday, 28

December 1989. Three days later, a guard in Northampton Park spotted a pair of ice-encrusted, black denim jeans in the snow. Identification found in the pockets identified the wearer as Felicia Stephens.

Later, during a more thorough search, police found her pleated grey boots and assumed she was buried close by. Indeed, a deer hunter telephoned 911 on Sunday, 31 December, after he had discovered the woman's body in a derelict farmhouse about 300 yards from where her clothes had been found.

Shawcross later claimed that, apart from wearing a fur coat and boots, Felicia was wearing nothing else when she stuck her head through his open car window in Lyell Avenue. 'She was running away from her pimp,' he said. 'I sorta got real scared and pushed the window button. I dragged her several blocks, then stopped, an' she just got in the car and asked about sex. I took her down to the river, and strangled her, too.'

* * *

The successful capture and subsequent trial of Arthur Shawcross was due to a combination of good luck and dogged police work in equal measure. Ultimately, though, it was the 'mind set' of this psychopath that ultimately sealed his fate for, on Thursday 4 January 1990, Shawcross literally offered himself up and, in doing so, he brought about his own arrest.

During that afternoon, a New York State Police helicopter was flying over the east corner of Northampton Park, some two-and-a-half miles from where June Cicero's clothing had been found just days beforehand. Senior Investigator, John P McCaffrey, was one of two observers in the aircraft. He spotted what he thought was a body frozen in the ice of Salmon Creek. At almost the same moment, the other observer's attention was drawn to a portly white male, who appeared to be urinating, or masturbating, over the bridge parapet. The man stopped, looked skywards and threw a plastic bottle into the creek before driving off in a grey Chevrolet saloon. The vehicle was soon traced to a nursing home in Spencerport, and the trail led to Arthur Shawcross.

On learning of their suspect's criminal past, the police questioned Shawcross at his home. He vehemently denied any involvement in the murders, and the decision was made to leave him alone overnight pending further enquiries. In the meantime, his house was kept under observation by a static police unit until morning. Early the next day, Detectives Lenny Boriello and Dennis Blythe took him in for a quiet chat in the police station. Within hours, Shawcross confessed and he is now serving two sentences of 250 years to run concurrently. The only way Arthur will leave prison is in a pine box.

* * *

From the time he was incarcerated, Arthur Shawcross consistently refused to be interviewed and it took several years of spasmodic correspondence before he changed his mind. When he did, the confirmation came in the form of a blunt, handwritten note, which said simply: 'I will see you.'

As part of the preparation for the interview, I set about talking to everyone who had been involved with Arthur's life and crimes, particularly Clara Neal, who, in her wisdom, feels that Art should be released.

'I will keep him on tablets so he won't murder again,' she promised. 'Besides, we are getting married soon. I really love him. He is such a wonderfully gentle man.'

At 10.15am, Monday, 19 December 1994, the first interview started at the Sullivan Correctional Facility. Before being admitted into the serial killer's presence, the guards explained to me that Shawcross was still considered a highly dangerous and formidable killing machine.

'He can revert to type within a microsecond,' they said. 'Should his features whiten, then tighten up, or should he break into a sweat, then get out of his way as fast as you can. He is strong enough to rip your head right off.'

Weighing in at around 20 stone, Arthur Shawcross is 5ft 11in tall. With a potato-shaped head topped with thin, silvery hair, a bulbous nose and small, black, ever-watery, pig-like eyes set close together, he is quite an intimidating sight. Massive arms hang from immensely strong sloping shoulders, his chest merging into a pot-belly which hangs over his belt. From his waist down, the shape of Shawcross is reversed. From the rolls of fat that circumnavigate his middle, he has short, stumpy legs that terminate in very small feet. All in all, one gets the impression that he is top-heavy and could topple over at any moment.

For the first of four interviews, we came face to face in a small locked cubicle. No one else was present while Shawcross was engrossed with eating his lunch. He greedily stuffed the food into his mouth, and his eyes were furtive, darting around as if someone was about to snatch his food away.

After he wiped the grease and food particles from his mouth, he was asked why he had eaten the body parts of many of his victims. Shawcross smiled, and said, 'Yes, sir, I have. The human meat, well, ah, it tastes like pork. I eat meat, uncooked meat, and it's like that. I eat hamburgers raw. I eat steak raw, an' I eat pork raw. I don't know why I ate parts of people, but I just did. Period.'

For a long moment, Shawcross fell silent. His podgy fingers fiddled nervously with a Styrofoam cup. His eyes scanned the ceiling as if he was searching for an invisible fly, then he added, 'Yeah, an' I ate another one with the bone. I just remembered that.'

God, I thought. How can someone 'just remember that'?

Although the truth of the matter is that Shawcross never fired a gun in anger while serving in Vietnam, he nevertheless wanted to boast about his service career during this period. Talking about his favourite subject was a good way of gaining his confidence and, true to form, Shawcross came up with the goods. He explained that he had killed up to 50 people while out on what he called 'search and destroy missions'. He claimed, that he was tasked to destroy any living human he came across.

Despite the improbability of Arthur's gruesome acts, Arthur obviously enjoyed talking about them if only to cause shock waves. When pressed, this intellectual pygmy came up with a multitude of often-conflicting reasons in his efforts to mitigate his heinous behaviour. These ranged from various types of child abuse, especially incest, to his self-perceived Rambo-type activities carried out in Vietnam: 'The Army taught me how to kill, but it didn't teach me how not to kill. I have been a god unto myself. I've been the judge, the jury and the executioner. I have murdered, butchered and totally destroyed 53 human beings in my lifetime. I just wanna know why.'

Arthur's excuse for murdering prostitutes was equally bizarre. At first, he stated that he was ordered by God to murder them because they all had AIDS. When questioned about the obvious fact that he had also raped and killed two young children, and two quite decent women, he clammed up and could not provide an answer. And, as the interviews progressed, he tripped himself up at every turn.

He admitted that he had murdered many of the women after having had sex with them. On another occasion, he strangled his victim because she bit his penis during fellatio, all of which somewhat flies in the face of him being ordered to kill them because they had AIDS. Another luckless soul he battered to a pulp after she had accidentally trapped her head in the window of his car. He went further to say that after dragging her two blocks, he stopped, and she calmly climbed into the car and asked him if he wanted sex. But, then, he changed his excuse once again: 'I went out with 80 to 100 women, including hookers. I was trying to find out why I was impotent, something like that.'

One girl had been murdered because she allegedly accused Art of stealing her purse. Another was slaughtered because she had stolen money from his home, and then threatened to tell Mrs Shawcross that her husband was having an affair. Then Arthur argued that he was suffering from a rare genetic disorder, and this was why he turned to serial homicide, changing tack almost immediately to blame his four wives for denying him sex so that he had to go out and find hookers to kill. Finally, he said that bright lights give him terrible headaches, and this is the cause of his problems.

In an effort to tap into the black abyss of Shawcross's mind, I questioned him about the emotions he experienced prior to, and during the acts of murder. True to form, he did not disappoint with his answer.

'It was a combination of the quietness of the area, the starlight, an' I got sweating an' stuff. I can't control that. I strangled most of them, an' it ain't like on TV where they just drop dead. In real life, they can hold their breath for three minutes, and up to seven minutes before they susscumm [*sic*]. One woman, well, just as I was strangling her, she said, "I know who you are." Then she went limp an' she didn't feel nothing. She just went limp.'

Asked why some of his victims' bodies bore multiple bruising, while some had been disembowelled and others had had vegetation debris forced into their body orifices, he started to become agitated. His fingers and hands constantly fidgeted, and his eyes darted around the room.

After a few moments, he regained his composure, replying, 'Yes, sir. Some of the bodies, yeah, they had bruises on them.

That's where I knelt over them with my body weight, or I dragged 'em into the rushes down by the water's edge. I cut 'em open so's they'd rot a lot quicker that way. Kinda gutted 'em like fish an' stuff. The other stuff. Well, I just don't need to talk with you about this just yet.'

Then he had the gall to ask me to be the Best Man at his forthcoming marriage to Clara Neal!

* * *

Lynde M Johnston, Captain of Detectives of the Rochester Police Department, took considerable interest in the progress of my interviews with Shawcross, who is also suspected of murdering 30-year-old Kimberly Logan, a black girl whom he had befriended. Now behind bars, Arthur is smug enough to refuse to answer police questions and, with the case still open for investigation, the police needed all the help they could get.

The Rochester PD allowed me access to the Logan file as part of the research for this book. It was apparent from the scenes-of-crime photographs and the autopsy reports that there were disturbing similarities between the Logan murder and the confirmed kills committed by Arthur Shawcross.

Special interest focused on several witness's references to a suspect who matched Shawcross's description. This man had been wearing a red T-shirt around Megis Street at the time in question. At the time of his arrest, Shawcross denied ever knowing Kimberley Logan, and he rejected the assertion that he owned a red T-shirt. With the police unable to find such a garment when they searched Shawcross's home, this item proved to be the missing link because no other evidence, forensic or otherwise, was found.

Kimberly was a trusting, young mute, and the sort of person who could make friends with anyone, including Arthur. For his part, Shawcross had established the set pattern of a serial murderer by the time of Kimberley's death; indeed, her demise was sandwiched between the murder of Frances Brown on 11 November 1989 and that of Elizabeth Gibson on 25 November 1989. Moreover, Kimberley's murder was distinguished by several hallmarks of Shawcross's *modus operandi* – battery, strangulation, no evidential signs of rape, heavy bruising, nose and mouth stuffed with vegetation debris, clothes found neatly folded near to the corpse, and an attempt to cover the body to prevent premature discovery. Of course, these attempts to hide the bodies did not always pay off, but Arthur knew that the longer the victims were exposed to the elements and the ravages of animals, the faster forensic evidence would deteriorate. In other words, he was 'forensically aware'.

With Shawcross in the 'frame', so to speak, it was perhaps more by luck than good detective work that brought to light a photograph of Shawcross wearing a red T-shirt. The bearer of such a piece of good fortune was none other than Arthur's fiancée, Clara Neal, who in her genuine efforts to prove that Arthur was a 'loving and caring man', produced a photo album containing pictures of Arthur taken around the time of his homicidal spree. Flicking through the pages I saw a Polaroid photo of her man wearing a bright red T-shirt; a garment he has denied owning, and one that fitted the witness's descriptions. When the photograph was shown to Shawcross, he responded by declaring: 'That's fuckin' bullshit. I ain't never had one of them, and now you're getting' on my fuckin' nerves.'

With this point-blank denial recorded on audiotape and effectively in the bag, the Rochester police were able to close the Logan file.

As it turned out, this particular matter raised more questions than it solved. Why, when he had admitted to all of the other Rochester murders, did Shawcross deny murdering Kimberley

Logan? The Rochester police had never released the gruesome details of the Logan murder to the media, so the chances of a copycat crime being committed with an identical MO at the same time in the same city, were millions-to-one against. It was a puzzle indeed.

The answer to this riddle rests with the fact that Shawcross is a racist. Time and again over the years, he has expressed hatred for the black population. He has said that to have sex with a black woman is repugnant to him, but, suddenly confronted with the red T-shirt, Shawcross back-tracked and, in one of his letters, he explained:

I had sex – good sex – with 5 black ladies and they are all alive today. [Notwithstanding the fact that he murdered Felicia Stephens who was black-skinned]. *Some may get stoned, but what the hell, it's their choise* [sic]. *I do not hate blacks, only some of them, whites as well plus Spanish! You can tell the Rochester police to kiss what the sun does not shine* [sic]. *Kimberley Logan did not enter my life. I've never seen her or met her in real life. I'll grant a polygraph test to anyone on this subject and talk to the cops. She is not my victim or body.'*

When I offered Shawcross the facilities of a lie-detector test along with the opportunity to speak to the police, he flatly refused. Nevertheless, having completely contradicted himself all over again, he then went on to write another letter:

'None of the women and girls did I mess with near where I lived. I went with about 6 to eight ladies near home and never killed them. Mostly with the mute. I felt sorry for this one. We got along as friends.' [Author's underline.]

Even a cursory examination of this categorical statement shows that Shawcross is lying again. In reality, he murdered 30-year-old Dorothy Keeler who cleaned his apartment. Darlene Trippi knew Shawcross well enough to exchange small gifts. And no one has ever told Shawcross that Kimberley Logan was a mute, the fact being that she was the only mute killed.

From the outset, Shawcross had made it perfectly clear that he would not, under any circumstances, discuss the 1972 murder of Jack Blake. Arthur is by no means an intelligent man, but he possesses a certain animal cunning, and has the instinct to smell a rat a mile away, so broaching the subject was not a simple task. But it needed to be done for, although Mrs Blake has been confronted with incontrovertible proof that her son was dead, she still believes that, one day, Jack will return home.

'They say Shawcross killed my boy,' she sobbed during a sensitive interview at her home. 'I believe in God, I am a good woman, Christopher, and I will only rest if I hear the truth from Mr Shawcross. Then I can sleep.'

During a third interview with Shawcross, reference was made to the 14-and-a-half years he had previously spent in prison. I put it to him that to document his life thoroughly, as indeed he wished, just rubbing those years out, as if they didn't exist, was not good enough. What follows is taken verbatim from this audiotaped interview, and it makes for disturbing reading:

AS: 'So, whaddaya wanna know about it?'
CBD: 'Fourteen years jail time, Art. How do we deal with this?'
AS: 'We don't. You ain't taking me there, so don't fuckin' try. DON'T FUCKIN' GO THERE.'
CBD: 'OK. So, I take out an eraser and out goes 14 years?'
AS: 'Yes, sir.'
CBD: 'What about Jack Blake?'

By asking this question, I knew that I was treading on unsafe ground because if the prison population heard that in the past Shawcross had raped and killed two little children, then his problems with other inmates, who would kill him at the drop of a hat, could surface all over again.

Within the blink of the eye, Shawcross's expression changed. His skin tightened and a curious paleness washed over his face. Beads of perspiration formed across his brow, running in glistening rivulets to stain the collar of his prison-issue shirt. Then, in anger, he suddenly reached out and grabbed my arm in a vice-like grip.

'You don't know who ya dealing with, fuck-face,' he snarled. 'You don't know WHO I am, or WHAT I am.'

'You don't need to do this,' I replied. 'Okay, you have a problem with Jack, and now you have a problem with me. You mess this interview up and Clara will climb the wall, pal.'

At the very mention of Clara's name, it was as if someone had flicked a switch inside his head. Shawcross's expression reverted to normal and he relaxed his grip, letting his hand fall away. Now, he looked confused as he shook his head, negatively from side to side. The killer's eyes started to moisten, and he began to mouth a mumbled form of apology:

AS: 'OK,' he said, his voice shaking. 'Yeah, I killed him, okay. I told him to go home, and he wouldn't. An' then I got kinda mad at him. Yeah, I killed him, an' I buried his body under the dirt, and went fishin'. It was his fault he died. It ain't got nuthin' to do with me…I'm sorry.'

CBD: 'And, the clothes. What about Jack's clothes?'

AS: 'He took 'em off, an' I told him to just fold 'em up, an' stuff.'

CBD: 'Why?'

AS: 'Dunno. Maybe to keep him shut up, ya know. Let him think he's gonna put 'em again. Stuff like that. I dunno. Just went back and did stuff to him the next day.'

Asked if his parents made him fold his clothes up when he took them off as a child, Arthur replied that it was one of the rules of the house.

I then returned to Jack Blake.

CBD: 'What did you do to his body, Art?'
AS: 'I ain't going there.'
CBD: 'Why?'

Again I reminded him that if I walked out of the interview, Clara would be furious with him because she was expecting him to be totally honest during the interviews.

CBD: 'What about little Karen Hill. Why did you murder her?'
AS: 'Same reason, ya know. She kinda wanted it, ya know. Sex, an' stuff like that. Then, I get started, an' she starts cryin' and wants her mom, so I suffocated her. Not with my hands. Covered her mouth with dirt and stuff.'
CBD: 'But you did have sex with her. Vaginally and anally, Arthur.'
AS: 'Yeah. But that was after she was dead. Then I went home.'

Then came the final question:

CBD: 'Art, how come you stuffed leaves and twigs into your victims' ears and noses. Things like that?'
AS: 'I dunno, really, I dunno. Just don't want to make a mess, I s'pose.'

With that, the interviews were completed. Shawcross rose slowly to his feet and shook my hand for the last time. Meekly, he allowed himself to be body-searched by the guards after his 'full-contact visit' with the outside world. Then 'The Monster of the Rivers' was led shuffling back into the depths of the prison. He never looked back and didn't say goodbye.

* * *

At the root of this evil is Arthur Shawcross, for without his antisocial behaviour, the world would have been a much safer place. Having apprehended Shawcross and placed him in custody for the murders of Karen Hill and Jack Blake, the responsibility for his welfare, and society's common good, fell upon the shoulders of others.

The trial judge for the Rochester homicides was His Honour Donald J Wisner. During a meeting with him during a court recess, he said, upon reflection, that the prosecution should have pressed a first-degree murder charge against Shawcross for the two earlier murders when they had had the opportunity. Indeed, the prosecution could have gone even further and pressed for an aggravated charge, which would have ensured that he would never have been released again.

'He most certainly would have received a natural life sentence, had that been the case,' said the judge. 'Instead, in an effort to save the state the expense of such a case, they opted for a lesser charge and, in doing so, they behaved like Monday morning quarterbacks.'

The State Prosecutor for the Rochester murders felt much the same way, supporting Judge Wisner's sentiments to the hilt. Charles 'Chuck' Siragusa – now a Justice of the Supreme Court, was, and still is, disgusted that Shawcross was released after 14-and-a-half years to kill again and again. Perhaps the most damning indictment of the entire episode came from the pursed lips of Edwin Elwin, the Director of the State Division of Paroles. On learning of Shawcross's murderous spree of terror after his release from prison, Elwin casually stated that 'he [Shawcross] did a comfortable adjustment to parole. We simply hate it when one of our people goes sour.'

Greenhaven Prison psychiatrist, Dr Robert Kent, had formed the opinion that 'Shawcross was possibly the most dangerous individual to have been released to the community for years', and this evaluation was supported by Dr Y A Haveiwala, another of Greenhaven's psychiatrists who had completed several evaluations on the killer. Shawcross, who had refused group therapy sessions, could not tell Dr Haveiwala why he had murdered the children, and raped Karen after she was dead; more to the point, Shawcross even expressed his concerns that he might kill again when he was released. Dr Haveiwala had concluded that Shawcross was 'a grave parole risk with an antisocial personality disorder [sociopath] and schizoid personality disorder with psychosexual conflicts'. Unfortunately, Dr Kent and Dr Haveiwala's colleagues thought they knew better.

Shawcross's prison psychiatric records show a hotchpotch of so-called professional interpretations laced with educated and uneducated guesswork with just the one inconsistency; that he might, or might not, murder again. Yet, still this monster was released ten years before his full 25-year tariff had expired.

But was justice done on the cheap as the judicial system anticipated? The answer must be a categorical 'no', for the cost in the human lives extinguished by Shawcross is immeasurable. While a figure cannot be placed on this degree of suffering, the cost to the public purse can be estimated, and these figures are truly astronomical. Aside from the estimated $35,000 spent to bring Shawcross to justice for the two earlier killings, and the $250,000 to keep him under lock and key at Greenhaven, plus incidentals such as psychiatrists' bills, there is also the invoice for the Rochester murders to tally up. The Rochester Police conducted 2,210 interviews during this investigation. 3,255 licence plate enquiries were made at $12 a time, and the police developed leads on 150 suspects. On-duty personnel costs added $420,447,00. Overtime costs were $121,916,00. Non-personnel services added $27,196,00. In total, these costs reached a staggering $893,612.

However, the Rochester Police Department added a rider to these figures, noting that the total would have been dramatically inflated – by perhaps an additional $2 million – if factors such as 'patrol time/area altered to a specific pattern; training of investigative personnel; administrative staff time in managing the project, and volunteer hours spent on the investigation by RPD employees' were included. Finally, to keep Shawcross in prison until he is 80 will cost the state a further $750,000, making him a very expensive serial killer indeed.

Today, Arthur Shawcross repairs locks for the prison, cooks for fellow inmates and he has, once again, wheedled his way into the psychiatric unit, where he counsels other prisoners. Currently, he claims to be suffering from what he calls, 'a rare genetic disorder', and first impressions of this claim may lead us to believe that this is simply one more convenient peg to hang his hat of mitigation upon. But is it? This claim, which is substantiated by many of America's leading authorities in the field, who subscribe to the theory that XYY abnormalities may be the cause of violent and homicidal behaviour, is that Shawcross is certainly suffering from an extremely rare biochemical imbalance linked to a rare XYY genetic disorder. It is contended that this mix could be the cause of at least part of the reason why he turned to commit such antisocial acts of violence.

Looking back to his formative years, there is well-documented evidence, even then, to show that Shawcross was showing signs of antisocial behaviour. We know he was bullied, before the worm finally turned and he became a bully and sadist himself. The roots of his evil had already been planted at this time; indeed, this genetic disorder was within him at conception, and might account for his being the only member of his immediate family to turn to such extreme practices.

The prison authority medical officer, when approached on this issue, declined to confirm that Shawcross has any such problem. But Dr Kraus, who spent months evaluating Shawcross, found solid evidence that he has an XYY disorder. Approaches to several of the world's leading authorities, seeking clarification on the XYY phenomenon linked to antisocial behaviour, not surprisingly, brought no clear answer. There are two camps, each with its own strongly felt views. With our present level of knowledge, it seems that chromosomal abnormality can only have a bearing on a minute fraction of the criminal population. It is necessary to consider the millions of people throughout the world who have an XYY abnormality and who exhibit no antisocial tendencies whatever. Consequently, while an XYY disorder might partly account for Shawcross's behaviour, it cannot provide the total picture.

There are a hundred million brain cells in the average person, and the presence of one extra chromosome in each cell equates to the presence of an additional one hundred million chromosomes in the XYY male, which are not present in the normal XY male. World-respected geneticist Dr Arthur Robinson once screened 40,000 newborns for XYY, and he has claimed that about 2,000 XYY males are born in the United States each year. His research shows that two-thirds are thin, tall and awkward, with an IQ range of 80 to 140. Robinson says, 'These people are excitable, easily distracted, hyperactive and intolerant of frustration. Fifty per cent are learning-disabled (compared to 2 to 8 per cent in the general population) and most suffer delays in speech development.' Many of these personality characteristics, uncannily, match Shawcross's profile.

Dr Kraus has commented: 'Studies report that the XYY male has a 10 to 20-fold increase in his lifetime risk, as compared to their incidence in the population, of being institutionalised in a mental hospital or prison – a risk that is not trivial. XYY males have a much higher average rate of learning disability and are described as 'problem children' who cause serious behavioural and management problems at home and school. Studies describe how 'at least some XYY boys show behavioural disability that makes them not only a great problem in family management, but also quite disparate from other family members in their behaviour altogether.'

This is a finding consistent with the early life history of Arthur Shawcross and his own frequently reported belief that he was 'different' from all of his family members. Personality characteristics associated with these children also include descriptions of them as drifters or loners, disposed to running away from home, who, as they grow up, are frequently agitated, experiencing paedophilic urges, arson, threatening to kill others, molesting children, stealing and exhibiting moments of sudden violence and aggression. These are all the personality traits well documented in Shawcross's life.

In an article entitled; *Human Behavior Cytogenetics*, published in the *Journal of Sex Research*, Dr John Money, adds weight to Dr Kraus's claim. He wrote, 'It seems perfectly obvious, that an extra chromosome in the nucleus of every cell of the brain, somehow or other, makes the individual more vulnerable to the risk of developing mental behavioural disability or abnormalities.'

So, it seems that, at the very least, an XYY chromosome disorder is part of Shawcross's problems. But what of the biochemical imbalance? In searching for a diagnosis in Shawcross's case, Dr Kraus turned his attention to blood and urine testing where he hit upon a little-known fact revolving around kryptopyrrole. Indeed, so little was known about kryptopyrrole, that half of the authorities Dr Kraus spoke to for advice had never heard of it, and the biochemistry laboratory at the University of Rochester didn't know how to spell the word, replying, '… it sounds like something out of a *Superman* movie, doesn't it.'

During laboratory examination of Shawcross's bodily fluids, Dr Kraus found that while the concentrations of copper, zinc, iron and histamines were all within the normal range expected to be found in a healthy person, one of the results from an analysis of urine showed unexpected findings. Kryptopyrrole showed 'H 200.66mcg/100cc' against an expected value 0–20. The 'H' was laboratory shorthand for 'High'. Kryptopyrrole comes from *kryptos*, the Greek word for 'hidden', while 'pyre' is a prefix for fire. The derivation is both Greek and Latin, and 'pyrrole' is a combination word meaning 'fiery oil'. Thus, kryptopyrrole becomes 'hidden fiery oil', the chemical structure of which resembles other chemicals known to be toxic to brain function, such as LSD. The presence of kryptopyrrole, in elevated amounts, although not considered a sign of a particular, or, specific disease entity is, in abnormal amounts, considered a biochemical marker of psychiatric dysfunction, much like the reading of an elevated clinical thermometer. This biochemical metabolite (5 Hydroxy-kryptopyrrole Lactam) is normally present in humans in either very low amounts, or not at all, and it can be detected in the urine, which may have a mauve-coloured appearance.

Feeling now that he was finally on to something, the indefatigable Dr Klaus burned even more midnight oil, and, in doing so, learned that any kryptopyrrole reading of 20mcg/100cc was a cause for concern. Shawcross's readings were ballistic, at up to 200mcg/100cc. Kryptopyrrole is also related to bile, and when excessive amounts are present, can combine with vitamin B6 and zinc to cause a metabolic defect called 'pyroluria'. This proved to be another clue to understanding Shawcross, for pyrolurics function well in controlled settings of low stress, proper diet and predictability. Apart from the initial settling down periods, which are common to all prison inductees, Shawcross has always been quite at home within the structured prison system where he enjoys a balanced diet. Conversely, pyrolurics appear to suffer poorly, outside controlled conditions. Unable to control anger, once provoked, they have mood swings, cannot tolerate sudden, loud noises, are sensitive to bright lights, and tend to be 'night people'. They usually skip breakfast, have trouble recalling night dreams, and they suffer poor, short-term memory, so they make bad liars. Sometimes, they lack pigment in the skin, and are, therefore, pale. The hair is prematurely grey, and they have a diminished ability to handle stress. As such, they may be very dangerous and constitute a risk to the public.

All of this shows Shawcross's personality and behaviour in an interesting light. Dr Kraus argues that the symptoms manifested by Arthur Shawcross correlated in every way with one suffering from the abnormally elevated levels of this toxic chemical invasion. Parental disorientation, abnormal ECGs, general nervousness, progressive loss of ambition, poor school performance, and decreased sexual potency, all of which are embedded in his personal history.

The abnormality also correlated with marked irritability, rages, inability to control anger once provoked, mood swings, terrible problems with stress control, violence and antisocial behaviour, all aligned with the high risk of becoming violent, which is evident in this man's behaviour.

* * *

There seems little doubt that Shawcross was born handicapped, certainly in the genetic and biochemical sense. The 47 XYY chromosome disorder, linked to the abnormally high levels of kryptopyrrole, had formed a human time bomb from conception, and this would certainly account for him being the only rotten seed in the family of four children, and the undeniable fact that he demonstrated antisocial behaviour at a tender age. Of course, Shawcross always knew that he was somehow different from everyone else, especially the rest of his family, but never, in his worst nightmares, could he have known why, or just how different he might be. For the first 25 years of his life, his sexual history highlights an inclination towards children far younger than himself. He certainly enjoyed sexual fantasies about making love to his sister, Jean, and with his inbred predisposition towards violence, perhaps it was inevitable that paedophiliac behaviour leading to rape and homicide was pre-programmed into him like a faulty computer chip. Murdering Jack Blake and Karen Ann Hill serve as grim testimony to that.

A sexual inadequate throughout his life, Shawcross blamed his wives for letting him down in that department. Millions of men use prostitutes for one reason or the other, so perhaps on his release from prison, Shawcross graduated to the seedier side of prostitution to fulfil this need, too.

There is also evidence suggesting that people with the genetic and chemical disorders ascribed to Shawcross can metamorphose into extremely dangerous individuals who thrive during the hours of darkness. 'The Monster of the Rivers' came out at night and, when the beast surfaced, it was the prostitute population that suffered its homicidal wrath.

Looking back, with all the gifts of hindsight, couldn't it be argued that Shawcross's rationale and *modus operandi* were predictable? Clothing – not only his, but that of his victims – was important to him. Garments subconsciously obsessed him, and he always mentioned clothing in his police statements and in letters and during interviews. Maybe we will never know why clothing was so important to this man, but the folding up of the garments was an indelible hallmark of his crimes, perhaps for the reason he gave during one of his interviews: 'Fold the clothes up and they'd think they were going to get dressed again' was his calculated remark. As a young child, Arthur's mother demanded that he be neat and tidy, more especially with regard to his clothes, so this was possibly a learnt legacy from childhood, and a trait that he carried through to form part of his *modus operandi*.

What is the explanation for his disgusting – yet quite unique – practice of forcing vegetation debris into the ears, nose, mouth, vagina and anuses of many of his victims? Again, this may be an echo from his early days when he indulged in torturing and killing small animals, fish and birds. Back then, as a child, he learned that by forcing material into his victims, he could not only prevent them from screaming out in pain, but also stop their urine and excrement from leaking out and spoiling his clothes. Shawcross murdered all of his victims near water, and this part of his MO is far easier to explain for he had been a keen angler since childhood, and during these isolated periods down by the rivers, he had ample time to fantasise about sex. Hence, Shawcross had an affinity with water. The riverbank was his territory, where he felt safe and secure.

Shawcross also returned more than once to the bodies of his victims. Often, he would sit with the rotting corpses and discuss his life with the remains. He told them how his wives disgusted him. He explained that he did love children, and that it wasn't his fault that he killed little Jack Blake or, for that matter, Karen Hill.

On at least two occasions, Shawcross cut open his victims and ate their most intimate body parts. With June Cicero, his penultimate victim, he returned three times, the second time to cut into the frozen corpse, as it lay in a creek, to take his gruesome trophy.

'It took some getting out,' he explained. 'I hacked it some, then I thawed it under the car heater as I drove along. I ate it raw. I wanted to show the police where the bone was, but they didn't want to know.'

One rather feels that even Stephen King could not better that scene in one of his horror novels. And then, on his third visit to the body of June Cicero, Shawcross masturbated over the bridge parapet, an act observed by a police officer and which sealed his own fate.

Shawcross feels no remorse for his crimes; indeed, he always, without exception, lays the blame for his antisocial acts at the feet of others – his wives, God, the Army and, more recently, what he feels is his genetic and biochemical abnormality. In shifting blame in this manner, he is able to justify his behaviour to the extreme point of grand appraisement, which finds him standing on a plinth in the serial killers' hall of fame, arguing that he is a very special human being and, as such, he is worthy of scientific study. He may be right about that, if only for the possibility of examining more closely his genetic and biochemical make-up in the hope of furthering our understanding of what he is.

The following extract is taken from a letter written by Shawcross to the author. It is published here with his permission:

I have been asked, Did I kill? Yes, too many times for any one person to do so! It is said I have partaken of human flesh. Think back in history: You will see that man hunted man (still do in some remote parts of the world.) Think about the animal we call pig or boar. Why does it say in some books we can't eat this animal? Because it tastes just like human flesh. I have eaten flesh of man or woman … So the next time any of you sit down to eat bacon, ham or a nice juicy pot roast or pork chop, think about the taste, the flavour of eating human flesh. But this only effected me when I got very angry – the hunger of the predator.

I have been a god unto myself. I've been the judge, the jury and the executioner. I dear people, have murdered, butchered and totally destroyed 53 human beings in my life time. Why?

Picture in your mind: I was taught to sit for hours at a time and not move; I was taught to seek out and destroy the enemy as I received them to be.

The prostitutes I am accused of killing were the enemy to me in their own fashion, because they can kill with social diseases and AIDS and get away with it! Do I regret it, I have been asked? My answer is, I very much regret it, to the point of wondering why I was chosen to carry out this assignment.

The United States government taught me how to kill; what it did not teach me was the desire not to so! I still get those feelings – but the pills I am now on dampen them to the point of calming me down. Why not before?

Why am I like I am? Study it – seek the answer before too many people get killed! I am like a predator, able to hunt and to wantonly destroy at any given time or moment … I have been pushed and threatened, but somehow the pills stop or slow down the desire to fight. I know that when I do fight there will be no control – I'll be the predator again.

Most people tell me I will die in prison! (So what.) Do you have a choice of when and where you will die? … Many people believe that when they die they will go to heaven. Not so! Your soul waits to be called: Read your Bible if that is what you believe in. As for me, I will live again and go on to the next transition. I am a spiritualist … Death is but a transition of life. The people I have killed are in their next transition. They will live again, but in a much better way than the one they left behind! … I have lived in many parts of the world, even in England, Kent to be exact. The fens were home to me 700 years ago.

What went on in the home I grew up in is better left unsaid, but I cannot do it! I, as a child, had no control on who my sex partner was! I cannot say I did not enjoy it, be it a cousin, sister or the old girl herself.

Every man, woman or child from 10 years of age and up is able to kill knowingly. How did I kill without the use of drugs or a struggle! Let me explain this further. The body has many pressure points: some to relax you, some to excite you and some to give pain or remove it. A few of them to stun you and, be that as it may, to kill you! Many of you humans portray me as mad-crazy. This is your free will. What you think may not be so.

Look to the heavens, I came from there! So did you but you wont admit it! My time is near in this transition. I will move on shortly, I feel what I feel. If every man, woman and child had the same as everyone else, then crime and war would be nonexistent.

Remember: watch the heavens, we are coming to rescue you from you.

I am, or am I?'

SIGNED BY ARTHUR SHAWCROSS
SEPTEMBER 19, 1994

This chapter is based on exclusive television and audiotape interviews between Christopher Berry-Dee and Arthur John Shawcross within the Sullivan Correctional Facility, Fallsburg, New York State, on Monday 19 and Friday 30 September 1994, and correspondence covering three years.

Shawcross welcomes correspondence, and his address is: Inmate # 91-B-083, Sullivan Correctional Facility, PO Box AG, Fallsburg, NY 12733-0016.

JOHN MARTIN SCRIPPS

UK

'They won't hang me. I'm British.'

JOHN SCRIPPS FOUR DAYS BEFORE HE
WAS EXECUTED AT CHANGI PRISON,
SINGAPORE, 19 APRIL 1996

Describbed by the media as 'The Tourist from Hell', Scripps became the first Westerner to be hanged in Singapore for murder, and only the second for any offence. Dutch citizen Johannes van Damme was executed by the Singapore authorities, for drug-trafficking, in 1994. He was arrested on 27 September 1989, when he was found to be carrying 4kg of heroin. He was sentenced to death on 26 April 1993.

Scripps is the last British murderer to be hanged since the abolishment of capital punishment in 1964. The last executions in Britain took place on 13 August of that year. Peter Anthony Allen, aged 21, was hanged at Walton Prison, Liverpool, and John Robson Walby, alias Gwynne Owen Evans, aged 24, was hanged at Strangeways Prison, Manchester. They had been jointly convicted of the murder of John West, a van driver from Workington, Cumberland, in the course of robbery.

John Martin Scripps was born in Hertford, on 9 December 1959. The family moved to London when he was a small boy and he remembered a happy childhood, in which he was close to his sister Janet. When he was nine years old, he experienced the loss of his father, who committed suicide after he learned that his wife was leaving him for another man. John found his father at home with his head in the gas oven. At about the same time, his mother was diagnosed as having throat cancer and, although she recovered, John's world fell apart.

According to the FBI, 70 per cent of multiple murderers have undergone trauma at some point in their childhood.

'The trauma festers away and becomes a fantasy of getting revenge,' says Ian Stephen, a forensic psychologist who works for the police and the prison service in Strathclyde. 'In Scripps's case, the anger might have been directed against the fact that he has been deprived of a father, deserted.'

John became increasingly introverted. He cut himself off from his friends and found it impossible to concentrate on learning to read and write. He acquired these skills later on, in prison, although his handwriting always remained very childish.

At the age 14, he disappeared while at a training camp in France organised by the Finchley unit of the army cadet force. A year later, he was in juvenile court for burglary and theft.

His first adult conviction was for indecent assault in 1978, when he was fined £40 at Hendon Magistrates Court. Thereafter, it was a grim catalogue of offences including burglaries in London, followed by jail in Israel, for stealing from a fellow kibbutz worker. In 1982, he was jailed again for burglary and assault in Surrey.

He managed to abscond from the prison system and embarked on a crime journey throughout South-East Asia and America. In Mexico, he met and married 16-year-old Maria Arellanos, but, by 1985, he was back in Britain once again, facing a prison sentence for committing burglary. Prison could not hold him and he absconded, yet again, to return to his drug-smuggling activities in South-East Asia and America.

Justice caught up again with Scripps in 1987, when was jailed for seven years in London for heroin offences. The following year, his young Mexican wife divorced him. While on home leave from prison in June 1990, he disappeared for the third time and flew to Bangkok.

When later interviewed by Customs and Excise officers, Scripps said that he had flown out to Bangkok to meet a girl he had been writing to. On arrival in the Thai capital, he booked into the Liberty Hotel for three days, taking a cheap room, costing about £10 a night. Accompanied by his girlfriend, he frequented a few bars and visited the local tourist attractions. Romance seemed to be in the air and they made a trip to Ayuthaya, the historic former capital, where they stayed for two days. The couple then moved on to Pattaya, known as 'Sin City', and from there, to Phuket, where they lived at Nilly's Marina Inn, at Patong Beach. Scripps spent ten days in Thailand before deciding to fly back to London. He had spent £1,000 during his sojourn in the East, including £270 on clothes and just over £100 buying 48 phoney watches. He also bought a quantity of heroin.

* * *

At 1.20 local time, Scripps boarded Gulf Air Flight GF 153, destination Muscat in the Sultanate of Oman. On arrival he proceeded to the transit area of Seeb International Airport to await his connecting flight to Heathrow, London. He was travelling on a UK passport issued in the name of Jesse Robert Bolah. This travel document, #348572V had been stolen.

While killing time, in an airport bar, he met Christopher Davis, and the two men conversed as they waited for their flight. As Scripps prepared to board Flight GF 011 to London, he was subjected to a routine security check, which included a body frisk. Police Corporal Saeed Mubarak of the Royal Oman Police, found two packages wrapped in red tape in his pockets. Thinking that the packages might contain explosives, he summoned assistance from Inspector Saeed Sobait. The two police officers went through Scripps's hand baggage where they discovered a larger packet containing white powder. The dilemma for the authorities was that, the white powder could not be tested without detaining the passenger. It was therefore decided to give one of the packets, which, as it later turned out, contained 50g of diamorphine, and the passport to the captain. Scripps was then allowed to proceed to London, effectively under detention and the responsibility of the Gulf Air flight crew.

Scripps nervously boarded the Tri-Star aircraft and settled into seat 39H. Mid-way through the flight, schoolteacher Gareth Russell, sitting in 39K, noticed his fellow passenger drop something on the floor and kick it under the seat.

As soon as the aircraft entered British airspace, the pilot contacted HM Customs & Excise and, moments after the plane had taxied to a stop, a rummage team headed by David Clark boarded the aircraft. The packet, which Scripps had kicked under seat, was found. After a field test for opiates had proved positive, he was charged under Section 3(1) of the Misuse of Drugs Act 1971, contrary to Section 170(2) of the Customs & Excise Management Act 1979.

John Scripps was held in custody that night to allow Customs and police officers to search 6 Gordon Road, Farnborough, where he stayed, with his uncle, Ronald White. A folder of documents was found, containing a West German passport, in the name of Robert Alfred Wagner and a Belgian identity card, in the name of Benjamin George Edmond Stanislas Balthier, with Scripps's photograph attached to it. The men named in these documents had been reported missing, many years previously, and there has been no trace of them since.

Later that day, Scripps was interviewed again, and he was asked how he earned his money, how he could afford to travel all over the world, and how he could afford a very expensive Samsonite suitcase. He cockily replied, 'It may be very expensive to you, but it isn't to me. If you can't afford a suitcase like this, it's because you're working as minor subservients of the State for a standard wage, and you're not willing to go out and work all hours.'

At 10.00pm on 31 August, Scripps was released in the name of John Martin, and instructed to answer bail on 29 October 1990. He failed to report and, on 28 November, he was arrested by Detective Constable Malone at his mother's home at 11 Grove Road, Sandown, on the Isle of Wight. Police found more drugs and he was charged with possession of 50g of diamorphine at 80 per cent purity. The street value of this amount was estimated at around £9,473, while the remaining

191.5 grams of heroin he had tried to smuggle through the airport was valued at £38,551. Given the knowledge that Scripps possessed drugs valued at over £48,000, the police now understood how he could afford his jet-set lifestyle.

Because Scripps had previously absconded from a seven-year custodial sentence for drugs offences, he was held on remand in Winchester Prison until his trial. He instructed his solicitors that he would plead 'not guilty'. His defence was simple enough. His case would stand or fall by his claim that he had found the red-taped package containing heroin on the ground at Muscat Airport and had handed it in to the police. He categorically denied that any drugs were found on his person at Muscat. Further, he argued that the traces of heroin found in the pockets of his jeans he was wearing at the time resulted directly in him being asked to open the package he had found containing drugs. He denied any knowledge whatsoever of the traces alleged to have been found in the pocket of a shirt. If he managed to wriggle out of that, he was still not completely out of the woods, for the police had found heroin on him during his arrest in Sandown and his wallet had been stuffed with £2,000 in cash. The implication was that he intended peddling drugs on the Isle of Wight, yet another allegation that Scripps denied.

Prisoner V48468 Scripps was given legal aid, and case #T910602 was held at Winchester Crown Court on 6 January 1991. Represented by Bruce Maddick QC, Scripps suddenly changed his plea to 'guilty' in an effort to gain leniency. Despite this ploy, he was sentenced to 13 years' imprisonment. Amazingly, he spent just three years and ten months in jail before contriving another escape.

Scripps started his prison term at Albany Prison on the Isle of Wight and, during a six-week period, between March and April 1993, he was instructed in butchery, by Prison Officer James Quigley.

'He was shown how to bone out forequarters and hindquarters of beef, sides of bacon, carcasses of pork, and how to portion chicken,' James Quigley said, adding, 'He was a quick learner, and very fast on picking up on how to slaughter, dismember and debone animals.'

What the authorities could never have guessed was that, while they were training an inmate in butchery skills, they were also equipping him to slaughter and dismember humans, the gruesome calling to which he subsequently set his hand.

Scripps's ultimate odyssey began on 28 October 1994, when he failed to return to the Mount Prison in Bovington, Hertfordshire, after four days' leave. Throughout the week before he walked out of the open prison gate, he had been openly selling his possessions to finance his escape. He had even bragged to fellow inmates that he was going on the run. This was picked up by the prison staff, who failed to act on it.

When he failed to return, the Governor, Margaret Donnelly, said, 'He was no longer considered a risk. He had no history violence. He was quiet and reserved.'

What, it appears, the Governor did not know, was that Scripps had absconded from every home leave he had ever been granted. And, far from being quiet, reserved and no longer a risk, the smooth-talking drug-dealer, was about to become a vicious serial killer.

After absconding, Scripps embarked on a globetrotting, three-nation murder rampage. His first port of call, before the killing started was Holland, where he met a former drug-dealer whom he had encountered, while on remand, in Winchester Prison. He travelled next to Belgium and Spain and reached Mexico in late November, where he attempted a reconciliation with Maria Arellanos. He told her that he had been released from prison on a technicality, and that he was returning to Thailand to buy silk clothes and wanted them both to set up a boutique in Cancun.

He told her that he was now a deeply religious man and, to convince her, became a devotee of the Virgin of Guadeloupe, Mexico's patron saint.

To finance this venture, Scripps befriended Timothy McDowell, a British backpacker who was holidaying in Belize and had travelled to Mexico in 1994. It is believed that he beat the 28-year-old Cambridge graduate and management consultant to death, dismembered his body and dumped it in an alligator-infested river. Shortly after the murder, the victim's bank account was milked dry to the tune of £21,000; the money being transferred to Scripps's account in London. This sum of money was later moved to another account, in the United States, under the name of Simon Davis, one of Scripps's many aliases.

* * *

Thirty-three-year-old Gerard George Lowe arrived at Singapore's Changi airport on the morning of 8 March 1995. Dressed casually, in khaki Bermuda shorts and an orange T-shirt, he was indistinguishable from all the other international travellers as they stumbled wearily off the plane and on to the moving walkway. He was just another tourist, and that was the point. Travelling alone in a strange country, Lowe was looking for a friendly face. And, as people do in airports, when they are trying to establish their bearings, he found himself talking to a complete stranger. The tall, soft-spoken Englishman, in his thirties, politely introduced himself as Simon Davis. As they chatted, Lowe explained that he was a South African brewery design engineer who was on a shopping trip to Singapore to take advantage of the low cost of video recorders and cameras. When Scripps caught sight of Lowe's gold credit card, he knew he had found another victim.

It was apparent to Scripps that his new acquaintance was thrifty, so he suggested they share an hotel room. The River View Hotel was suggested by Scripps. This is a middle-class businessman's stopover, with a greying marble reception area and a tacky boutique selling plastic orchids and 'Hong Kong Girl' perfume. The hotel was full and the two men had to wait several hours before they were given a room. 'They seemed very normal,' as Roberto Pregarz, the hotel's manager, later testified at Scripps' trial. 'They were smiling and laughing together. There was nothing strange.'

Within minutes of booking in, the two men made their way to room 1511. After unpacking their cases, Lowe settled down at a small, round table, from which he could admire the panoramic view of Singapore and, picking up a pen, started to compile his shopping list.

Scripps chose this moment to steal up behind Lowe and brought down a 3lb camping hammer on his victim's head in a single, crushing blow. After his capture and subsequent detainment in Changi Prison, Scripps said of the murder, 'I think he [Lowe] was a bit surprised when I hit him. At first he thought I was mucking about. That made me mad with him because I thought that he was a homosexual. I threw him against the wall and he started to fall down. He was shaking and then he pissed himself. I knocked him about a bit, and got him to tell me his bank card PIN number. When he was in the bathroom, he was conscious. There was water dribbling from his mouth. He gurgled, or something like that.'

Without a trace of emotion, Scripps added, 'Well, I cut his throat an' left him to bleed to death like a pig.'

The following exchange between John Scripps and myself took place when he was in prison and under sentence of death:

CBD: 'So, let's get this right, John. You smash this innocent man against the wall of the room, then beat him half-senseless, or something like that. Then you drag him into the bathroom, lift him into the bath, forcing his head down to his knees. You turn on the taps, and cut through the back of his neck to paralyse him. Then, you stab him in the neck, or whatever, and let him bleed to death. Did he know what was going on, John?'

JS: 'Do you want the fucking truth?'

CBD: 'Yes.'

JS: 'Yes.'

CBD: 'Yes, what?'

JS: 'Do you want blood out of a fuckin' stone?'

CBD: 'Did Mr. Lowe know what was going on?'

JS: 'Yes! He pissed and shit himself. It made a stink. He was shitting himself. Yeah. Right. Oh, fuck it. Yeah. Really, I can't say about it. It wasn't good and I spewed up. He really shit himself, but he couldn't do much about it, could he?'

CBD: 'I suppose not, John. What did you do after you'd killed him?'

JS: 'I cut him into parts so's I could dump the body.'

CBD: Is it true that you used the little saw that went with your Swiss Army knife?'

JS: 'That's bollocks. I have a knife like that for camping. But, anyone will tell you can't use a little saw like that for cutting carcasses.'

CBD: 'Okay. What did you use?'

JS: 'A six-inch boning knife. I was taught how to look after knives, you know.'

CBD: 'Now, I know you're telling the truth. Go on.'

JS: 'Well, after the blood had been washed away, I took his head off. Just like a pig. It's almost the same. You cut through the throat and twist the knife through the back of the neck. There ain't much mess if you do it properly … I cut off his arms at the elbows. Then, I cut off his upper arms at the shoulders. You just cut through the ball and socket joints. You don't saw anything.'

CBD: 'And?'

JS: 'Well, the legs. Um, on a pig you have the legs, and you have to use a saw to make … I think it's called a "square cut". But, honest … I just stuck the knife in and twisted and cut until the legs came away at the hip joint, I suppose. When I got to the knees, I just cut through and they snapped back so's I could fold them up. Fuckin' heavy stuff, right?'

After packaging the body parts in the black bin-liners Gerald Lowe had brought with him to wrap up his duty-free purchases, Scripps deposited the bundles in the room's only wardrobe. He liberally sprayed Lynx deodorant around the room in an attempt to mask the smell of his own vomit: It proved inadequate, for a couple who stayed in room 1511, in the days that followed, reported a strange fishy odour lingering around the room. Finally, Scripps washed his hands and cleaned up the bathroom. Again, he was not absolutely thorough and missed a few tiny spots on the shower curtain, door and toilet bowl. These traces were to provide crucial evidence when he was eventually brought to court to answer the charge of murder.

Murder, committed in this meticulous fashion, can rarely be a crime of passion. It is an eminently practical business, carried out with the studied objectivity of a professional. It requires thought, planning and an ability to attend to every detail with cold-blooded efficiency. Scripps may have left traces of his butchery in the bathroom, but he demonstrated a clinical, unhurried persistence after the event. He started by practising the forging of his victim's signature on tracing paper.

His next move was to visit a computer shop, where he told the sales assistant he was Gerald Lowe and he wanted to buy some lap-top computers. By 9.00pm, he was back in the hotel's River Garden Restaurant, sitting down to a plate of fillet steak and a bottle of white wine. It was a balmy evening. The string of multi-coloured lights around the patio reflected in the waters of the nearby Singapore River. John Scripps was at peace with the world.

The next morning, Scripps informed the hotel receptionist that his companion had checked out and that he would settle the bill when he left. He then went on a spending spree in Singapore's glittering shopping malls. He threaded his way from one air-conditioned shop to another, using Lowe's Gold card again and again. His first purchase was a pair of Aiwa speakers, and then came a pair of Nike shoes and socks, as well as a video recorder, which he arranged to be sent to his sister in England.

On the morning of 9 March, Scripps used the credit card for another shopping bonanza. He also drew S$8,400 in cash from a local bank and made a telegraphic transfer of US$11,000, to one of his accounts in San Francisco, in the name of John Martin. He used the Gold card to buy a S$30 ticket to attend the Singapore Symphony Orchestra, where he heard a programme of Brahms and Tchaikovsky. Finally, in an extraordinary whimsical but callous bid to maximise his gains, he bought five Big Sweep lottery tickets.

Later that night, he packed the dismembered body parts into a suitcase and caught a taxi to Singapore Harbour where, under the cover of darkness, he dumped the gruesome contents into the waters swirling around Clifford Pier. The next day, flush with cash, he flew to Bangkok.

* * *

Sheila Damude, a 49-year-old school administrator, from Victoria, British Columbia, had flown into Bangkok for a two-week stay with her son who was on a 'gap' year tour of the world. 22-year-old Darin had broken his leg while travelling with friends, and she wanted to give him some motherly attention. They had decided to take a tourist trip to the Thai 'Paradise Island' of Phuket.

On 15 March, mother and son arrived at Phuket Airport and were collecting their thoughts, in the usual arrival turmoil, when Scripps sidled up to them.

'I was on the same plane as you. Do you have a problem?' he enquired.

Within minutes, Scripps gleaned the information that Sheila and her son wanted to get to Patong Beach, but they were not sure how much to pay for a taxi.

With his marauding instincts fully attuned, Scripps, ever the experienced traveller, told them about 'Nilly's Marina Inn', where a room would cost them about US$18 a night. The small luxury hotel lay on the quiet southern end of Patong Beach, one of the most popular beaches on the island. He suggested that they share a taxi with him which would give them all a cheap ride. Mother and son exchanged glances and nodded their agreement. They were clearly very impressed by this helpful young man and soon they were on their way along the dusty roads to Patong Beach.

Scripps signed himself in, at Nilly's Marina Inn, as Simon Davis, a shopkeeper from London. No one noticed, in a revealing slip of the pen, that he had inadvertently signed his name 'J' Davis. The consummate traveller, he had stayed there before, always drawing admiring looks from the pretty female staff who deferred to him as 'Mr John'.

The Damudes caught the lift to the second floor and were shown into a spacious deluxe suite overlooking the bay, a *Miami Vice* view with jet-skis and speed boats swooping on to white sands. Scripps took a nearby room, just across the corridor, which overlooked scrubland at the back of the hotel.

The Damudes had two king-sized beds, a well-appointed mini-bar, IDD telephone, colour television, air-conditioning and a kitchen area. There was a separate bathroom and shower and even a safe, in which they could store their valuables.

If the room was quite luxurious, especially at the low cost, the view from their window was priceless. Situated across from a long, sandy beach and a narrow road, was the crystal clear water of the Andaman Sea. Looking out from their balcony, two tall palm trees grew out of the sandy soil, where two of the local girls were breaking open the coconuts. The girls looked up and when they saw the handsome young Darin, they broke into giggles. At that moment, the Damudes thought they had found Heaven but, as the next day approached, they would be pitched into Hell.

Meanwhile, after a short walk to Patong's exciting nightlife, the Damudes spent the evening exploring the shops for silk garments. Scripps hired a high-powered 450cc Honda motorcycle, and ended up on the seafront at The Banana Bar. Throbbing with music, the place was full of good-time girls, who would sell their young bodies for less than the price of a meal. He danced the early hours away and had sex with a young woman on the beach before retiring for the night. The Tourist Police admired his yellow and green motorcycle parked on the double-yellow lines outside the hotel and decided it was not good policy to issue a parking ticket to a holiday-maker.

During the next morning, Sheila and Darin came down for breakfast, which they ate in the sunshine. After the meal, they searched the rather dismal fish tank for signs of life, and Sheila flicked through the postcard rack for something suitable to send to her husband back home. This was the last time they were seen alive. It is believed that they returned to their room to make plans for the day ahead.

At about 11.00am, people wandering about outside the small hotel next door noted a large flood of red-coloured water flushing down an open drain that led from Nilly's Marina Inn to the sewer under the road.

Because John Scripps has never been charged with the murders of Sheila and Darin Damude, he refused to discuss the case with me. Nevertheless, using the known evidence, it is possible to reconstruct what happened when the Damudes returned to their room at the Inn.

Scripps knocked on the door and entered their room on some pretext and, within seconds, he had stunned them with a stun-gun. Such a weapon was found in his possession when he was arrested. With his victims immobilised, he took out his hammer and beat them to death – swabs from his hammer matched bloodstains on the carpet in the room occupied by the Damudes – after which he dismembered their bodies, using the butchery skills he had learned so adroitly at Albany Prison.

After stealing his victims' travel documents, passports and credit cards, he went on yet another shopping spree. The skulls, torsos and several limbs, belonging to the Damudes, were found between 19 and 27 March, scattered around the local countryside. Also, during this time, a Thai woman, out walking her dog in the area, found other gruesome remains, partially tipped into a disused tin mine shaft. The identity of the victims was later confirmed using dental records.

The Western world has become hardened to this kind of cold-blooded multiple murder. The gruesome details of the killings perpetrated by, for example, Kenneth McDuff, Harvey Carignan and Peter Sutcliffe, have become all too familiar. When the latest sensational murder case features in the headlines, we have the feeling that we have read it all before. Dismembered corpses, anonymous victims, apparently motiveless crime and bizarre acts of violence have become common currency.

But this is not so in Singapore where violent crime and murder are unusual. In this draconically ordered City State, where even the pavements seem to have been scrubbed clean and where the glass of the skyscrapers sparkles spotless in the sun, crime comes in rather more sanitised forms.

Famously harsh punishment awaits those who dare to drop litter or carelessly discard chewing gum. Here, taxis are fitted with a warning bell, which rings automatically if the driver exceeds the 50mph speed limit. It is not that Singaporeans have not encountered murder before. They have their share of domestic homicide, averaging fewer than 50 murders a year in a population of two-and-a-half million. Murders committed in the heat of the moment always seem to be more understandable.

It fell to Acting Superintended Gerald Lim to lead the investigation into the crimes committed by John Scripps. At the time of Lowe's murder, he was the senior investigating officer with the Special Investigation Section of the CID, and his work began on 13 March 1995, in Singapore Harbour, with the discovery of a pair of feet, which were poking out of a black bin-liner and tied up with a pair of large, blue, Woolworths underpants.

A boatman made the next discovery, for, bobbing among the pleasure boats, off Clifford Pier, were two thighs – white, hairy and bound with strips of orange fabric.

Finally, on 16 March, a plump, male torso was retrieved from the water. These gruesome remains belonged to the same male Caucasian body but the head and arms of the body have never been recovered.

Lim had dealt with fatal fights between immigrant building workers and he had come across domestic murder, but this was something completely and horrifyingly different. He examined the green-tinged, rotting flesh and wondered at the person who could be responsible for such cold and calculating destruction of another human being. And this body was not just headless and armless, it was nameless.

As most visitors to Singapore were registered as hotel guests, the detective's first stop was the centralised hotel registration computer. Within hours, a fax had been sent to every hotel in Singapore, asking if any guests were missing, or who had left without paying their bill. The Riverview Hotel responded immediately. Two guests – Gerard Lowe and Simon Davis – had checked out of Room 1511 without paying. But there was something else, the manager said. His duty reception staff recalled that the Englishman had been seen lugging a heavy suitcase through the foyer, the night before he and his companion disappeared. It was also noted that when he returned to the hotel, several hours later, he was empty-handed.

On 14 March, the police in Johannesburg, South Africa, received a report from a distressed Mrs Vanessa Lowe, who said that her husband was missing. He had not called her from Singapore to say that all was well which, she explained, was totally out of character. Her concerns soon reached Gerald Lim, and he invited her to fly to Singapore, to view the disarticulated body and a few items of wet clothing.

Before Vanessa Lowe arrived, Lim had determined that 'Simon Davis' had been using his victim's Gold credit card. Davis was now the prime suspect and a warrant was issued for his arrest. Police now believed he had murdered Lowe for his money.

When the distraught woman arrived, Superintendent Lim met her at the airport and, as delicately as he could, he asked her to identify the corpse. She bravely pointed out various marks on her late husband's body. She recognised the appendectomy scar on the abdomen, the freckles on the back and the bony lump just below the right knee. She also identified the underpants, used by Scripps to tie up his victim's thighs, and the orange strips were from here husband's T-shirt.

For some inexplicable reason, Scripps returned to Singapore on 19 March and, after a short struggle at Immigration Control, he was arrested and taken into custody. When officers opened the backpack of the man calling himself Simon Davis, which had been seized during his arrest, they were amazed at what they found. There, along with an 'Enjoy Coca-Cola' beach towel, a Pink Floyd cassette, a bottle of Paul Mitchell shampoo and some featherlite condoms, was what they came to describe as a 'murder kit'.

Scripps was carrying a 10,000-volt 'Z-Force III' stun-gun, a 1.5kg hammer, a can of Mace, two sets of handcuffs, some thumb cuffs, two serrated knives and two Swiss army knives. And that was not all. Another of his bags was filled with clothes, suitable for a middle-aged woman, consisting of skirts, dresses and even some pearl earrings. Hidden among them were passports in the names of two Canadian citizens, Sheila and Darin Damude, each of them containing crudely pasted-in photographs of Scripps. He was also found to be carrying more than US$40,000 in cash and travellers' cheques, together with the passports, credit cards and other belongings of Lowe and the Damudes.

* * *

In the Singapore equivalent of Committal Proceedings, the preliminary enquiry saw written statements from as many as 77 witnesses for the prosecution supporting the murder charge, and 11 other charges ranging from forgery, vandalism and cheating, to possession of weapons and small quantities of controlled drugs. Douglas Herda, representing the Royal Canadian Mounted Police, also wanted to question Scripps about the murders of Sheila and Darin Damude in Phuket. The Singaporean authorities refused his request.

The trial of John Scripps started on 2 October 1995 in Singapore's new high-tech court. Security was heavy throughout the session, with Scripps sitting between two armed uniformed officers in a glass and metal cage. His legs were shackled to a metal bar. He had entered no plea but 'claimed trial' which, under Singapore law, means he was contesting the charges. Singapore does not have trial by jury, a judge alone hears the evidence.

The first witness was James Quigley, who testified that he had taught Scripps butchery in Albany Prison. Chao Tzee Cheng, a government pathologist, said that the manner in which Lowe's body had been cut up indicated that only a doctor, a veterinarian or a butcher could have dismembered it. 'I told the police, "Look, you are dealing with a serial killer," ' he said in his evidence.

The prosecution alleged that Scripps, using a false name, had checked into the same hotel room as Lowe and killed him.

In what amounted to a confession, Scripps told the court he met Lowe at Changi Airport on 8 March, and they had agreed to share a hotel room. He admitted killing him in the room after he was awakened by a half-naked Lowe, who was smiling and touching his buttocks.

'I am not a homosexual,' claimed Scripps, 'and at that time it appeared to me that Mr Lowe was a homosexual. I freaked out; I kicked out and started swearing. I had experience of such things in the past and I was very frightened.'

Scripps said he used the hammer 'to hit Lowe several times on the head until he collapsed on to the carpeted floor. My right hand was covered with blood. Everything happened so quickly.'

After realising Lowe was dead, Scripps testified, he sought the help of a British friend, whom he refused to name. The friend disposed of the body without telling him how. He denied that he cut up the body.

The defence, led by Joseph Theseira, tried to show that Scripps had not intended to kill Lowe, and that the murder was an act of manslaughter, which carried a maximum penalty of life in prison.

The prosecution claimed that he committed premeditated murder with the intention of robbing the dead man.

On the fourth day of the trial, prosecutor Jennifer Marie said that Scripps had practised forging Lowe's signature, suggesting that the murder was premeditated. She showed the court items seized from his luggage, including a notebook and tracing paper with practised signatures of Lowe's name.

In a nit-picking exercise, the defence questioned two police officers, trying to show how they conducted an inadequate search for blood traces next to the hotel room bed where, Scripps claimed, Lowe fell and bled to death. Both officers said there were no traces of blood on the carpet, only in the small bathroom. The prosecution argued that this evidence supported their contention that the killing was premeditated. Clearly on a losing wicket, Pereira implied that if the police found no blood traces on the carpet, it could have been because they did not conduct sufficiently thorough tests, and not in the exact spot where Lowe fell.

During the court proceedings, on 24 October, Scripps said that while in police custody, after being arrested, he had tried to commit suicide, by slitting his wrists with a small, sharp piece of glass, to escape being hanged.

'I believed I was going to be hung,' the 35-year-old man said on his fifth day in the witness box. 'I kept thinking about Lowe and the Filipino lady that got hanged.' He was referring to the Filipino maid, Flor Contemplacion, who was hanged, on 17 March 1995, after she confessed to two murders.

Now, digging his own grave, Scripps agreed with the suggestion, by Judge TS Sinnathuray, that it would take about five minutes for a skilled butcher to dismember an animal. Then the prosecutor jumped in.

'Could your skills be used to dismember a human?'

'The bones look similar,' Scripps replied.

Cutting to the chase, Jennifer Marie asked again, 'Did you dismember Mr Lowe?'

Scripps looked down at his shackled legs, and replied unconvincingly, 'No, I don't have the all the skills you mentioned.'

On his sixth day on the stand, Scripps was asked by the prosecutor why he did not report killing Lowe to the police.

'Because this man died at my hands,' he said, 'and under Singapore law that is an automatic death sentence. That's what I understood at the time.'

'So who is the mystery man who dismembered Mr Lowe?' asked the prosecutor.

'He is a British friend staying at a hotel on Sentosa. While he was doing it I fled.'

Scripps said he had known this 'friend' for eight to ten years, and remembered that he had once worked at an abattoir. 'He's a very dangerous man,' he said meekly. 'I fear for the safety of my family.'

The Judge then cautioned Scripps that his reluctance to give even basic information on his friend could harm his defence.

'Here you are facing a murder charge,' the Judge reminded him, 'which carries the death sentence in this country. I have to ask myself, at the end of the day, this question – 'did the accused, John Scripps, go to a hotel on Sentosa?'

Sitting back in his seat, the Judge sighed as Scripps still declined even to describe the hotel, a refusal which prompted the prosecutor to accuse the defendant of lying, and that the activities of his friend were all a 'complete fabrication.' Discrepancies between Scripps's earlier statements to the police on 29 April, and his testimony from the witness stand, were also highlighted.

'You made no mention of attempted homosexual assaults while in prison in 1978, and the alleged 1994 assault by Mr Lowe, did you? I am suggesting that this 1994 incident never occurred,' said Marie. 'It's yet another fabrication of yours.'

With Scripps now firmly on the hook, the prosecutor started to reel him in. Pressed about his movements between 8 and 11 March, Scripps said that his memory was hopeless.

'You have got a good memory?' he was asked.

'I haven't,' he replied nervously. 'I'm dyslexic. I get things mixed up.'

On 6 November, Jennifer Marie told the court in her closing arguments, 'The conduct of the accused after the killing suggests that he was cold, callous and calculating, a far cry from the confused, dazed, forgetful man walking in a dream world, the picture he gives himself. He is a man very much in control of his faculties. When he embarked on the shopping spree using Lowe's credit card, buying a fancy pair of running shoes, a video cassette recorder, and a ticket to a symphony orchestra concert, he becomes a man who has no qualms about lying continuously, consistently, and even on the stand.' She added, with rare touch of venom, 'This man's excuse that he killed Mr Lowe because of a homosexual advance is just one of a string of lies to mask a premeditated murder by a greedy serial killer who preyed on tourists. And Mrs Lowe has stated on oath, a decent loving wife has come here to say that her husband had come here on a shopping holiday. He most certainly was not a homosexual. The accused has not only murdered and dismembered her husband; he now rubbishes his good name. '

In his closing statement for the defence, Edmond Pereira said, 'We urge this court to come to a finding that the accused is not guilty of murder, but is guilty of culpable homicide not amounting to murder. The killing occurred in a sudden fight in the heat of passion upon a sudden quarrel,' and he added, 'He is not a man prone to violence.'

Pereira also urged Judge Sinnathuray to ignore the information from Thailand. 'There is no evidence to suggest that the accused is responsible for the deaths of the two Canadians,' he said, calling the Thai information 'nothing more than circumstantial and prejudicial'.

On 7 November 1995, Scripps, dressed in khaki, with a prison-style crew-cut and standing in the court's glass cage, was said to be laughing and joking with his guards, before the verdict.

'Karma is karma. It's in God's hands now,' but his attitude changed within minutes.

The Judge told the packed courtroom, 'I am satisfied beyond a reasonable doubt that Scripps had intentionally killed Lowe. After that, he disarticulated Lowe's body into separate parts, and it was he who subsequently disposed of the body parts by throwing them into the river behind the hotel.' Having announced the guilty verdict, Judge TS Sinnathuray sentenced Scripps to death by hanging. The condemned man was less glib as he was taken away to a place of lawful execution.

After the verdict, defence lawyer Edmond Pereira told reporters, 'Scripps has a right to an appeal, which he can exercise within 14 days, and he shall be advised of that right.'

Privately, in an interview for the research for this book, the Judge said that he was convinced that Scripps had killed the Damudes, but added that he decided Scripps's guilt independently of the Thai evidence.

'On the evidence, I had no difficulty to find that it was Scripps who was concerned with the deaths of Sheila and Darin, and for the disposal of their body parts found in different sites in Phuket. The disarticulation of the body parts of Lowe, Sheila and Darin, had all the hallmark signs of having been done by the same person. The Thai evidence was materially relevant because it rebutted Scripps's defence that he killed Lowe unintentionally during a sudden fight.'

Upon hearing the news, at her home in Sandown, Isle of Wight, his mother, 58-year-old Jean Scripps, said, 'I brought John into this world. I am the only person who has the right to take him out. I cannot believe how my boy could have changed from a kind human being into the monster described in court.'

On 4 January 1996, John Martin Scripps virtually signed his death warrant when he wrote to the prison authorities to withdraw his appeal, which was scheduled to be heard on 8 January, but confirmed he would file for a clemency plea. This was the only sensible avenue open to him, and he had a brief six to eight-week window of opportunity to complete the paperwork.

* * *

The death penalty was in use during the colonial period in Singapore, and was retained after the City State became an independent republic in August 1965. Today, death sentences may be imposed for various offences under the Penal Code – the Internal Security Act, 1960; the Misuse of Drugs Act, 1973 as amended in 1975; and the Arms Offences Act. Capital offences include murder, treason, hurting or imprisoning the President, offences relating to the unlawful possession of firearms and explosives, and perjury resulting in the execution of a person indicted on a capital charge. The 1975 amendment to the Misuse of Drugs Act made the death penalty mandatory for possession of over 15g of heroin, or fixed amounts of other drugs.

Capital offences are tried before the High Court. The defendant has the right of appeal against conviction to the Court of Criminal Appeal and legal counsel is guaranteed by law. On the dismissal of an appeal, prisoners may seek permission to appeal to the Judicial Committee of the Privy Council in England, which serves as the final court of appeal for Singapore. If the Privy Council upholds a sentence, prisoners may submit a clemency petition to the President of Singapore.

On 14 February 1996, a spokesperson from the British High Commission in Singapore, visited Scripps in prison. Afterwards, she told reporters, 'He won't be putting in an appeal. He's eager to get it over and done with. He's just waiting for the day,' she said.

This comment surprised Edmond Pereira who was moved to say, 'There are some instructions Scripps has given to me, but I'm not at liberty at this stage to make any comment because the matter has not been finalised,' he said, adding, 'but, even if a prisoner refused to petition for clemency, the matter still has to go before the President. However, if we don't request clemency, they won't exercise clemency.'

While he was being held in solitary confinement at Changi, Scripps spent most of his time watching television and reading. A priest visited him weekly, and, once a fortnight, a consular representative went to check on his welfare and to pass on messages from his family.

The Singapore *Sunday Times* newspaper reported, on 10 March, that Scripps had declined to seek a pardon from President Ong Teng Cheong. 'It was his wish to let the law take its course,' the story concluded.

* * *

It was announced that John Scripps was to die, at dawn, on Friday, 19 April. He had turned down a request by Scotland Yard detectives, to interview him about the murder of British backpacker, Timothy McDowell, in Mexico in 1994. He spent his last two days writing garbled love poems to his former Mexican wife, Maria, described as the one true love of his life, from his cell. He was confined in a windowless cubicle measuring 8ft by 6ft, illuminated 24 hours a day and kept under continuous surveillance by a camera. There was a hole-in-the-ground lavatory and a straw roll-mat to sleep on.

His sister Janet and mother Jean said their farewells to him in his cell, 12 hours before his execution. They had turned down an offer to be present at his death. Janet said, in an interview with the author, 'How do you say goodbye to your own brother like that? We didn't actually say the word. I just couldn't.'

In a semi-literate scrawl, on a scrap of paper, Scripps wrote that he had given himself to God, who had betrayed him. 'You may take my life for what it's worth, but grant thows I love, pease [sic] and happiness.'

For his last meal, he asked for a pizza and a cup of hot chocolate. He then requested another scrap of paper and left a final, rambling note which read:

> *One day poor. One day reach. Money filds the pane of hunger but what will the emteness inside? I know that love is beyond me. So do I give myself to god. The god that has betrad me. You may take my life for what it is worth but grant those I love peace and happiness. Can I be a person again. Only time will tell me. What really upset me was when you are told every day that you are not a member of the uman rase.*

In accordance with the execution procedure, hangings are carried out in private on a large gallows, in Changi Prison, which can accommodate up to seven prisoners at a time. Hangings are carried out with a black hood covering the head and the use of the 'long drop' method.

The recommended drop is based on the need to produce a force of 1,260lb on the neck and upper spine region of the condemned person as he plunges through the trap. This figure, divided by the prisoner's weight in pounds, gives the length of drop in feet. Therefore, to kill instantaneously, it is crucial to get these calculations correct.

It is also normal practice in Singapore to hang several prisoners simultaneously, although no specific details of the executions are released to the media. The 'official' version, which is issued for every execution as a matter of policy, was that:

> *John Scripps was woken by guards at about 3.30am, and escorted to a waiting room where he, and two other prisoners,*

*two Singaporean drug-traffickers, were prepared. He spoke to
a priest and a prison chaplain before his time came when he
walked bravely to his death.*

The relatives of Scripps's partners on the gallows received
identical letters, with only the names being changed.

The apparently smooth procedure was later thrown into disarray
when the priest, who had been in attendance at the execution,
unexpectedly resigned. As part of his clerical duties, he had
witnessed most of the executions at Changi during the previous ten
years, but he was so horrified by the death of John Scripps that he
resigned immediately afterwards. And, far from walking bravely to
his death, Scripps had put up a fight to the bitter end.

The guards did indeed come for John Scripps at 3.30am. He
was ordered to step out of his prison-issue shorts, to avoid soiling
them with urine and excrement, and told to dress in his civilian
clothes. John refused, so his prison garb was torn from him.

He should have been weighed to calculate the drop; however,
he had told me that he would give his jailors an execution to
remember, for he hated his prison guards who daily reminded
him that he was not a member of the ' 'uman rase'. Crucially, he
refused to be weighed for the drop, with all the consequences that
might have for the efficiency and humaneness of his execution.

Too long a drop, and he could be decapitated; too short a drop,
and he could strangle to death at the end of the rope. In the event,
it took 12 guards 20 minutes to drag him to the holding cell next to
the gallows. During this struggle, he sustained a broken nose,
cheekbone, jaw, two black eyes and multiple bruising.

As the appointed time drew near, John was heard to be
sobbing. The two other doomed men were already pinioned and
hooded on the trap when he was prepared. Again, he lashed out
before being bound with leather straps. Now 'neutralised', naked
and tightly buckled, he lost control of his body functions. Quickly,

a rubber bung was forced between his teeth. Then came the hood, followed by the rope, which was snapped tight under his left ear; a pull on a lever, and John Scripps plunged into eternity.

For half-an-hour, his body swung silently in the pit before being taken down. The consequences of the failure to calculate a proper drop were only too obvious, for his head had almost been ripped from his body.

At 10.30am, Scripps left prison for the last time. Wrapped in a white sheet and placed in a cardboard coffin, his body joined the other two corpses in an old, green, tarpaulin-covered truck, and taken to a funeral parlour in Sin Ming Drive. The two Singaporeans were dropped off for cremation en route. When Jean Scripps, with her daughter, viewed the body, she almost fainted. With the press pack beating on the funeral parlour door, they finally made good their escape and John was cremated, later that afternoon, at the Republic's expense.

In a final irony, John Scripps spent that night at The Riverview Hotel. The urn containing his ashes was in the charge of one of the representatives of the Scripps family, lots having been drawn to decide who should have this responsibility. On their arrival in England, and at a private service, attended only by relatives and close friends, the ashes were scattered, at a secret location.

* * *

John Martin Scripps had followed the tourist trail to Thailand and Phang-Na, popularly known as 'James Bond Island', which was one of the film locations for *The Man with the Golden Gun*. While there, he had his photograph taken and printed on a souvenir plate.

'I can't believe he killed them,' said Nipa Eamsom-Ang, the receptionist at Nilly's Marina Inn. 'He was not crazy. I liked him very much,' she added. 'He was always smiling, smiling, smiling.'

Locals say she has become nervous about ghosts since Scripps was convicted, though she seemed non-plussed when asked whether hotel business had suffered in the aftermath of the murder.

Everyone who knew Scripps agrees he seemed 'a really nice guy'. During his trial, he looked sensible, decent even, and chatted politely to his guards about the weather. Once, when the judge sneezed, he turned around and said quietly, 'Bless you.'

The Roman Catholic priest, whom John called 'Father Frank', said, 'I try to imagine how his face would have looked when he was chopping up the bodies,' concluding, 'It's impossible. I can only see him as he was with me – young, handsome, soft-spoken and gentle.'

This is an all-too-familiar perception. When people meet serial killers, they often think they are shy, quiet, nice people who are not easily upset. The reality is that of the over-controlled personality, which may well lead to occasional outbursts of rage in appropriate situations.

So, what was Scripps's motive? Was it the lure of money that drove him to kill? Strangely, in view of his actions, many observers think that this was unlikely. He robbed his victims, but there was more to it than that, as Brian Williams, liaison officer for the Royal Canadian Mounted Police in Bangkok, said. 'You can rob without killing, and you can kill without cutting up the body into bits. This man went to such an extreme and I can only think that he relished what he was doing.'

Brian Williams may well be correct in his commonsense appraisal but, ultimately, it comes down to a common enough motive and, this I believe, boils down to financial gain.

Scripps was a cold, calculating killer, who had planned his MO almost to perfection. His butchery skills merely added to the clinically efficient way he disposed of the bodies. That he 'relished' the dismemberment is open to debate.

John Scripps was neither insane nor mad in the medical or legal sense. When he killed Gerard Lowe, in their hotel room in Singapore, he was deluding himself if he believed that the island Republic's system of justice would not hand down a death sentence to an Englishman. As an experienced traveller in South-East Asia, he must have known that some countries in the region have an unequivocal attitude to murder and drug-smuggling, crimes which carry a mandatory death sentence.

For their part, the Singapore authorities are tough on criminals. The Deputy Superintendent of Police, Chin Fook Leon, said to me during an interview, 'We impose the maximum sentence of death without concern for race, colour or creed. Break the penal code in Singapore,' he warned, 'and suffer the consequences.'

The deterrent value of the death sentence in Singapore is there for all to consider, if there is an intention to break the law. It is even printed on red-and-white notices, prominently posted around the city. Singaporeans argue that it is effectively the individual's own choice. Go against the law of the country and suffer the consequences, and this uncompromising attitude is always applied.

Five Thai men who entered Singapore illegally as labourers and were held as 'guests' of the Republic took it upon themselves to abuse their hosts by robbing construction sites between November 1991 and January 1993. In committing their crimes, they murdered a citizen of Myanmar and two Indian nationals.

Panya Marmontree (22), Prawit Yaoabutr (22), Manit Wangjaisuk (31), Panya Amphawa (29) and Prasong Bunsom (32) were sentenced to death on 16 January 1995. Their appeals against execution were dismissed on 10 July and they were duly hanged at Changi Prison on Friday 16 March 1996.

Thai Ambassador, His Excellency Adisak Panupong, told me, 'My countrymen were aware of the laws and punishments of

Singapore and, in breaking them, they also knew what the consequences might be. The decision was theirs to make.'

John Scripps had made visits to the Far East before he killed Gerard Lowe, and therefore knew and understood the law very well. He was aware of the risks of committing serious crime in both Singapore and Thailand, and of the consequences of being arrested and found guilty of drug-smuggling and committing murder. When he killed Gerard Lowe, he did so for financial profit and the Singapore authorities took the view that, by committing this murder on their soil, he merely validated his own execution. It is consistent with this outlook that he demonstrated, by his unlawful behaviour, that murder was permissible. As far as the Singapore authorities were concerned, those were *his* standards, and he was treated accordingly.

Consideration of punishment, whether it meant life in prison or execution, was also determined by John's own actions. It was not his victim, the police, the Singapore judicial system, the department of prisons, or the executioner, who initiated the sequence of events leading to his death by the judicial process. It was down to John Scripps himself. And if he had escaped the noose in Singapore, what would have been his fate in Thailand? It would have been execution by machine-gun.

Legislation in Thailand has now been extended to include imposition of the death penalty for offences other than murder. The Royal Act on Habit-Forming Drugs (1979) introduced an optional death penalty for the possession of more than 100g of heroin, while maintaining a mandatory death sentence for its production, import or export. Although Thailand is reluctant to implement the death penalty in respect of convicted Europeans, who usually receive commutations by Royal pardon, the number of people under sentence of death and the number of executions carried out on Europeans have been rising steadily.

It seems, therefore, that John was playing a lethal game, with his own life also at stake. Not only did he risk the death sentence, for international drug trafficking, he had committed two counts of aggravated homicide, which carries the mandatory death sentence in Thailand.

A final dimension to his recklessness was provided by Singapore Drugs Squad Officers who discovered a substantial amount of heroin in a safety deposit box he had rented in the city. This was his stash which, on its own, was enough to send him to prison for the rest of his life. It seems that he was doomed in any event.

This chapter is based on an exclusive interview between Christopher Berry-Dee and John Martin Scripps at Changi Prison, Singapore, in the week prior to his execution on 19 April 1996.

MICHAEL
BRUCE
ROSS

USA

'There was nothing they could have
said or done. They were dead as
soon as I saw them. I used them. I
abused them, then I killed them. I
treated them like so much garbage.
What more do you want me to
fucking say?'

MICHAEL ROSS IN AN INTERVIEW WITH
THE AUTHOR

Suddenly, there he was, Connecticut's only convicted serial killer, shuffling along, surrounded by three immaculately-dressed prison officers wearing starched shirts, knife-edge creased trousers, and spit-and-polished boots. He was handcuffed and shackled at the legs, his loose-fitting prison uniform covering a plumpish physique. Michael Ross stands around 5ft 10in, and weighs about 140lb. He appears bookish, with his spectacles perched high on the bridge of his nose, and is polite.

Michael has the intellect. He has a bright intelligence and, with an IQ of 150, became an Ivy League student at Cornell University. He has a fresh complexion, with a chubby face, a cheeky smile and mischievous eyes, giving the impression of a stereotypical 'All-American' homespun boy. At face value, Michael is very much the boy next door; the type a father might approve of his daughter dating. But, as all fathers know, appearances can be deceptive. In real life, he is a sexual sadist and serial murderer who has raped six precious daughters before killing them.

During the course of several interviews, for this book, he added to his murderous record by confessing, for the first time, to raping and killing two other girls, and having anal intercourse with the dead body of another.

* * *

Michael Ross was born in Brooklyn, Connecticut, on 26 July 1961, under the sign of Leo. He was the first of Daniel and Patricia Ross's four children, the others being Donna, Kenneth and Tina. The marriage was a stormy one, and Patricia, a borderline schizophrenic, who would, later, twice run away from her husband, never hid the fact that she was forced to get married because she became pregnant with Michael. From the outset, her baby was an unwanted child.

Family and friends have described Patricia as a woman who could be charming one minute, and cold and calculating the next. She had spent time in the state mental hospital at Norwich. A number of people who knew her had witnessed at first hand a volatile, manipulative woman who would take out her resentments on her family, especially Michael, whom she blamed for ruining her life.

Michael remembers his mother's mood swings, which all of the children feared. They couldn't understand how she could laugh after making them ill by feeding them bad meat. Or why she would ruin her two daughters' clothes with a box of dye. Spiteful, vicious and sadistic, Patricia tried to trick young Michael into shooting his pet dog, after convincing him that it was suffering, after a short illness. She even set his mattress on fire on the front lawn because she had caught him masturbating. So, by all accounts, Patricia was 'The Mother from Hell'.

Yet the four kids loved their mother, simply because she was their 'mom'. They grew to accept her mood swings, and learned to keep out of her way when she was angry. Like unwanted pets, which return even meagre scraps of affection with devotion and loyalty, the children had to love her just to survive.

Michael Ross explained this in an audiotaped interview, and the authenticity of his account has been verified by one of his sisters:

'We had what we called 'Mom drills'. The first person up in the morning would go downstairs while the rest of us kids would wait and be real quiet and listen to what type of reception we'd get from our mother. And, if we got one kind of reception, we'd know how to act. An' I'll give you an example. See, one day my sister, Tina, was setting the table, and, uh, there was six of us in the family, you know. So, she opened up the dishwasher to get six glasses, three in each hand. You know *how you do it. You know, the glasses clink together. My mother went off. She was screaming and yellin', so we knew that was a bad day coming. You just knew how she was but we loved her.'*

The Ross children had little time for fun and games, and they were even discouraged from having any friends, or participating in after-school activities. With these restrictions in place, they had bonded into a tight-knit group, for self-preservation and mutual support, although Michael was alienated because his brother and sisters erroneously believed that he was favoured as a 'mommy's boy'.

For his part, young Michael was very proud of his father, and the family egg farm business in Brooklyn, Connecticut. Eggs Inc would become the most important part of Michael's formative years. Indeed, by the age of ten, he had his own set of chores, which included wringing the necks of sick and deformed chicks. Michael was a hard worker, a mixed-up kid who desperately wanted to live up to his father's high expectations of him, while, at the same time, he was very much seeking the approval of his schizoid mother, and constantly vying for her rare affection. When asked if he was physically abused as a child, he had this to say:

'It's hard for me to tell you what was wrong with my family because I don't know anything different. That's how I was raised. I was beaten sometimes but I don't think that was it. It was more emotional abuse, an' like I mean with my dad when we were beaten, we would have to go out an' pick up a stick out of the garage where we had a wood pile. An' what you would do was to go out and you couldn't pick one that broke 'cos if it broke he'd get pretty mad. But, you didn't pick yourself a club. You know, you didn't want to get the hell

beaten outa you. An', so I had my own stick put away, hidden away in the back so that people coming in to get firewood wouldn't inadvertently take it. But, I mean there is something wrong there when a kid goes to the wood house and picks up his stick; his own special stick for getting beaten. And, he hides it so no one accidentally takes it. And, you know if you got beat you didn't scream because my father just got madder.'

Michael loved his parents despite the physical and psychological abuse they handed out, but the effects of such treatment on the developing mind are often irreparable unless drastic counter-measures are taken to remedy the problems.

Many psychiatrists and psychologists now generally agree that if contact and interaction with others in a peer group are restricted during the early stages of infant development, the ability to interact successfully at a later stage in life is retarded. That is, the infant and child must experience love and feel valued, or the limbic nuclei in the brain will not develop normally and gross mental abnormalities may result. Children will lose the ability to form emotional attachments with others, or, any attachment that does come about may only be superficial, and this abnormality may last for the rest of their lives.

Michael Ross certainly had this problem, and it is not surprising to learn that, during an FBI study of serial sexual murderers, 53 per cent of the subjects' families had a history of psychiatric problems, 42 per cent of the subjects had been subjected to physical abuse, and 74 per cent had a psychological abuse history.

* * *

In September 1977, after a period of schooling, at the ironically named Killingly High School, Michael's future looked decidedly bright as he drove his car on to the Cornell University campus in Ithaca, New York. He had overcome long odds, and was justifiably proud of himself, as only 10 per cent of Killingly High's vocational agricultural (vo-ag) students went on to college. Fewer still attended Ivy League schools.

At Cornell, Ross enrolled as an Animal-Science major, and he started a course of study that would well suit his ambition to become the third generation to run the family poultry business. This was an obsession with Michael and, for a time, his fraternity brothers even called him 'The Egg King'.

Michael joined AgPAC, the Agricultural Student Union Council, and attended the Collegiate Future Farmers of America. He was a student teacher, counsellor, researcher teaching assistant, and a study group leader around this time. Alpha Zeta, one of the two campus fraternities dedicated to agricultural activity, recruited Ross, and he pledged to them in 1977. He lived in the fraternity house, throughout his sophomore and junior years, with his brothers, who were mostly young men, with small-town farming backgrounds.

Since his incarceration for serial murder, a number of Michael's old Cornell friends have said that he enjoyed the house, its social life, and the chance to share common interests. His classmates, though, also recall that Michael was a loner, aloof and somewhat arrogant at times.

The student body of Cornell was three times larger than the entire population of his hometown of Brooklyn, and the campus became a large playground for Michael Ross. Now free from his mother's unpredictable influence, he could do whatever he wanted, without fear of reprisal. He literally went crazy with all the fun he was having, plunging headlong into the party life to the extent that he started taking Ritalin three times a day to control his hyperactivity. He would continue to use this drug for a further six years. He drank heavily and he started to experiment with sex, often sleeping with different girls four nights a week.

During his first junior year at Cornell, Michael met his first true love, a pretty girl called Connie Young. They met at a party, and he walked her home through the moonlight, and they kissed as they watched a team of divers swimming in the shimmering silver water of Beebe Lake. They strolled to the statues of the college's founding fathers, and he explained how they were supposed to move together and shake hands when a virgin passed between them. On this occasion, the statues apparently did not move, for 'Connie was hotter than a kitchen stove', Michael recalled.

Connie remembers Michael as a 'go-getter', and a guy who always liked to be 'the centre of attention'. At first she accommodated this behaviour because he seemed a worthwhile prospect. She certainly overlooked his arrogance and constant boasting about his father's egg farm. In Connie's eyes, he was handsome, if just a little nerdy. He was articulate, took her dancing and dined her out. She remembers that he always had money when he needed it and, for his part, he enjoyed taking her to places to show her off. To everyone who knew them, they seemed the perfect couple, and most were thrilled when they became engaged to be married.

For a short period, Connie shared his bed, and then the arguments started. Michael's fraternity brothers threw him out of the house because he was breaking the rules by sharing his room with a female. As a result of this, the couple rented a small apartment where Michael withdrew into himself. The schooling pressure and the demands made by the close relationship with Connie had started to take their effect. Added to this were his parents' escalating marital problems, and these were clouding his judgement over the future, as home issues were never far from his mind.

Connie's distress over her lover's change of attitude came to a head when he started to miss classes. She was a dedicated student, trying to cram four years of education into three, but Michael Ross seemed to have lost interest, and he started to hang around their apartment all day, watching television and reading pornographic magazines. He changed his major, to Agricultural Economics, and his grades plummeted. He became bone idle, expecting Connie to do all the housework and cooking and, despite the fact that she was exhausted after studying, he demanded sex with her at least four times a day.

Initially, Connie complied with Michael's demands, for fear of rejection. She loved him deeply, and even allowed him to have rough sex with her, although it hurt her badly. Then, as the day-to-day events became even more unpleasant, she now started to wonder if marrying Michael was such a good idea at all. He was, she now believed, sex mad, and getting worse. With his graduation approaching in the spring of 1981, Michael could not face the prospect of leaving Connie behind at Cornell, and he became even more restless and agitated, withdrawing for much longer periods into a fantasy dream world of his own.

Even as a pre-teen, he had experienced constant fantasies about women when he would take them to what he called 'a special, underground place', where he hid them, and kept them so that they could fall in love with him. From juvenile criminal records, it is known that, at the age of 15, he molested several neighbourhood girls. Now an adult, Michael's fantasies grew more sexually extreme and progressively more violent. During these fantasies, he says that he was always the assailant and, by the time of his graduation, Connie had joined his faceless dream victims. He terrorised his fantasy girls and humiliated them by forcing them to undress and drop to their knees in front of him. Michael gained enormous sexual pleasure and relief from raping his fantasy victims. He savoured the sense of domination that accompanied their fear, and he reasoned that he had control over real women, too, even though these bizarre thoughts were still locked away inside his mind.

Whatever dreadful thought patterns were developing inside Michael's head during that period in his life, it seemed that there was a meeting between his distorted subconscious thinking and the bland reality of everyday life. This is where the two roads met, for not only did Ross overlay the beautiful face of Connie on to his fantasy victims, his demands for kinkier sex from her began to spiral out of all control. Added to this, he masturbated himself raw. Although he did not know it, he was suffering from 'satyriasis', an abnormally intense and persistent desire in a man for sexual intercourse. In women, the compulsion is called 'nymphomania'.

More and more, Michael found himself wandering aimlessly around the campus. He became titillated by stalking female co-eds, staying just far enough behind them to remain undetected. He explained, 'This turned me on so much I always had a hard on.' To release this almost uncontrollable compulsion, he had to masturbate ever more frequently, or else tip right over the edge, and act out his fantasies in reality.

Michael Ross crossed that threshold in April 1981, when he found himself running up behind a co-ed, grabbing her and dragging her into a small copse where he forced her to act out his fantasy of stripping naked before him and giving him oral sex. After he ejaculated, he ran off into the night, swearing to himself that he would never do such a terrible thing again.

Just three nights later, he was revisited by the same uncontrollable demons and, overcome with sexual compulsion, he attacked a second girl. During this assault, he slipped a rope around the student's neck, enjoying the heightened power this form of restraint bestowed on him. The terrified co-ed was like an animal he could control with a quick tug of his hand. Fortunately, someone approached the scene before he raped her and he fled into the shadows, his sexual frustrations still boiling inside him.

Michael has said that he firmly believed that these outrageous acts would cease after he left Cornell, and that he prayed that he could last out the final month without attacking anyone else. At the same time, he says he also felt cheated of the ultimate sexual satisfaction, which had been denied him during the previous attacks. Weighing up the pros and cons on his mental balance sheet, he said he was compelled to satisfy himself fully, at least once before he graduated, but he promised himself that this would have to be the final attack, after which he would never hurt a woman again.

* * *

On Tuesday, 12 May 1981, Ross stalked a pretty 25-year-old student called Dzung Ngoc Tu. He followed the delicate young woman from her class, and raped her in a secluded area of the campus. During the attack, she recognised her assailant and, when she told him this, she effectively signed her death warrant. To avoid arrest, Michael now had no option other than to kill her, so he strangled her before throwing the body over a bridge and into Beebe Lake.

A chilling fact of this murder was that, during the autopsy, the medical examiner determined that the cause of death was by drowning, indicating that Dzung had been alive when she plunged into the icy water. Although Ross has always been suspected of committing this murder, he has never allowed himself to be interviewed by the police. The case was finally cleared up when he admitted to the murder, during one of the interviews which form the basis of this chapter.

* * *

Michael believed that his parents attended his graduation ceremony only for appearance's sake and he decided, from that moment, not to return to the family farm. By a stroke of good fortune, despite his poor grades, he managed to land an enviable job in June 1981 with Cargill Inc, of Minnetonka, on the outskirts of Minneapolis.

Cargill is an international agricultural business best known for grain sales, and Ross was employed at one of the company's more modest operations, in Louisburg, a country town about 30 miles north-east of Raleigh, North Carolina. As a production-management trainee in the poultry products division, Michael was taught how to supervise the care and management of a quarter of a million laying hens. It was a job well suited to him and, by all accounts, his career prospects with Cargill were excellent.

During the transitional period between graduation and full-time employment, Michael tried to convince Connie to transfer to the North Carolina University, where, he suggested, she could complete her studies. Over the preceding months, their relationship had so deteriorated that he was now paranoid about the separation and feared that she would soon be gone for good. Nevertheless, he was secretly hopeful they would marry one day. Connie had ideas of her own, and marriage was no longer one of them; besides, she was now dating someone else.

Then a bomb dropped on Michael's world when he learned over the phone that his mother and father had separated for the third time, with Mr Ross leaving the family home and business to its own devices. Patricia flew to Louisburg, and Michael was pleased, if not surprised, to see his mother so quickly after learning the bad news. Mistakenly, Michael thought this visit was a sign that his relationship with his parents might improve. At the very least, he wanted to believe that his mother could keep the egg farm going until he returned home to take charge, if only for his father's sake. This thought was the furthest thing from Mrs Ross's devious mind, for she had, in fact, come to visit her son for one reason only. She needed Michael to sign over his shares in

Eggs Inc so that she could dispose of the company, while becoming rich into the bargain.

Having been duped into signing the share transfer, and soon after learning of the true reason behind his mother's impromptu visit, Michael felt that he had betrayed not only his father but himself.

Then life was made even worse when Connie flew to North Carolina with more bad news. For her, the trip was a short one. She explained that she didn't like Michael's parents, and even if he did end up running the egg business, this wasn't exactly her idea of a future. The finality of the relationship hit home on Tuesday, 25 August 1981 when, at Raleigh Durham airport, the couple fell into each other's arms, sobbing their farewells. Michael could not bring himself to believe that his relationship with Connie was finished, so he was understandably distraught as he drove back down Highway 401 to Louisburg.

At around 6.30pm, he passed through the small town of Rolesville where he spotted a young woman pushing her seven-month-old child, in a buggy, along Main Street. Within milliseconds, his uncontrollable sexual urges surfaced again and, after parking his car, Ross ran up to the woman and offered to carry her groceries.

Rolesville was a friendly place, with just 353 residents, and violent crime was virtually unknown, until Ross drove down Main Street. The young mother, used to such a secure environment, did not hesitate when this helpful and decent young man approached her. She thanked Ross for his offer and passed over the heavy bags. They walked to her home several blocks away and, as they entered the backyard, Ross suddenly dropped the bags, whipped off his leather belt, and threw it over the woman's head. He dragged her into a nearby soya bean field, while threatening to smash the baby's head against a tree if it didn't stop crying.

This innocent woman now became a repository for the months of Ross's pent-up anger and sexual frustrations. He smashed his fists into her face, and he choked her with the belt, forcing her to her knees to beg for mercy. Then, with his hands tightly clasped around her neck, he ejaculated.

After regaining his breath, Ross sat back on the ground with his victim squirming around in front of him. Somehow he felt cheated, for he had wanted to satisfy his perversions by ejaculating as she died, not beforehand. Enraged, acting like a wild animal, he ripped off the woman's clothes, beating her again and again before strangling her with his bare hands while the baby screamed close by. And, as suddenly as he had appeared, Michael Ross vanished. It was over an hour before the woman regained consciousness. Painfully, she crawled across the street to a neighbour who summoned the local police chief, Nelson S Ross. Officers arrived almost immediately and roadblocks were set up to the county line, but Michael was long gone. He was not charged with this offence until he was arrested in Connecticut, three years later.

When asked if he recalled the Rolesville attack, Michael said, 'I don't really remember her, or any of my victims for that matter. It's like an old, black and white movie; a collage of strange faces, that's all. Nope, I couldn't remember this woman if you had showed me her photograph the next day. There was nothing she, or any of them, could have done when I zeroed in on them. They were dead. All over. That this one lived ain't got nothing to do with me. That she lived? Well, that was purely an act of God.'

When I asked him if the Rolesville victim fought back, and tried to escape, Ross said, 'Nothing. She could have got away or something, but it never happened. I can't remember. I can't remember any kind of struggling with her or anything like that. I can't remember, uh, any kind of fighting at all. I do recall, with the Rolesville victim, saying that I would smash the baby's head into a tree or a wall. So, I would imagine I probably said things equally horrible to, uh, the other ones that would make them stop and think not to do anything.'

Ross simply carried on his daily existence as if nothing untoward had happened at Rolesville. Then, on Tuesday, 17 September 1981, his parents filed divorce papers at the Windham County Superior Court. A week later, Michael's employer, Cargill, sent him on a field trip to Illinois, where he would visit the Chicago Commodities Exchange. Before this trip was over, Ross would be arrested for the first time.

He decided on Monday, 28 September, to look over the Cargill operation in La Salle, which is about 11 miles south-west of Chicago. He rented a car at Chicago's O'Hare International Airport, and headed west across the flat, central Illinois farm country. Just before 11.00pm, an attractive 16-year-old La Salle girl was walking along a road that threaded through a cluster of houses, when she noticed a car slowly creeping past her. She had noted the vehicle several times beforehand, and she was now becoming frightened for her safety.

Without warning, the teenager was suddenly grabbed from behind and a handkerchief was stuffed into her mouth. She was dragged into nearby woods where the attacker wrapped a belt around her neck and asked her for money. She gave him the 22 cents she had and, when he loosened his belt, she screamed. She was now moments from a terrifying rape when salvation arrived. A woman living nearby, had just switched off her television, with the intention of having an early night when she heard a noise that made her blood chill. Opening her kitchen window, she heard a gurgling sound and rustling noises in nearby bushes, so she called the police. Luck was now on the teenager's side, even more so because a patrol car was only 100 yards away, and it arrived at the scene in a flash. When Ross saw the beams of police torches illuminating the woods, he hurried back to his car but, this time, his luck deserted him.

Sergeant Lewis of the La Salle Police explained how Ross got himself arrested. 'What happened is, when we took the girl home, Ross had his car parked on the same street she lived on. And, on the way home, she saw the car, and said, "That's the car, that's the car." And, so pretty soon we were looking at the car, and he comes up and says, 'What's the problem?" '

After Michael's arrest, for 'unlawful restraint', Sergeant Lewis said that he was puzzled by the contradiction, between Ross's demeanour, and what he had done.

'He was real humble,' Lewis recalled. 'He wouldn't look you in the eyes when you talked with him. He was a very educated and a talented kid. He didn't appear to be the kind of guy who would go out to other towns and do this kind of stuff. He more or less kept his mouth shut, and he was subdued and spiritless when we took him in.'

The downside of the La Salle attack was that Ross was fined $500 after pleading guilty and on Tuesday, 8 October he was fired from his job. On the upside, and with no alternative, he returned to Brooklyn where he attempted a reconciliation with Connie. Indeed, he was very pleased when she invited him to spend Christmas with her at her parents' home in Vermont. He was even more delighted that they had also been invited to share the New Year with his mother in Brooklyn.

Unfortunately, the visit to Mrs Ross was an unmitigated disaster. His mother could not stand the sight of such a beautiful young woman in her house, and Michael was very upset by the fact that his father had been reduced to living in a run-down shed nearby. The hoped-for rekindling of his relationship with Connie failed, for the second time, and she went off to Ithaca, New York, to visit a 'friend'. This was the catalyst that precipitated Ross into rape and murder again.

* * *

Seventeen-year-old Tammy Lee Williams lived with her family on Prince Hill Road, Brooklyn, which was only a mile or so from the Ross's egg farm. That Christmas, among the gifts from her parents, she received a pocketbook. A free-spirited young woman, who had quit high school, she came and went as she pleased, and it wasn't unusual for her walk along Route 6 to visit her boyfriend who lived in Danielson, about three miles away.

At 10.15am, on Monday, 4 January 1982, Tammy left her boyfriend's apartment and started to walk home, after first promising him that she would telephone him to let him know that she had arrived safely. She did not fulfil this promise because she encountered Michael Ross on her journey. He was surprised to see the young woman walking along a busy road on such a bitterly cold day. Seizing the moment, which distinguishes the opportunist killer, he parked his car and ran up to Tammy offering her a lift. When she declined, he dragged her screaming and struggling into nearby woods, where he forced her to strip and get to her knees. He raped and strangled her before hiding the body, under a pile of rocks and brush, in a swamp. He said it took him all of eight minutes to throttle her to death, because he kept getting cramps in his hands. Each time this happened, he had to release his grip and massage his fingers before finally throttling the life out of her.

Tammy's father reported his daughter missing the next day and, on 6 January, a motorist found Tammy's pocketbook, lying along Route 6, at the junction of Brickyard Road. Michael Ross explained that he had thrown the item out of his car moments before arriving back at his mother's place, shortly after the murder.

On Saturday, 30 June 1984, he guided police officers to the decomposed corpse of Tammy Williams, and said later that she had recognised him and that she pretended to enjoy the violent rape to avoid being killed. He also said that he returned to the corpse several times, during the weeks following the murder, in order to masturbate over the body.

During January and February, 1982, Ross's thoughts continually returned to Connie. Acting on impulse, he decided to drive to Ithaca to visit her, without prior warning of his intentions. On arrival, he found Connie in bed with another man. He stormed out in a rage and headed south in search of a victim to kill.

* * *

May Day fell on a Monday, in 1982, and Paula Perrera left Valley Central High School early because she didn't feel well. With no money for a bus fare, she started hitch-hiking, and she was last seen alive near the Montgomery Auto Shop, on Route 211, during the early afternoon. Paula's mother, Christine Canavan, reported her 16-year-old missing, to the Crystal Run Police, later that day.

Although Ross has always been the prime suspect in the Perrera killing, there has never been enough evidence available to charge him with her murder, a situation exacerbated by the fact that Ross has refused to be interviewed by the police investigators. This changed when Ross was subsequently interviewed in prison as part of the research for this book. Confronted by me with police documents and a newspaper article, Ross made a full confession on videotape, giving details of the murder that only Paula's killer could have known. The case is now classified as solved.

He said that he had seen her walking along Route 211, and had offered her a ride home. At a spot near a marshy wooded area, and close to a rest stop, he pulled over and raped his victim before strangling her. He hid the body near a low stone wall, and then drove home. His confession closed the file on this murder enquiry.

Asked during the interview what Paula had been wearing, he said he could not recall the details and tossed the documents to the floor, saying, 'Well, it's just another murder, isn't it?'

* * *

Ross started work at Croton Egg Farms on Friday, 5 March 1982. The world's largest poultry operation, based in the small town of Croton, north-east of Columbus, Ohio, hired him as a co-supervisor for 30 employees. He was also responsible for 14 hen houses and over one million birds.

A fellow supervisor, Donald Harvey, remembered Ross, saying, 'He was a disaster in the job, and we were planning to fire the guy pretty soon. He was very bossy. And he just didn't relate to you in giving an order. He just didn't know how to come across. He wanted everyone to know that his education was much higher than theirs, and they were hourly workers and high school drop-outs.'

On Sunday, 25 April 1982, Ross spotted Susan Aldrich in a laundromat in Johnstown, a town close to Croton, and followed her home. She was completely unaware that she was being stalked and he was completely unaware that she was an off-duty police officer. He knocked on her door and told her that his car had broken down and asked if he could use her telephone. As soon as Susan turned her back, he reached over her shoulder, cupped his hand over her mouth to prevent her screaming, and forced her to the floor. She struggled, and managed to shout out, saying that her husband was a policeman, and that he would be home at any moment. After giving her a severe beating, Ross ran back to his car, ripped a parking ticket from the windscreen and drove off.

Ross's car had been parked close to the laundromat, and it was there that he got the ticket. Police also found a witness who saw him running from the direction of Susan Aldrich's home towards his vehicle, so they put two and two together and traced the owner through the Vehicle Licensing Office. In an act of poetic justice, it was Susan's husband who arrested her attacker.

Ross was sacked from Croton Egg Farms on 3 May, and bailed to his mother's home before sentencing. While there, he visited a psychiatrist, at the Learning Clinic in Brooklyn. He was trying to win a little sympathy from the doctor, who might have influence with the Ohio court.

The following month was another disaster for Michael Ross, for, although he had returned a number of photographs to Connie, she still had his engagement ring and he wanted it back. However, the day before he turned up to collect it, she set off across country to marry her new boyfriend. When Ross learned of this, he went crazy with anger. But, if that slap across the face was hard to take, a family development enraged him even further.

Financially, his mother's divorce had paid off handsomely. When Patricia flaunted her new lover before speeding off in her flashy new Cadillac, it was too much for Michael. These emotional setbacks coming so close together were sufficient to set him off on the murder trail again.

* * *

The last time anyone could recollect seeing 23-year-old Debra Smith Taylor alive was around midnight on Tuesday, 15 June 1982. She was driving home with her husband when their car ran out of gas, on Highway 6, near Hampton, just eight miles east of Mrs Ross's home. A state trooper came across the stationary car, and drove the couple to a service station in Danielson, where the boyfriend of one of Ross's earlier victims, Tammy Williams, had lived. The trooper recalled that the Taylors were arguing, and that Debra was so annoyed that she said that she would find her own way home. After leaving her husband to his own devices, she walked across Danielson Town Green, to the bandstand, where she gratefully accepted the offer of a ride home from a bespectacled young man who had walked up and spoken to her.

Two hunters discovered the skeleton of Debra Taylor on Saturday, 30 October, in one of the large tracts of woodland east of Route 169, in Canterbury. The spot was less than ten miles from the Ross's farm. The body was so decomposed that identification was only possible by means of dental records and items of jewellery.

* * *

During the first week of August 1982, Ross returned to Ohio for sentencing over the assault he had committed four months previously. The psychiatrist who had examined him earlier said that Michael was an 'over-achiever', and had 'too much spare time on his hands'. In his report, the psychiatrist also suggested that he should find a hobby, such as learning how to fly an aeroplane. The judge nevertheless packed Ross off to the Licking County Jail, where he would serve a six-month jail term for the assault on Susan Aldrich. He was ordered to pay a $1,000 fine. Daniel collected his son from prison on Wednesday, 22 December, drove him back to Connecticut, and offered him a place to stay.

Michael Ross had misrepresented himself when he applied for work at Croton Egg Farms by declaring that he had never been in trouble with the police, and he did exactly the same thing again in May 1983, when he applied for a job with the Prudential Insurance Company of America. He would become one of the 40 agents selling health, life, automotive, property, casualty insurance and securities, from the company's office in Norwich, Connecticut. With steady money in his pocket, Ross rented an apartment at 58 North Main Street, in Jewett City. He settled in, and his landlady remembers him as a decent, smart and extremely affable young man, whom she enjoyed having around her large, Victorian-style house.

Ross's female work colleagues also took an immediate liking to him. They thought of him as sweet, and inexperienced in romance. He dated when the opportunity arose, and when he met recently-divorced Debbie Wallace, while out canvassing for business, he reasoned that his past problems were well behind him.

During this relationship, Ross says he spent a great deal of time masturbating, fantasising and stalking women. Some he followed at random. With others he set out to learn their daily schedules. He slipped into apartments, just to watch women undress and get into bed. And he raped once during this time, allowing to his victim to run away.

Although he was often out until all hours of the morning, Debbie Wallace was totally ignorant of Michael's perverted behaviour. She believed that he would make a good father for her three children; however, like Connie, Debbie was stubborn, independent and strong-willed. She was a spitfire, full of energy, and sex with Michael was excellent. Their relationship was volatile, too, and their frequent arguments often ended in physical violence. During Thanksgiving 1983, the couple had a furious fight over dinner arrangements.

From the outset, Patricia Ross had never liked Connie, and she didn't approve of Debbie either, so she invited her son for a meal but refused to extend the invitation to Debbie. Ross did not know what to do. He felt torn between the two women, so he and Debbie fought and the outcome was that he spent the holiday alone.

Around the time Ross was learning the insurance business – giving a new meaning to the term 'The Man from the Pru' – 19-year-old Robin Dawn Stavinsky was moving from Columbia to Norwich, where she hoped to find a job that paid enough that would allow her to go to college.

In August 1983, she took a job as a switchboard operator at DPM Enterprises. At 9.30pm on Wednesday, 16 November 1983, she disappeared after apparently arguing with her boss. Although it was cold and dark, Robin refused a ride from a workmate and, in what proved to be a fateful mistake, decided to walk to her boyfriend's house.

That evening, Ross was driving along Route 52 between New London and Norwich, when he saw Robin storming along the roadside. He stopped, climbed out of his car and approached her with the offer of a lift. When she rebuffed him, he became angry and dragged her struggling into a patch of dense woodland just a few hundred yards from the office of the Connecticut State Police Major Crime Squad. Ross had started to strangle Robin as soon as he grabbed her, and by the time he was ready to rape the young woman, she was barely conscious. Ross recalled that by now he was no longer excited by the idea of sex, and his satisfaction came about only from the act of killing, and by reliving the moment, occasionally driving by the murder scene and masturbating, until the body was discovered eight days later.

A jogger, running through the grounds of the Uncas-on-Thames Hospital in Norwich, found the partially-clothed corpse of Robin Stavinsky under a pile of leaves. Police retrieved the remainder of the dead woman's clothing, from a river, after Ross's arrest.

The brutal murder of Robin Stavinsky was to prove a dreadful watershed in Ross's killing career. Previously, he had murdered out of the fear of recognition if his victims survived. However, he had always hoped that one day he would achieve his ultimate sexual thrill, that of ejaculation as his victim's death supervened. So far, the murders had provided him with only part-realisation of this fantasy. The overwhelming emotions, topped up with feelings of power, domination and the act of murder were there, but he reasoned that Robin Stavinsky had short-changed him. She had provided him with none of the sickening criteria because she had collapsed limp and helpless as he dragged her into the scrub. Nevertheless, he strangled her and raped her after death. He said later, 'I was surprised, ya know. It was a pretty good thrill, but not the best.'

* * *

Two more young women, both 14, disappeared in eastern Connecticut on Easter Sunday 1984. Leslie Shelley and April Brunais, inseparable friends and neighbours in Griswold, had decided to walk into Jewett City. Both girls were aware that their parents would not permit them to walk back during the hours of darkness, so each said that the other's parents had agreed to drive them home. It was this childish deception that would cost them their lives.

As darkness fell, the girls phoned their homes; both were ordered to walk back as punishment. At 10.30pm, when neither girl had returned, their distraught parents called the police who made the initial mistake of listing the youngsters as 'runaways'.

The exact time Ross stopped and offered the girls a lift is unknown. It is known, however, that April, who was the more assertive of the two, climbed into the front passenger seat, while the petite and fragile Leslie sat behind. Both were understandably startled when Ross drove right past the end of their street, and despite their protests that he had missed their turning, he wouldn't stop. April pulled out a small pocketknife, with which to threaten their abductor, but Ross easily disarmed her. Driving east out on Highway 138, he headed for Voluntown, and the nearby Beach Pond, a vast expanse of water with a dam holding back the Pachaus River, which separates the states of Rhode Island and Connecticut.

Parking up at a still undetermined location, Ross tore off April's jeans, cutting them into strips which he used to bind his victims' hands and feet. He shut Leslie into the trunk of his car, and then dragged April a few yards and forced her to her knees. There can be no doubt that the terrified Leslie overheard her friend arguing with Ross. April put up a spirited fight for her life before he raped and strangled her to death.

Ross now turned his attention to Leslie. He said later that the girl made a great impact on him.

'She [*Leslie Shelley*] was delicate with wispy blonde hair,' he stated. 'She was calm as I talked to her in the car. I told her I didn't want to kill her, and she cried when she found out that her friend was already dead. Yes, I suppose she started shaking and appeared resigned to her fate when I rolled her over. This is the murder that bothers me. I can't remember how I strangled her, but her death was the most real and hardest to deny. With the others, it was like someone else did it, and I watched from afar through a fog of unreality. This was real but somehow not real. It was fantasy but not really fantasy. Her death? Leslie? It wasn't someone else and for the first time I saw it was me. I watched myself do those things and I couldn't stop it. It was like an invisible barrier was between us. I didn't want to kill her.'

At this point during his interview with me, Ross showed the first signs of stress and remorse. He stopped talking, lowered his head, and sucked in a lungful of stale prison air. When he resumed his sickening account of the murder of Leslie Shelley, there were crocodile tears in his eyes:

'I couldn't do anything but watch as I murdered her, and you want to know something outrageous? Well, I cried afterwards. You know something else? Well, ah, I don't know but nobody knows this. Well, I wanted to have sex with her straight after I raped and killed April, but I couldn't get it up. So, I had to sit back with Leslie for an hour, just talkin' an' stuff. Then, because she started crying, saying that she would be in trouble for being late home, I had to kill her. But, I anally raped her, after death, to release the tension. You see, nobody has been told this before.'

Then he smiled sheepishly before adding, 'You know, they call me a serial killer, right? Well, I've only killed eight women. Big deal. There are a lot more guys you could meet and they've killed dozens more than me. An' in that context, I'm a nice guy. I'm such a nice guy really.'

With that, he burst into an uncontrollable fit of laughter, before explaining that he had dumped the bodies of April and Leslie at another location near Beach Pond, occasionally revisiting the site to masturbate over their remains.

'I'd just sit there, just to look at their decomposing bodies. Like my childhood fantasies, they were there for me and they gave me pleasure when I needed it.'

Ross took police to the bodies of April Brunais and Lesley Shelley shortly after his arrest on Tuesday, 28 June 1984, although the precise location of the murder scene was never established. This was put down as an 'oversight' by the Connecticut State Police, and later proved in court to be a deliberate attempt by them to avoid a jurisdictional boundary dispute with the Rhode Island law enforcement agencies who had to foot the bill for this murder enquiry.

* * *

Ross was now nearing the end of his run, he was mentally out of control, and his work at the Prudential Insurance Company was suffering as a result. Faced with the prospect of dismissal, as he was failing to bring in new business, Michael was also coping with his turbulent relationship with Debbie Wallace which had taken a more active turn. Debbie's father had died while she and Michael were on vacation and, after the funeral, on the return journey home, they had argued. A major rift followed and, once again, he felt alone and rejected.

* * *

For 17-year-old Wendy Baribeault, Friday, 15 June 1984 was the final day of examinations at Norwich Free Academy where she was a junior student. She stopped at her mother's home after studies before catching a bus back to Jewett City to visit a convenience store. It was a fine afternoon, so she decided to walk back and, at around 4.30pm, she was seen, by a passing motorist, walking along the fairly busy Route 12. But she was not alone, for other witnesses later came forward to say that she was being followed rapidly by a man on foot. He was about 6ft tall, white, clean-shaven, of medium build and had dark hair. Other witnesses saw this man get out of a blue, compact car with a rear window wiper, and they recalled that he walked briskly off in the direction of the young woman who answered Wendy's description.

When Wendy failed to return home, her mother reported her missing the following day. Hundreds of police and local residents launched a search of the immediate area, and, two days later, her body was found by a fireman. The corpse was in dense woods and hidden in an ancient stone wall just a quarter-of-a-mile from her home. She had been raped and strangled.

Ross explained later that he had intended to go to work that day, but had cut himself while shaving, and blood seeped on to the collar of his only clean shirt. After phoning in with the excuse that he was ill, he dressed himself in smart, casual clothes, and hung around his apartment, reading pornographic material and masturbating. At around 2.00pm, he went for a drive, and later on he saw Wendy walking along the road towards her home.

After swinging his car around and parking up at the entrance of a gravel track, he dashed across the road and asked Wendy if she would like to go to a barbecue that night. When she turned him down, Ross her dragged into a clearing in nearby woods, where he rolled her over on to her stomach before strangling her. He ejaculated almost immediately, so he throttled her again. She struggled and kicked, and her body twitched. Michael had cramp in his hands as he fought to strangle the life out of his victim. When he stopped to massage his fingers, she heaved and squirmed under him until re-applied his grip. Finally, a kick of her legs told him she was dead.

* * *

Known for disarming suspects, using his boyish smile and supportive manner, State Police Detective Mike Malchik has used his investigative skills to crack even the toughest of homicide enquiries, including 40 or more which were considered 'unsolvable' by his colleagues. A legendry figure in Connecticut, the fair, blue-eyed cop often worked alone and unpaid on these jobs, such was his dedication to law enforcement. The case of Wendy Baribeault was no exception.

Mike had already found solid links between the murders of Debra Taylor and Tammy Williams, and when he placed Robin Stavinsky and Wendy Baribeault into the equation, he knew he was looking for a sexual psychopath and serial killer who would not stop murdering until he was arrested and brought to justice.

Mike Malchik's experience in homicide cases was such that he did not need to consult the FBI for advice, but, to confirm his belief, he spoke to a colleague at the National Centre for the Analysis of Violent Crime in Quantico, Virginia. Malchik already knew what type of suspect he was looking for. He would be a young, dark-haired Caucasian male in his late twenties or early thirties. He would be of the 'white-collar' type, who worked in

Norwich yet lived further south, and this man would frequently travel along Route 12 between his place of work and his home. Griswold was a good bet for the suspect's locus and now there was the extra bonus of knowing that the man drove a blue, foreign make of sedan car.

Using what Mike calls 'basic common sense', he reasoned that whoever had murdered Wendy Baribeault would want to flee the crime scene and get home as quickly as possible, so he reasoned that his target was a local man. He called the Vehicle Licensing Department and asked them for a print-out of all vehicles, and their owners, in the locality. For this service, the VLD charged the police department \$12, which proved to be a cheap investigative tool. When the list rolled out of his fax machine, Malchik started looking for a blue, foreign make of car. At number 27 on the list was the vehicle owned by one Michael Bruce Ross who lived in Jewett City.

Ross seemed intrigued when Malchik arrived on his doorstep on Thursday, 28 June, to question him. He invited the detective in for a cup of coffee and enjoyed the attention of the police. For his part, Mike actually felt that the personable young Ross could not have been a serial killer. As he was about to leave to rejoin his colleague, Detective Frank Griffen, outside in their car, Malchik was asked a question. Ross wondered if such a murderer would be declared insane, and escape the electric chair, if he was convicted? It was such a pointed question that it prompted Malchik to return to Ross's sitting room.

The sleuth knew that the description of a blue car didn't exactly match that of Ross's vehicle, which was parked outside. The cop was looking for a hatchback with rear wipers and, while Ross certainly had a blue Toyota, it was a sedan and had no rear wiper blades. After a few more minutes of general conversation, Malchik got up to leave, for the second time. He had only walked a few yards before a gut instinct prompted him to turn around and ask Ross a question of his own.

In the manner of television actor, Peter Falk, acting out his role as Columbo, Mike asked, 'What were your movements on Friday, 15 June, the day Miss Baribeault went missing?'

Amazingly, thought Malchik, Ross immediately reeled off his movements for that day almost to the minute, with the exception of the hour encompassing 4.30pm. This was the time when witnesses had seen Wendy walking along the road, with Ross following her. Malchik thought it remarkable that anyone could recall his or her exact whereabouts, along with solid timings, two weeks after an event, so he reckoned that 15 June must have been a special day for Ross. He then asked him what he had been doing on the two days either side of this crucial date. Ross couldn't remember a thing and the detective was stunned, for the implication was now obvious. Ross had tried to alibi himself for the day of the murder, and in doing so had proved himself too clever for his own good.

Malchik then asked his suspect to accompany him to the nearby murder incident room, which had been set up in the Lisbon Town Hall. Ross thought that a ride in an unmarked police car would be 'fun', so he changed into a white, short-sleeved shirt, and dark, lightweight slacks for the ten-minute journey, the very same clothes that he had worn when he killed Wendy Baribeault.

Once he was seated in the police interview room, Ross was soon rambling about his life to the amiable cop. By now, Malchik was privately convinced that he had a serial killer sitting in front of him. But in the bustling confines of the command post, obtaining a full confession was another matter entirely. At one point, just as Ross was about to make some serious admissions, a cleaner burst into the room and started to mop the floor. This unexpected intrusion broke the spell and Malchik had to begin coaxing his suspect again.

Suddenly, Ross asked: 'Mike, do you think I killed Wendy?'

Malchik said that he believed so, and with that, Ross admitted 11 sexual assaults and 6 murders.

Recalling that first meeting, during a subsequent prison interview, Ross said, 'I remember the detective coming to the door. He was looking for a blue hatchback with wipers, and I didn't have a blue hatchback. I had a blue sedan with no wipers. And, uh, he was getting ready to leave, and I told him something. I don't remember exactly what I said, but something that made him pause. And he said he had better ask me a few more questions and then afterwards he was getting ready to go. An' I said something else, so I guess I didn't really want him to leave.'

Remembering the interview with Mike Malchik, Ross explained, 'You know, it's not exactly the easiest thing in the world to do. You know, 'Hello, Mr Police Officer, I killed a load of people.' You know, it was hard for me. If you actually listened to the audiotape confessions, ah, it was very difficult for me to admit that I did it, and then I had one got out. Then, he would have to kinda get the next one out. Then I could talk about that one. Yes, it was hard at first saying I killed this one, or that one. I mean I told 'em about two they didn't know about. I mean they didn't even question me about them 'cos they thought they were runaways.'

When I asked Ross why he had confessed to the murders of April Brunais and Lesley Shelley, when he hadn't even been asked about them, the killer complained, 'Well, the police said that there was something wrong with me, and there was a place called Whiting for insane criminals. Yeah, I fell for that one, an' I thought I was going to get the help I needed and that's what I wanted to hear. "Hey, you know you have got something wrong with you and we are going to do something about it cos the murders have stopped." Yeah, Malchik said all the right things, so I thought, What the hell, and I gave 'em everything.'

To be fair to Mike Malchik, he did honour his promise to Ross, for the murders did stop, and the law eventually did something about Ross's problem. If possible, they would execute him.

* * *

Wyndham County prosecutor, Harry Gaucher, only charged Ross with the 1982 murders of Tammy Williams and Debra Smith Taylor. Whether it was because of lack of physical evidence to support the rape portion of an aggravated capital felony charge, which carried the death sentence, or Gaucher's anxiety about losing his case at trial, he allowed Ross to plead guilty solely to murder.

Sitting on Saturday, 13 December 1986, the trial judge sentenced Ross to two consecutive life terms. He would serve no less than 120 years behind bars. However, the murders of Wendy Baribeault, Robin Stavinsky, April Brunais and Lesley Shelly fell under the jurisdiction of a more tenacious prosecutor. New London County State's Attorney, C Robert 'Bulldog' Satti, of the 'hang-'em and whip 'em' brigade, wanted to be the first prosecutor for decades to send a murderer to Connecticut's electric chair.

Satti also knew that he was up against a death penalty statute that tipped the balance in favour of life imprisonment. But the counsel stuck to his guns, for he strongly believed that if ever there was a man worthy of the chair, it had to be Michael Bruce Ross. Apart from the morality of executing a man in liberal Connecticut, there was another cost to consider. 'Old Sparky' had not been used since Joseph 'Mad Dog' Taborsky had been electrocuted in it on Tuesday, 17 May 1960, since which time it had fallen into disrepair. If they wanted to kill Michael Ross, the state would have to pay out at least $30,000 to make the chair serviceable, and redecorate the witness viewing area and death house suite.

For their part, the defence attorneys had to convince a jury that Ross was not legally responsible for the crimes to which he had confessed. Making their job tougher was the fact that Ross didn't qualify for an insanity defence. Moreover, the case had received so much pre-trial publicity that, in the summer of 1987, the venue was moved to Bridgeport, where the prosecution would argue that Ross was a rapist, a cold-blooded, calculating monster, who had planned his assaults and murdered his victims, simply to stay out of prison.

In June 1987, after four weeks of testimony, the eight men and four women of the jury took just 87 minutes to convict Ross of capital felony murder. At the penalty phase, three weeks later, it took them under four hours to prove that Connecticut's death sentence could be imposed. On Monday, 6 July, 20 days before his twenty-eighth birthday, Ross was condemned to death. Under Connecticut law, he would have been spared this sentence if the court had found even one redeeming factor or quality, that the jurors believed to indicate remorse or mitigation. They could not, for Ross, it seemed, did not have a conscience and didn't give a damn.

* * *

Ross explained to me that he is not afraid of dying in the electric chair. He says that living is too good for him, but he is worried that, if that fateful day does arrive, he will say the wrong thing, or show weakness in the face of death. He is also afraid of something he says is worse than death.

'I've always felt that I had to be in control of myself and, even to this day, I feel the need to be in control. What scares me the most isn't life in prison, or the death penalty, but insanity. I'm scared of losing touch with reality. Sometimes I feel I'm slipping away and I'm losing control. If you are in control you can handle anything, but if you lose it, you are nothing.'

When asked if he had any feelings or remorse for his crimes, he replied bluntly, 'Nope! I don't feel anything for them. I really wish I did. I don't feel anything. I feel really bad for the families. I mean, I feel lots of times. Like I can see Mrs Shelley, the mother of one of them girls I killed, on the witness stand crying. And, then there's Mrs, ah, I can't remember her name, but I can think of another one on the stand describing her daughter. She went to the morgue and saw her at the morgue. But the girls themselves I feel nothing for, and I never have.'

Ross then explained why he hadn't turned himself in to the police when he started to commit his earlier offences, way back at Cornell University, when he knew he needed help.

'I made myself believe that it would never happen again. And, I know it sounds hard, but looking back, I can't understand how I did it. It was a fluke because I really didn't do those things. Even sitting here now, I know if I was released I'd kill again. There's no reason to think otherwise. But, I can't, as I sit here now, picture myself wanting to do that. I can't really see myself doing it. I mean, it's like being on different levels.'

When asked if he had any detailed memories of the murders, Ross chuckled, and then said, 'Yes and no. I used to fantasise over the crimes every day and every night. I would masturbate to the point of, um, actually having raw spots on myself from the masturbation. I would bleed. It's weird. I get a lot of pleasure from it. It is really a pleasurable experience. But, when it's all over, it's a very short-term thing. I guess it's like getting high. You know I've never used drugs, but you can get high, then you come down and crash. That's almost how it is. It's just not any easy thing to live with.'

An inevitable question was to ask him what had been going through his mind when he was raping and killing his tragic victims. His reply was, 'Nothin.' But, after a moment's reflection, he added, 'That's what's so weird about this thing. Everybody seems to think, you know, the State's theory that I'm a rapist and I kill them so they can't identify me. Look, most of the time it's broad daylight. I mean, I'm not a stupid person. As sure as hell, if I was going to do something like that, I sure as hell wouldn't do it that way. There was nothing going through my mind until they were already dead.'

'And then it was like stepping through a doorway. And, uh, I remember the very first feeling I had, was my heart beating. I mean really pounding. The second feeling I had was that my hands hurt where I always strangled them with my hands. And, the third feeling was, I guess, fear, and the kind of reality set in that there was this dead body in front of me.'

'And, again, I don't want to mislead you because I knew what was going on, but it was like a different level. I mean it was like watching it. And, after it was all over, you know, it kinds of sets in, an' that's when I would get frightened and stuff. I would hide the bodies and cover them up, or something.'

Ross lives in his death row cell which is truly an ancient dungeon painted a muddy brown colour. 'Death Row' is stamped in white stencil on the steel door leading to the tier which houses Connecticut's seven condemned men. On my final visit to the prison, only Ross and Robert Breton were at home. Sedrick Cobb, Ivo Colon, Richard Reynolds, Todd Rizzo and Daniel Webb were enjoying fresh air in the exercise yard, and taking in a little sun.

Ross is proud of his cell. It is piled high with books and writing materials; indeed, he boasts about the fact that he has been allocated a second cell, where even more of his books are stored. Michael also brags about the dozens of pretty young women who court his attentions, one of whom is as pretty as a starlet and has even signed her photograph 'With Love'. Her letters show that she would marry him in a flash, but he would probably kill her in an instant.

Michael Ross is not unique among the serial killer breed but, to his credit, he is struggling to understand why he was driven to commit such terrible crimes on young women. Indeed, he is striving to understand the forces that propelled him into such severe antisocial behaviour in the first place. To this end, he volunteered for a series of treatment, which includes chemical and surgical castration, the latter being refused by the State.

Many acknowledged experts seem to believe that this treatment could separate the beast from the decent Michael Ross and, for an extended period, he was prescribed Depo-Provera to reduce his enormous sex drive. At the same time as he was taking this drug, he was being prescribed Prozac, a powerful anti-depressant, and this cocktail certainly reduced his abnormal sexual desires. Unfortunately, excessive use of Depo-Provera ballooned his weight by several stone and, as a result, he suffered pathological changes in liver function and hormone levels and his depression reappeared.

Before these drugs were prescribed, Ross claims he masturbated constantly. Occasionally, when in the company of a female correctional officer, he experienced an overwhelming desire to kill her. The Depo-Provera reduced his sex drive, and Michael said, 'You know that everybody has had a tune playing over and over again inside their heads. And, if you have this tune that plays all day, over and over, it can drive you nuts. An' just imagine having thoughts of rape an' murder, an' you can't get rid of it. Well, just like the tune, it'll be driving you nuts. No matter what you do to get rid of that tune, it's going to stay in your head. And that's how I am. I don't want these thoughts.'

Asked if he thought this tune was, in reality, the monster, he replied, 'No, I think he's separate. He goes to sleep for a while and, uh, you never know where he's gone, and that's very true. I mean, sometimes he's there, and especially with the Depo-Provera, I can feel him back here. [Ross touched the back of his head.] I don't know how anybody is going to understand this, but he used to be always in front of my mind, and always intruding, like an obnoxious roommate, always butting into your business and you can't get rid of him.'

In a letter, Ross described what happened to him when he became used to the drugs:

'I would do anything to clear my mind. The medication gave me some relief but my body has adjusted to it now, and the thoughts and urges have returned. Now, my obnoxious roommate has moved back in and things seem worse because now I saw what it was like without him. Today, I feel like a blind man from birth who was given eyesight as a gift, but was taken away a month later. It's really hard to understand what is normal for everybody else if you've never had it yourself.'

It is a rare thing for defence and prosecution psychiatric experts to agree on both a diagnosis and its ramifications, but the Ross case was unusual and, in this instance, there was a consensus that he was suffering from sexual sadism, a mental disease that resulted in a compulsion in Ross to 'perpetrate violent sexual activity in a repetitive way'. Unknown to the members of his trial jury, forensic psychiatrists from both sides had also agreed that the crimes committed by Ross were a direct result of the uncontrollable sexual aggressive impulses to which he was prey. But the State, aware of the damage that could be caused by their own psychiatrist, effectively giving evidence against them by concurring with the defence team, presented no psychiatric witness at all. Hence, the jury were kept in the dark as to a probable mitigating factor which would have removed the threat of the death penalty from Michael Ross.

Contrary to this line of argument, the State successfully argued that Ross was sane, and therefore totally responsible for his crimes. Their suggestion to the jury was that Ross had been examined by a psychiatrist who had found him not to be suffering from a mitigating psychopathology, which was patently untrue. Amazingly, the defence failed to ask why the State's expert was not made available to testify. Had they done so, it would have become apparent that he had withdrawn from the case, a damaging admission for the prosecution. This amounted to constructed deceit, for the jury had been led to believe that there was a difference of opinion, between the State and defence psychiatrists, when there was not. This resulted in rulings that improperly excluded evidence, disingenuous summations, and instructions that allowed the jury to draw inferences that were insupportable.

But what had happened to the State's psychiatrist? Again, unknown to the jury, Dr. Robert B. Miller had concurred with the defence expert's assessment and, in his report to the State's Attorney a year prior to the trial, had concluded, 'Were a specific diagnosis to be attached to Mr Ross's condition at the time of his offences, it would be, in DSM-111,302.84, Sexual Sadism.' He added that, notwithstanding this diagnosis, he believed that Ross could still conform his behaviour to the requirements of the law.

Some time later, Dr. Miller explained that he had suffered sleepless nights, having been influenced by the media reports of the case, and the awfulness of the crimes. This, he claimed, had coloured and tainted his otherwise professional opinion. His conscience now weighed heavily on him, for his diagnosis could help a man into the electric chair. This was something the doctor said he could not live with, and if the State had its way, they might as well be using him to push the switch.

To rectify his error of judgement, and to clear his conscience, just days before the trial, Dr. Miller wrote a letter to the Judge explaining his reason for having to withdraw from the case. In due course, this distasteful issue was brought before the State of Connecticut's Supreme Court for a ruling, and the prosecution came in for a roasting. In their summation, the justices ruled in Ross's favour, to the effect that his illness, that of sexual sadism, was a mitigating factor after all. 'The State' they said, 'was able to seize upon inflammatory connotations of the sexual sadism diagnosis to turn a legally mitigating factor into an aggravating factor ... and the judgment of the court is reversed.'

So, Ross had won the day, and with no experts to disagree with the defence, the law now pronounced that Ross had mitigation for his crimes, that he had been suffering from overpowering, uncontrollable, sexual urges, and that all of the rapes and murders were one continuous act.

Of course, Ross claimed successfully that he was not only unable to control his sexual desires, but also the need to inflict suffering as well. In other words, he was a walking time-bomb – 99 per cent unstable for most of the time, requiring the slightest jolt to set him off. But, is there any real substance to his claims that the problem is like an intrusive roommate who lives inside his head? There is some sense in thinking that people like Michael Ross are, simply, wrongly 'wired-up'.

The hypothalamic region of the limbic system is the most primitive and important part of the brain. The hypothalamus serves the body tissues by attempting to maintain its metabolic equilibrium and providing a mechanism for the immediate discharge of tensions. It appears to act rather like an on/off sensor, on the one hand, seeking or maintaining the experience of pleasure and, on the other, escaping or avoiding unpleasant, noxious conditions. Hence, feelings elicited by this part of the brain are very short-lived; neither can it bear a grudge, and the feelings generated may disappear completely after just a few seconds, although they may last much longer. This is much the way Ross described his thoughts.

So the limbic system mediates a wide range of simple emotions. Because it controls the ability to feel pleasure and displeasure, it is able to generate and use these emotions to meet a variety of its needs, be they sexual, nutritional or emotional. That is, it can reward or punish the entire brain, thus the individual. If, for example, the hypothalamus experiences pleasure, be it from satisfying a craving for chocolate, drugs or sex – even the need for sadistic sex and murder – it will switch on 'reward' feelings so that the person continues engaging in the activity desired. If it begins to feel displeasure, it will turn off the reward switch. But, if the switch jams half-way, so to speak, the limbic needs go unmet, and the individual will experience depression, anger or even homicidal rage.

The person who feels sexual desire, and abstains, may feel tension. Paradoxically, the only way to reduce this tension is by increasing it until orgasm, and thus tension release is obtained. Under normal circumstances, this would be considered quite acceptable; however, if satyriasis becomes linked with sexual sadism, a very different problem emerges altogether. Wrap this package up with an antisocial personality disorder, and an unstable situation is created which could erupt, for no apparent reason, at any given time.

Even in perfectly normal people, emotions elicited by the hypothalamus are often triggered reflexively and without concern or an understanding of the consequences. The hypothalamus seeks pleasure and satisfaction, and whether the stimulus is thirst or sexual hunger, the basic message from the hypothalamus is 'I WANT IT, NOW!' There is no consideration of the long-term consequences of its acts because it has no sense of morals, danger, values, logic or right and wrong.

If the limbic system is physically damaged, feelings of love, hate, affection and even sexual responsiveness and desire may be abolished, or become severely abnormal. It is not necessary to suffer physical damage to this area to experience these types of altered responses, for electrical stimulation of the limbic centre can also cause feelings of violence, which can lead to murder. Moreover, if certain regions in the limbic system (such as the amygdala) are damaged, heightened and indiscriminate sexual activity can result, including excessive and the almost constant need for masturbation. A need which Ross exhibits to this day.

It is interesting to note that the FBI found that 81 per cent of the serial murderers they interviewed indulged in compulsive masturbation.

Like the hypothalamus, the pleasure principle, or the drive to fulfil needs and obtain pleasurable satisfaction, is present at birth. Indeed, for some time after birth, the infant's search for pleasure is unrestricted and intense as there are no forces other than 'mother' and 'father' to counter it, or help it achieve its strivings. If the child's bonding with its mother is satisfactory, and it is brought up in a healthy environment, then the child goes through a healthy development process. If the opposite occurs, the child may be psychologically damaged beyond repair.

Put another way, imagine a complete amateur building a complex computer without any previous experience and little understanding of the complicated instruction manual. Inevitably in such a case, there will be a pile of chips, nuts, bolts and wiring left over, and when the computer is switched on it is bound to malfunction, and continue to produce erroneous calculations, no matter what inputs are entered via the keyboard. While the machine might appear quite normal from the outside, the electromechanical switching systems inside are inherently flawed. For basic functions, it might even work quite well for some of the time, but it will break down when more complicated calculations are required of it. This seems to illustrate what has happened to Michael Ross.

* * *

Michael Ross lives today in limbo because the Connecticut Supreme Court has reversed his death sentence after having found a mitigating factor in this killer's antisocial behaviour. But he is not yet off the hook. With the evidence Ross gave, during his interviews for this book, concerning the anal rape after killing Leslie Shelley, the State is asking for another trial.

For his part, he has volunteered for execution because, he says, he doesn't want to put his victims' families through a court case again. This begs the question – why did he allow his attorneys to argue the mitigation issue in the first place?

But will Connecticut execute their only convicted serial killer? The general concensus of opinion is 'no'. Of course, the supreme penalty is firmly on statute, but finding the will to use it is another matter. As a retired judge explained, 'Ross will probably outlive everyone else involved with his case. If he really wants to be executed that bad, then he should kill himself.'

Michael Ross is the boy-next-door who turned into a monster, and his own words leave an indelible mark: 'You know, they [medical examiners] found strangulation marks around the neck of Wendy Baribeault. They called them multiple strangulation marks 'cos they were kinda all around her throat. An' they got confused. I knew that she was struggling and my hands kept cramping up. I kinda laughed at them for that. I thought that was funny.'

Yet his chilling sense of priorities is masked by the impression he gives to outsiders. Karen B Clarke, an experienced New York journalist, who visited Michael in Somers Prison, said, 'Michael Ross looks so normal he could be the guy next door. If I was walking down a dark alley at night, heard footsteps behind me, and turned around, well, I would have been relieved to see Michael Ross. That's how normal the guy looks.'

This chapter is based on video and audiotape Death Row interviews between Christopher Berry-Dee and Michael Bruce Ross within the Osbourne Correctional Institute, Somers, Connecticut, commencing 10.15am, Monday, 26 September 1994, and several years correspondence.

Michael welcomes correspondence, and his address is: Inmate #127404, Death Row, Osbourne CI, PO Box 100, Somers, CT 06071.

RONALD JOSEPH 'BUTCH' DeFEO JR.

USA

'I've been fuckin' waiting for two

hours for you. Who'd do ya think I

am? I got better things to do.'

RONALD DEFEO'S LESS-THAN-
WELCOMING GREETING ON FRIDAY, 23
SEPTEMBER 1994, PRIOR TO HIS
INTERVIEW WITH CHRISTOPHER BERRY-
DEE AT THE GREENHAVEN CORRECTIONAL
FACILITY, STORMVILLE, NEW YORK

If it were not for a sensational best-selling book and a subsequent motion picture called, *The Amityville Horror* along with several sequels, the village of Amityville, Long Island, and the story of the slaughter that occurred at the DeFeo house, would hardly evoke any public interest. As it is, Amityville has become identified with what was marketed as an outstanding true horror story but which, in the final analysis, is only a well-publicised, run-of-the-mill haunted house story with overtones of mass murder. Did the evil spirit of a dead Indian chief haunt the house? Was the property built on the site of an ancient Indian burial ground? Did green slime ooze from the walls and blood pour from taps? Is Ronald DeFeo Jr the son of Satan?

Because of the horrific events that took place in Amityville during the night of 13 November 1974, one thing is certain – Amityville will never be the same again, so I set out on an equally terrifying journey to find out why.

My journey started in the sleepy, Long Island village of Amityville, then to call upon several of the drug-crazed friends of Ronnie DeFeo. I met with a bunch of crooked and brutal cops, a biased 'whip 'em and hang 'em' judge, and I examined vital evidence that the police had 'lost', then mysteriously found. Finally, I met the monster they call 'The Amityville Horror', behind the grim walls of his prison in up-state New York. This is the true story of 'The Amityville Horror' *and* you can believe every word.

* * *

Ronald Joseph DeFeo, Jr was born on 26 September 1951 at the Adelphi Hospital in Brooklyn, New York. He was the first of five children and, his father, Ronald Sr, then a textile worker, was 20 years old. His mother, Louise, was still a teenager.

A short and porky child, Ronald Jr's classmates nicknamed him 'Butch', a soubriquet that has stayed with him until the present day. He was a sullen, troublesome and lazy pupil who caused trouble, not only to his teachers, but also to other students with whom he was always fighting. He was always coming home bruised black-and-blue and, on one occasion, he suffered a superficial stab wound in the back when another lad attacked him with a knife.

In the early '70s, Ronald Sr started working for his father-in-law, and appears to have been well paid for his labours. Deciding that their Brooklyn apartment was now too small, and with Louise expecting her fifth child, they moved out to the more affluent surroundings of Long Island and, after a little house-hunting, they chose the sleepy waterside village of Amityville.

The name 'Amityville' suggests peace and contentment and, at the very least, friendship. The township is home to around 11,000 residents, many of whom commute daily to New York, 35 miles to the west. Amityville straddles the Great South Bay on Long Island, and is a popular boating centre because its proximity to ocean beaches attracts a large influx of summer residents.

Local history began in the 1650s, when settlers from Connecticut and eastern Long Island first came to what is now called Huntington. Before that, King Henry VII of England, and his successors, claimed tithe to the area by right of discovery, resulting from John Cabot's voyage of discovery in 1496. 'Until the DeFeo massacre,' said one resident, 'about the only crimes were when vandals ripped small boats from their moorings in the bay nearby.'

On 28 July 1965, Ronald DeFeo Sr attained a trophy-sized piece of the American dream when he purchased a two-and-a-half storey, Dutch Colonial-style house from Joseph and Mary Riley. Paying an unknown amount, he acquired the splendid clapboard property, at number 112 Ocean Avenue, with a swimming pool and private dock backing into a protected canal. Initially, the family was overwhelmed with the house and its amenities but they soon began to find their feet in their new surroundings and grew accustomed to life in suburbia. But not everyone in Amityville was happy that the loud and flashy DeFeo's had chosen to live in their quiet community, and gossip was rife that the family had links with organised crime.

Symbolising his family's new life, Mr DeFeo placed a sign in their front yard that read 'HIGH HOPES'. To distinguish themselves even further, he commissioned an artist to create life size portraits of the family, which eventually hung on the walls of the staircase. In one, father and son, Ronald Sr and Butch, sit side-by-side, smiling at the artist, while father pours a glass of wine for his son. In another, the two daughters pose on a love seat, half-smiles on their faces. In a third painting, the two young brothers pose with Mark's arm on John's shoulder. Appropriately perhaps for such a paternalistic family, there was no portrait of the mother, Louise.

The interior of the house was made even more explicit, with its expensive furnishings, crystal chandelier and alabaster fireplace. All of this gave solid substance to the DeFeo's middle-class family life. But if the façade the family presented to the outside world was a 'tasteful' expression of middle-class family values, the actual relationships within the family were quite the opposite.

Ronald DeFeo Sr was the son of Rocco and Antoinette DeFeo. According to those who knew him, Ronald was a physically imposing man who ruled his family with an iron fist and demanded respect. He would change from a civil person into a savage animal at the slightest infraction, and everyone in the household knew that nothing could stop the man when he lost his temper.

Louise DeFeo was the youngest daughter of Michael and Angela Brigante. She was a gentle person, and loyal to her husband. He did not share these warm feelings, believing that his wife was enjoying a string of affairs, including a dalliance with the painter who had produced the family portraits. Although there was no evidence of adultery, mere suspicion seemed to merit beatings, and she experienced these on a regular experience basis.

Beneath the veneer of success and happiness, then, Ronald DeFeo Sr was a hot-tempered man, given to bouts of rage and violence. There were stormy fights between him and Louise, and he loomed before his children as a demanding authority figure. As the eldest child, young Ronald bore the brunt of his father's temper and attempts to impose discipline. Bullied at school, his father encouraged him to stick up for himself. While this advice pertained to school problems, it did not apply to the way Ronald was being treated at home. DeFeo had no tolerance for backtalk and disobedience, keeping his eldest son on a short leash, and refusing to let him stand up for himself in the way he was commanded to at school.

After moving to Long Island, Ronald's first school was the Junior High in Riverhead. As he matured into adolescence, he gained in size and became less of a sitting duck for his father's abuse. There were frequent shouting episodes which often degenerated into boxing matches, as father and son came to blows with little provocation. While DeFeo Sr was not highly skilled in the art of interpersonal relations, he was astute enough to realise that his son's bouts of temper and violence were highly irregular, and of a different kind to his own. After Butch seriously beat up his sister, Dawn, he and his wife arranged for him to visit a psychiatrist. This was to no avail because Butch simply employed a passive-aggressive stance with his therapist, and rejected any notion that he needed help.

In the absence of any solution, his parents employed a time-honoured strategy for placating unruly children by buying Butch anything he wanted and giving him money. His father presented his 14-year-old son with a $14,000 speedboat to cruise the Amityville River. Whenever Butch wanted money, all he had to do was ask, and if he wasn't in the mood to ask, he just took what was lying around.

When this strategy failed, Butch was packed off to St Francis Prep in Brooklyn, where he was thrown out at the end of his ninth grade. Finally, he attended the Amityville High School and, at the age of 17, left the school system for good. On the same day, his father bought him a car.

By this time, he had begun using drugs, such as heroin and LSD, and had also started dabbling in schemes involving petty theft. His behaviour was becoming increasingly psychotic as well, and not confined to outbursts within his home.

One afternoon, while out on a hunting trip with a few friends, he pointed a loaded rifle at one member of the party, a young man he had known for years. He watched with a stony expression as the young man's face turned white before his fear made him take flight. At this point, Butch calmly lowered his gun and when they caught up with each other later that afternoon, Butch asked, sneeringly, why his friend had left so soon.

At the age of 18, Butch was given a job at his father's car dealership which was a sole agency for Buick. By his own account it was an easy job, where little was expected of him. Regardless of whether he showed up for work or not, he received a cash allowance from his father at the end of each week, which sometimes amounted to $500. This he used to run his car, and buy alcohol and drugs.

In January 1971, Butch DeFeo met a young woman called Geraldine, in the Ninth Bar in New York City. They dated for quite a while, then, in December 1973, she found out that she was pregnant. His father started hounding the couple to get married and, after their daughter, Stephanie, was born, they married on 17 October 1974, at the Garfield Grant Hotel in Long Branch, New Jersey.

Altercations with his father were growing ever more frequent and progressively more violent. One evening, a fight broke out between Butch's father and mother. In order to settle the matter, Butch grabbed a 12-gauge shotgun from his room, loaded a shell into the chamber, and charged downstairs to the scene of the fight. Without hesitation or calling out to the participants to break up the argument, Butch pointed the barrel at his father's face, yelling, 'Leave that woman alone. I'm going to kill you, you fat fuck! This is it.'

He pulled the trigger, but the gun mysteriously did not discharge. Ronald Sr froze where he stood and watched in grim amazement as his own son lowered the weapon and simply walked out of the room, with casual indifference to the fact that he had almost killed his own father. While that particular fight was over, Butch's actions foreshadowed the violence he would soon unleash, not only upon his father, but also his entire family.

This incident with the shotgun seems to have inspired in Ronald Sr something akin to a religious conversion. He became a devout Catholic, and built several religious shrines amid the manicured grounds of High Hopes, and neighbours often saw him saying his rosary in front of a shrine of St Joseph and the Christ child that he had built on his front lawn.

* * *

In the weeks before the Amityville slayings, relations between Butch DeFeo and his father reached breaking point. Apparently dissatisfied with the money he 'earned' working for his father, Butch devised a scheme to defraud his family further. Two weeks before the massacre, he was sent on an errand by one of the staff at the Buick dealership, charged with the responsibility of depositing $1,800 in cash and $20,000 in cheques at the bank. Accompanied by a fellow worker from the dealership, they departed for the bank at 12.30pm. They were gone for two hours. When they finally returned, it was to report that they had been robbed at gunpoint while waiting at a red light. Ronald Sr exploded with rage, berating the staff member who had sent his son in the first place.

The police were called and naturally asked to speak to Butch. In reality, he and his accomplice had kept the money and split it two ways. Instead of engaging in at least a pretence of co-operation, he concocted a description of the fictional robber, becoming tense and irritable with detectives. As the officers began to suspect that he was lying and focused their questions on the two hours he was away, his behaviour became aggressive.

'Wouldn't you have rushed back to the dealership once you had been robbed of so much money?' asked the police. 'Where had you been during that time?'

In response to their questions, Butch began to curse at them, banging on the hood of a car to emphasise his rage. The police backed off for a moment, but his father had already come to the conclusion that his son was lying and had stolen the money himself.

On the Friday prior to the murders at High Hopes, Butch had been asked by the police to examine some mug shots in the possibility that he might be able to recognise the robber. Initially he agreed, but pulled out at the last moment. When Ronald DeFeo Sr heard of this, he cornered his son at work, demanding to know why he wouldn't co-operate with the police.

'You've got the Devil on your back,' his father screamed at him.

This time Butch did not hesitate. 'You fat prick,' he screamed, 'I'll kill you.'

Then he ran to his car and sped off. While this incident had not resulted in an exchange of blows, a final confrontation was clearly imminent.

* * *

The still shroud of night blanketed the village of Amityville in the early hours of Wednesday, November 14, 1974. Stray house pets and the occasional passing car were the only signs of life as families and neighbours slumbered. But hatred and savagery were brewing beneath the seeming calm at High Hopes on Ocean Avenue. The entire DeFeo family had retired to bed, with the exception of Butch. He sat in the quiet of his room, brooding on what he wanted to do, which was to ensure that his father and family would trouble him no more.

Butch was the only member of the family with his own room. His violent disposition and the fact that he was the eldest had afforded him this small luxury. It also provided him with a private storage place for a number of weapons he collected and sometimes sold. On this particular night, he withdrew a .35-calibre Marlin martini-action rifle from his closet. He set off, stealthily but resolutely, towards the door of his parents' master bedroom. Quietly pushing the door open, he stood, momentarily observing them as they slept, totally oblivious to the horror that was about to engulf them. Then, without hesitation, Butch raised the rifle to his shoulder and pulled the trigger. The first of eight fatal shots fired that night, slammed into his father's back.

Just after 3.00am, Butch DeFeo completed the annihilation of his family. Each defenceless member had been brutally slain in cold blood. The family dog, Shaggy, tied up outside the boathouse, was barking furiously in reaction to the sporadic bursts of violence emanating from the house. The animal's barking did not distract Butch in the least. Aware that he had completed the task he had set out to do, he now turned his attention to cleaning himself up and establishing an alibi to throw off the inevitable police investigation that would ensue.

First, he showered, and trimmed his beard. Then, dressed in jeans and leather work boots, he collected up his bloodied clothing, the rifle with its scabbard, and retrieved one of the expended cartridge cases from the floor. Stuffing everything into a pillowcase, he drove off into the pre-dawn light. His first stop was at the end of Ocean Avenue, where he threw the rifle into the dock. From there, he drove to Brooklyn and disposed of the pillowcase and its contents by throwing them into a sewer. Then he reported for work, at his late father's dealership, as if nothing had happened. For him, it was 6.00am and business as usual.

Butch did not remain at work for long. He called home several times and, when his father failed to show up, he acted as though he were bored with nothing to do and left around noon. He called his girlfriend, Mindy Weiss, to let her know that he would be at her place early from work, and that he wanted to stop by and see her. On his way, he passed a friend, Robert Kelske, and recalled the incident later during a prison interview:

'In my drugged stupour, I was driving down the road in Amityville and Robert Kelske, a junkie strung out on heroin, pulled up alongside of my car and started asking off-the-wall questions. This didn't register then because Kelske was a junkie and a thief who had previously burglarized both of my neighbour's homes, so I paid his questions no mind.'

DeFeo reached his girlfriend's house at around 1.30pm. Mindy was 19 years old, an attractive and popular waitress at Longfellow's Bar. He casually mentioned on arrival that he had tried to call home several times and, although there were cars in the driveway, there was no response. To make the point, he called his home from Mindy's apartment with the same predictable result.

Acting as though he was puzzled but unconcerned, Butch took Mindy shopping during the afternoon. From the mall in Massapequa, they drove to see Patricia and Robert Geiger, where DeFeo bought five $10 bags of heroin and shot them up. He said, 'I was out of it and actually forgot about what had happened at my house … I sort of blacked out.'

Just after 6.00pm, Butch arrived at Henry's Bar in Amityville, where he met Robert Kelske. Once again, he feigned concern over his inability to reach anyone at home.

'I'm going to have to go home and break a window to get in,' he said.

'Well, do what you have to do,' his friend replied blithely.

Ronald left the bar on his supposed journey of discovery, only to return within minutes in a state of agitation and dismay.

'Bob, you gotta help me,' he implored. 'Someone shot my mother and father!'

The two friends were joined by a small group of patrons, and they all piled into Butch's car, driving off with Kelske at the wheel. Approximately 15 hours had elapsed since the murders were committed. Within moments of arriving at the house, Kelske had entered the front door and raced upstairs into the master bedroom. He retraced his steps to find Butch distraught with grief and dismay. Joe Yeswit found a telephone in the kitchen and called the police.

At precisely 6.40pm on 13 November 1974, Patrolman Kenneth J Greguski of the Amityville Village Police Department based at Greene Lane, received a call from his control room to attend 112 Ocean Avenue, where there had been a report of a shooting. As he drove up to the house, he saw a group of young men standing in the driveway, and one of them tearfully introduced himself as Ronald DeFeo. He said, 'My mother and father are dead.'

'I went into the house and climbed the stairs,' said the officer. 'In the master bedroom, I found a white male lying on his stomach, and he had been shot dead. Next to him was a white female in the same position, and she had been shot to death. I proceeded to a second bedroom where I discovered two young boys in separate beds. They were lying on their stomachs and they had been shot dead. I came downstairs and used the dining room telephone to call my headquarters and informed them that there were four bodies in the house, and they should notify the First Squad Detectives.'

Continuing his account, the policeman added, 'Almost immediately, Ronald DeFeo told me that he had two sisters. Evidently he had heard me talking over the telephone, and with that, I ran back upstairs and checked a bedroom door that had been closed. I found a young girl's body there. She was lying, like the others, spread-eagled on her stomach. She was shot dead, too. And I seen a staircase, that I thought led to an attic, which actually led to another bedroom upstairs on the third floor, and I found another female body there. I immediately came back downstairs, re-called my headquarters and advised them I had two more bodies. After that call I went into the kitchen. I stood there with Ronald DeFeo and his friend Robert Kelske, and I put my hand on his shoulder and just told him to take it easy. I stood there and waited until Detective Sergeant Cammaroto and Lieutenant Edward Lowe turned up. They just checked the scene and they came back downstairs, too, and it was shortly thereafter that the homicide detectives arrived. It was a scene that I'll never forget, and it haunts me to this day.'

At the autopsy, the medical examiner, Dr Howard Aldeman, determined that, Ronald DeFeo Sr, aged 43, had been shot twice in the lower back. The bullets went through the kidney and spine. One stopped in the neck and the other ploughed through the body and on to the mattress. Death was most likely instantaneous since he had stayed on the mattress and did not crawl out of bed.

Louise DeFeo, aged 42, had been shot twice. The gunfire that had killed her husband seems to have awakened Butch's mother, and she was turning in her bed towards the doorway. The first bullet entered her back, exited through her chest, re-entered her left breast and wrist before landing in the mattress. The second bullet destroyed her right lung, diaphragm and liver. Death most likely occurred in a matter of seconds, since she never put up a struggle.

Mark DeFeo, aged 12, and John DeFeo, aged 7, had been shot once. From the evidence, the medical examiner determined that their killer stood less than two feet from the boys when he discharged the gun. Bullets penetrated the heart, lungs, diaphragm and liver of each victim. In addition, John's spinal cord was severed, causing involuntary movements of his lower body.

Allison DeFeo, aged 13, had been shot once. Like her mother, she had awakened and turned her head towards the doorway. The bullet smashed upward from her left cheek to her right ear, entering the brain and skull. The bullet exited, hitting the wall and bounced on the floor where it came to rest. Death was instantaneous, and powder burns on Allison's eyes indicated that she was awake at the time of her murder and staring down the barrel of a gun.

Dawn DeFeo, aged 18, had been shot once. Her killer had stood less than three feet away and fired at the back of her neck. The bullet entered the left ear and collapsed the left side of her face. Brain particles soaked the pillow and the sheets were covered with menstrual blood.

In Dr Aldeman's opinion, it appeared from the evidence that this was a gangland-style execution, and that at least three or four people had been involved with the control of the victims and their murders.

* * *

From the outset, Ronald Defeo was known to have a police record. He was a drug user, currently on probation for stealing an outboard motor. He was first interviewed at the scene of the shootings at 6.55pm by Detective Gaspar Randazzo, who had been working with the First Squad Detectives for eight years. Randazzo asked the sole survivor to account for his movements that day. DeFeo replied, 'I went to work and, upon coming home, I found the door locked. I figured there might have been something wrong because the doors were locked and I saw my parents' cars outside the house. I went back to the bar and spoke to Robert Kelske. I went back to the house, forced a window, and found the bodies of my family. I was scared, so I ran out and drove back to the bar for help. Then we all drove back and Joe called the police.'

Shortly after the interview began, Reverend McNamara arrived to administer last rites to the victims.

At 7.15pm, Detectives Gozaloff, Napolitano, Shirvell, Grieco, Harrison, Reichert and Detective Sergeant Barylski, all of the First Homicide Squad, arrived on the scene. They obtained permission to use the house next door, home to the Ireland family, as a command post. DeFeo was asked to leave the scene, and he was escorted next door where Detective Gozaloff spoke to him.

Asked who might have shot his family, Butch told the detective that a man named Louis Falini had a grudge against his folks. He was a Mafia hit-man, and he could be the murderer.

'I had an argument with Falini,' he said. 'I called him a cocksucker and that caused problems between him and my father.'

DeFeo pledged his full co-operation and agreed to go to the First Precinct, calling beforehand at the Amityville Police Station to complete the paperwork that relieved the Amityville Police of jurisdiction over the murders.

On arrival at the First Precinct, Detective Gozaloff interviewed DeFeo in more depth. Butch explained that he worked for his father, who was the Service Manager of Karl-Brigante Buick in Brooklyn, and that his grandfather, Mike Brigante, was the owner.

He described the layout of his home in some detail. That night, he said that he was up late watching a film called *Castle Keep*. He fell asleep watching the television around 2.00am, and awoke at 4.00am with stomach pains. He remembered walking past the upstairs bathroom, and noticed that his brother's wheelchair was in front of the door. Mark could only walk on crutches following an injury playing football, Butch explained. He also claimed to have heard the toilet flush. Since he couldn't get back to sleep, he decided to go to work early, and went on to describe what he had been doing until the time he discovered the bodies.

After Butch submitted his signed statement, the detectives continued to question him about his family and the suggestion that Falini might be the killer. Butch replied that Falini had lived with them for a period of time, during which he had helped Butch and his father carve out a hiding place in the basement where Ronald Sr kept a stash of gems and cash. His argument with Falini had stemmed from an incident during which Falini criticised some work Butch had done at the auto dealership. Butch also voluntarily confessed to being a casual user of heroin, and admitted that he had set one of his father's boats on fire so that an insurance claim could be made rather than paying for the motor, which Butch had originally blown up. The detectives finished their questioning at around 3.00am and Butch went to sleep on a cot in a filing room at the back of the police station. DeFeo had given every appearance of a co-operative witness and, so far, the detectives had no reason to hold him under suspicion of murder.

The circumstances began to change, though, as investigators intensified their examination of physical evidence, both at the crime scene and in the police laboratory. A crucial discovery was made ataround 2.30am on 15 November, when Detective John Shirvell conducted a last sweep through the DeFeo bedrooms. The rooms where the murders had taken place had been scoured thoroughly, while Ronald's room had, up to that point, been given only a cursory once-over. But, on closer scrutiny, Detective Shirvell spotted a pair of empty rectangular boxes, each with labels describing their contents as .22 and .35 Marlin rifles. Shirvell was unaware that a .35-calibre Marlin had been the murder weapon, but he took the boxes anyway in the event that they may become important evidence. Indeed, they were!

Shortly after returning to the police headquarters, with the boxes, he learned exactly what make of weapon had been used in the shootings, because a firearms examiner had identified the calibre of the murder weapon. Detective Sergeant Della Penna had wasted no time in examining the spent shell casings and the bullets used to kill the DeFeo family. He had determined that powder residue found at the scene was partially burnt particles of nitrocellulose gunpowder. The spent lead-jacketed bullets were of .35-calibre Remington Arms manufacture, and were originally components of Western Co .35-calibre cartridge cases.

Detectives leading the murder investigation now began to consider the possibility that Butch had been lying to them and, indeed, that he may be their prime suspect, knowing far more about the killings than he had so far told them. At 8.45am, Detectives George Harrison and Napolitano shook DeFeo awake.

'Did you find Falini yet?' was his first question. As he quickly found out, the officers were not there to answer Butch's questions, but to read him his rights. Butch protested that he had been trying to co-operate all along, and that it wasn't necessary to read him his rights. He went so far as to waive his right to

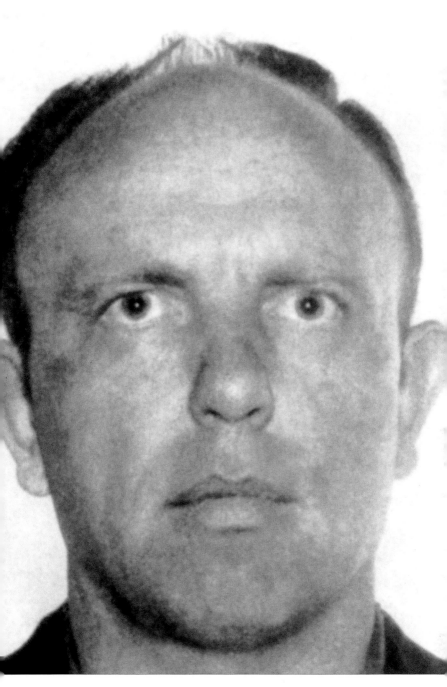

'I hate women with a passion … they always played mind games with my head.'

Harvey Louis Carignan

'The human meat, well, ah, it tastes like pork … I don't know why I ate parts of people, but I just did.'

Arthur John Shawcross

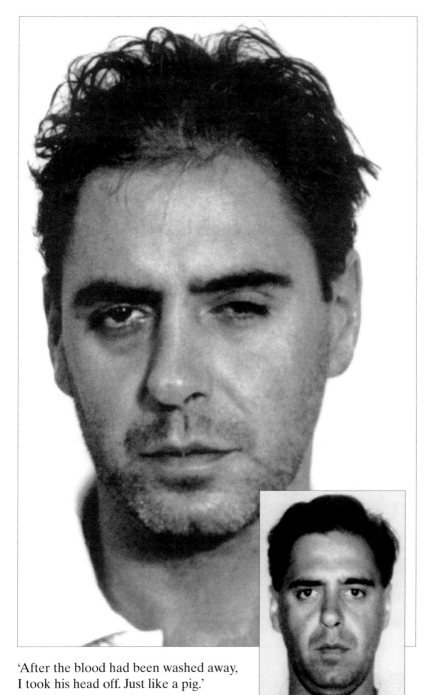

'After the blood had been washed away,
I took his head off. Just like a pig.'

John Martin Scripps

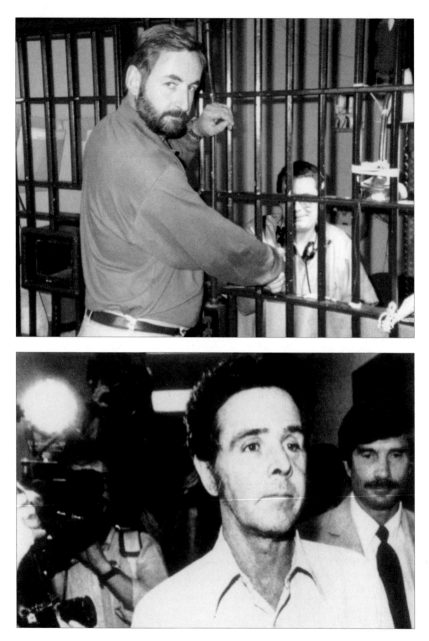

Top: 'There was nothing they could have said or done. They were dead as soon as I saw them.' The author with Michael Bruce Ross on Death Row.

Bottom: 'I had no intention of killing her. I don't know whether it was me or what. That was my first, my worst, and the hardest to get over.' *Henry Lee Lucas*

'It all happened so fast. Once I started,
I just couldn't stop. It went so fast.'

Ronald DeFeo Jr

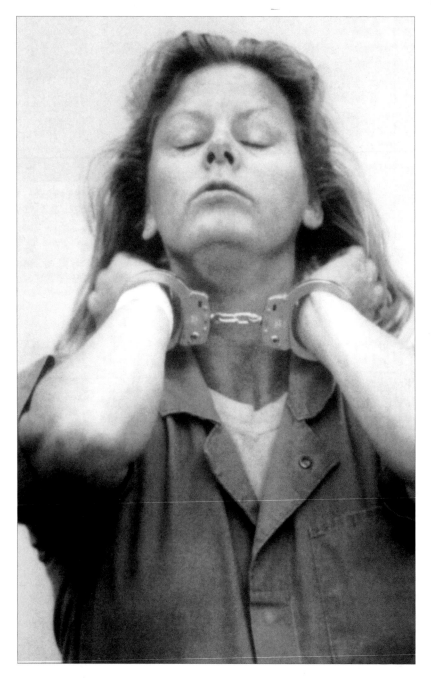

'Look, I can't remember their faces or their names ... but I'm telling you that he's got to be seriously dead by now.'

Aileen Carol Wuornos

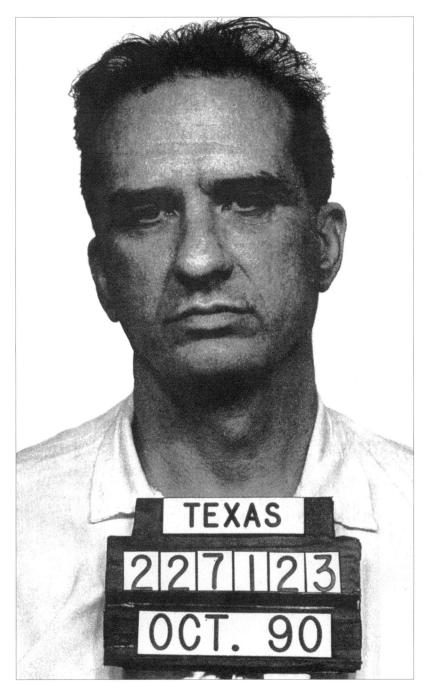

'Killing a woman's like killing a chicken. They both squawk.' *Kenneth Allen McDuff*

'I used to be a good-looking guy, ya know. But, see what they done to me in here. My hair is falling out, my teeth are rotten and still they want to kill me.'

Douglas Daniel Clark and Carol Mary Bundy

counsel, all to prove that he was an innocent witness with nothing to hide.

By this time, Gozaloff and Napolitano were due to go off duty and two other officers, Lt Robert Dunn and Detective Dennis Rafferty, took over. They meant business and, in the years following the Amityville shootings, both would be heavily criticised by a New York Commission of Investigation for using illegal practices to gain verbal confessions from suspects. Rafferty began by reading Defeo his rights, and proceeded to question him about his activities and whereabouts over the prior two days. Suddenly, Rafferty zeroed in on the time of the murders. Butch had written in his statement that he was up as early as 4.00am, and that he heard his brother in the bathroom at that time.

'Butch, the whole family was found lying dead in their bedclothes,' said Rafferty. 'That indicates to me that it didn't happen at, like, one o'clock in the afternoon after you had gone to work.'

Rafferty continued to press until he was able to pry Butch away from his earlier account of when the crime took place, establishing that the murders actually occurred between 2.00am and 4.00am.

With this slight fissure, DeFeo's crudely constructed story began to crumble. Dunn and Rafferty hammered at the discrepancies between Butch's stated version of the events and what the crime scene evidence indicated had actually happened. Once the time of the murder was established, Butch was implicated by his own statement, which confirmed his presence in the house at the crucial time. His response to this predicament was a desperate attempt to lead the detectives up the garden path. But they were not accepting the bait.

'Butch, it's incredible,' said Rafferty. 'It's almost unbelievable. You know we have a .35-calibre gun box from your room. Every one of the victims has been shot with a .35-calibre. And you've seen the whole thing. There has to be more to it. It's your gun that was used, so where's the fuckin' gun?' he shouted, just inches from Butch's face.

His desperation growing by the minute, DeFeo continued to lie, even though his lies sucked him in more squarely to the commission of the murders. He told his interrogators that at 3.30am Louis Falini woke him up and put a revolver to his head. Another man was present in the room, he said but, upon further questioning, he could not provide any kind of physical description to help the police. According to his new version of events, Falini and his companion led Butch from room to room, murdering each one of his family members.

The police allowed DeFeo plenty of rope and, as he continued talking, he eventually implicated himself with his account of how he gathered up and removed the evidence from the scene.

'Wait a minute,' said Rafferty. 'Why did you pick up the cartridge if you had nothing to do with it? You didn't know it was your gun that was used.'

Perhaps sensing that his position was deteriorating rapidly, Butch did not immediately respond to the question. The detectives played a waiting game and allowed him to keep talking. They had already obtained a good deal of evidence implicating DeFeo, particularly the absurd pretence that Falini and his accomplice had taken him along on their killing spree while sparing his life alone. Once they had been given a solid description of how, according to Butch, the murders had taken place, Dunn went in for the kill.

'They must have made you a piece of it,' he said. 'They must have made you shoot at least one of them – or some of them.' Butch tripped on the snare and the trap was sprung.

'It didn't happen that way, did it?' asked Rafferty.

'Give me a minute,' DeFeo replied, putting his head in his hands.

'Butch, they never were there, were they? Falini and the other guy were never there.'

At last came the confession. 'No,' said Butch, 'It all started so fast. Once I started, I just couldn't stop. It went so fast.'

On Wednesday, November 19 1975, a year and five days after the murders, the presiding judge instructed the jury in the deliberation chamber to return to the court with a verdict. On Friday, November 21 1975, Ronald DeFeo Jr was found guilty of six counts of second-degree murder. Two weeks later, he was sentenced to 25 years to life in prison on all six counts. He became eligible for parole in 1999 and insists that he is an innocent man.

* * *

Around the time of the Amityville murders, Suffolk County, covering the eastern portion of Long Island, beginning approximately 45 miles east of Manhattan and adjacent to suburban Nassau County, had a population of well over 666,500. It has one of the largest police departments in New York State after the New York City Police Department, the New York State Police and the Nassau County Police. Suffolk also ranks as one of the highest-paid police departments in the country. This police force also has something else to be proud of, for it enjoys the highest confession and oral admission clear-up rate of probably anywhere in the world.

In April 1989, a State of New York Commission of Investigation published its report on an *Investigation into the Suffolk County District Attorney's Office and Police Department*. In various sub-reports, the Commission unearthed a number of serious problems, which included misconduct and deficiencies in homicide investigations and prosecutions, misconduct and deficiencies in narcotics investigations and prosecutions, illegal wiretaps, failure by the District Attorney's Office to investigate and punish misconduct by agency employees and law enforcement personnel, deficiencies in the oversight of police personnel, and a whole host of other issues including corruption, the unlawful gaining of confessions by over-zealous police officers, police brutality, and 'precinct jumping', an unlawful police practice, used to stonewall lawyers trying to gain access to their clients. As a result of the Commission's damning findings, one senior police officer committed suicide and dozens of other ranks 'retired'.

From 7 to 11 December 1986, *Newsday* published a lengthy five-part series on deficiencies and misconduct in Suffolk County homicide prosecutions stretching back to the early '70s. The series included a statement that 94 per cent of Suffolk homicide prosecutions involved confessions or verbal admissions. This figure was confirmed to the Commission by the former Commanding Officer of Suffolk County Homicide, none other than Detective Lieutenant Robert Dunn, one of the two detectives who had obtained a confession from Ronald DeFeo.

This was an astonishingly high figure compared to other jurisdictions; so high, in fact, that it provoked scepticism regarding the police agency's use of confessions. For example, in *Newsday*'s study, which compared 361 Suffolk homicide defendants, from 1975 to 1985, to seven hundred cases from six other large suburban counties, Suffolk's 94 per cent confession rate far exceeded the 55 per cent to 73 per cent rate in the six other jurisdictions. The national average was 48 per cent.

There is no doubt that DeFeo had been 'precinct jumped', as two attorneys, Richard Wyslling and Richard Hartman, who had tried to see him were given a thorough run-around by the Suffolk County Police. Ronald DeFeo also says that his confession was 'beaten out of him' by Detective Lt. Robert Dunn and Detective Dennis Rafferty, who hit him with a telephone book. To verify this claim, it is only necessary to go back to the first day, when DeFeo appeared before District Judge Signorelli. The judge was so shocked at the defendant's appearance that he ordered a medical examination. The next day, a doctor reported that he had found black-and-blue bruises over different parts of the defendant's body and legs, a cut lip, and a great deal of swelling on his face. These injuries were not present when DeFeo was taken into police custody. During an interview for this book which took place at the Yaphank Police Headquarters on 27 September 1994, a smiling Dennis Rafferty said, 'Sure, of course we did a good job on him ... what do you expect?'

Ronald DeFeo Jr was not the only one to receive a good beating from the police. Robert Kelske, Chuck Tweskbury and Barry Springer also say that they were seriously assaulted and ordered to sign confessions for murder. Patricia and Robert Geiger were even accused of murder.

On 16 November 1974, DeFeo received a visit from a Reverend McNamara, the priest who had given the dead family their last rights. Within hours of McNamara's departure, jail records show that Butch's uncle, Vincent Procita, paid Butch a visit. Rocco DeFeo, Butch's grandfather, and his brother Peter, both members of the organised crime circuit, had asked Procita to get Ronald to sign a document, making Rocco administrator of his late father's estate. Butch was told that if he refused, he would be killed in prison. He deferred to his relatives and signed.

The following day, DeFeo received a visit from the FBI and was questioned for two hours about the DeFeo and Brigante families' links with the Mafia. Agent Robert Sweeney explained that his own daughter had been acquainted with Dawn DeFeo. He went on to say that the FBI had placed a legal wiretap on Michael Brigante's telephone. One of the conversations they recorded was between Brigante and Peter Defeo, who said that Butch knew too much, and they were going to have him killed. Sweeney offered

Butch the witness protection programme if he told them what he knew; he refused.

Jail records show that on 19 November, DeFeo received a visit from two more attorneys. Alexander Hesterberg and Jacob Sigfried told him that Michael Brigante wanted him to sign another document, this time making him the administrator for the late Mrs DeFeo's estate. Butch told them about the visit from the FBI, and Jacob Sigfried said, 'That's all the more reason to sign, then.' He was also told that his aunt, Phyllis Procita, was working for the District Attorney's office, which she was, and, unless he agreed to allow Sigfried to represent him with an insanity defence, he wouldn't get out of prison alive. Realising that his life was now in great peril, DeFeo agreed to both suggestions.

At his second court appearance, Sigfried failed to turn up. When the Judge asked DeFeo where his lawyer was, he told him about the prison visits and the Judge remarked, 'Even Stevie Wonder could see through this.' Events took an even more sinister turn, a few weeks later, when the Judge appointed William E Weber as DeFeo's defence attorney. Weber, who had never represented anyone in a murder case before, was also running as the Judge's campaign manager in the forthcoming surrogate court elections.

Weber collected a fat retainer from the DeFeo and Brigante families and moved on to prepare an insanity defence. Indeed, he started off with honourable intentions by employing the services of Herman Race, acknowledged as one of the most experienced investigators on Long Island. He had been a homicide detective for 20 years, and his first job was to examine the firearm and ballistic evidence on behalf of his client. He quickly discovered traces of 'backfire' on Dawn DeFeo's nightdress caused by unburned gunpowder blowing back on to her clothing. The only conclusion that can be drawn from this is that Dawn had fired the rifle, at least once, on that fateful night. Armed with this information, an excited William Weber was quick to inform DeFeo's relatives, who were not pleased.

The next afternoon, while the attorney was pulling up outside his home, two police officers stopped him and asked questions about unpaid parking tickets. They searched his car and, in the glove compartment, they found an unlicenced handgun and arrested him. Later, under the influence of the Brigante family, the police decided to drop the charge. Weber was left in no doubt that the matter of the nightgown should not be raised again.

With Butch protesting that he was not insane, William Weber, nevertheless, was carrying out his instructions from his client's family who were, as DeFeo said, 'calling the shots'. Counsel retained the services of a psychiatrist, Dr Daniel Swartz, for a fee of $8,000 and a professional opinion that was tantamount to saying that Ronald DeFeo Jr was insane.

Shortly before the trial started, the prosecutor, Assistant District Attorney Gerald Sullivan, asked Judge Signorelli to remove himself from the case, which he did. In turn, and quite illegally, Sullivan picked Judge Thomas M Stark, a tough, no-nonsense man whom the prosecution could rely on to bat for their side. Judge Stark later dismissed this matter with a wave of his hand.

'In hindsight,' he said, 'this was quite wrong, but things were different back then.'

With a psychiatrist in their pocket, the defence team now started to trawl elsewhere for people who knew DeFeo, and tried to coerce them to testify that they thought that Butch was insane. William Davidge, was approached, and in a sworn affidavit before Esther B. Hopkins, Notary Public for the State of Florida, dated 6 October 1988, he had this to say, 'I was a defence witness at the request of Attorney William Weber, defence counsel for DeFeo in Suffolk County, State of New York. Weber told me during consultations that DeFeo was guilty, but told me he would get DeFeo declared insane by fabricating a defence of insanity. Weber had me state facts to back up his defence. I was unco-operative with Weber over matters he stated to me about my personal friendship with DeFeo and his family that were not true.

'Weber startled me, because he was an officer of the Court and represented DeFeo. I wanted to help DeFeo by telling the truth. I was directed through Weber to describe Ronald DeFeo as insane, by testifying to acts to support the defence of insanity.

The acts described were purposely directed to me while testifying, by Weber's cross-examination at the DeFeo trial, in an attempt to place DeFeo in a mental hospital, and exonerate DeFeo from all criminal acts alleged in the indictment and proceedings. Weber advised me and ordered me to testify at his will, to support his insanity defence, and he refused to allow me to testify in any other manner, other than directed by him. At the time of my testimony, I did not know that I was violating any laws; nor could I appreciate a violation of any laws being violated, as I was completely unaware. I can also say that my brother, Frank Davidge, informed me that he and William Weber made a deal in a 'back-room' discussion in 1975.'

If William Weber was reluctantly breaking almost every rule in the book, the District Attorney had no compunction in breaking them all. Having schemed at standing down one judge, and illegally engineering the appointment of another, more 'suitable' judge to try the case, Gerald Sullivan now needed to find a motive for the defendant's crimes. He thought he had hit the jackpot when he learned that the DeFeos had a substantial horde of valuable jewellery in the house, which was now missing from the secret recess in the basement. He reasoned, therefore, that the accused had stolen it and, when his father had discovered the theft, Butch killed him and the rest of the family as well.

Unfortunately, from Sullivan's point of view, the jewellery had recently been placed in a safety deposit box at the European Savings Bank in Amityville.

In a desperate and quite illegal move to save the day, Sullivan called on the services of none other than Detective Rafferty who was told to visit a number of DeFeo's friends, including Lin and Roger Nonnewitz. After speaking to them over some quite spurious matter, the detective asked them to testify that the DeFeos had other jewellery, and that Butch had stolen it. Not only did the Nonnewitzes expose this in court, but they also signed sworn affidavits explaining that the prosecution had asked them to commit perjury. Judge Stark dealt with this serious issue with his usual air of casual indifference and that was the end of it.

There is no doubt that a confession had been beaten out of DeFeo by the Suffolk County Police, and it had done him no good trying to implicate the alleged hit-man, Louis Falini, who was able to provide a solid alibi for the time of the murders. There was also no doubt that Ronald DeFeo was in the house when the murders were committed. But with the absence of motive, what was his reason for killing his family? The answer is that he did not have one, whereas his sister, Dawn, had a very strong motive indeed. After considerable research, it has been possible to disentangle the web of lies spun by DeFeo surrounding the murders, and arrive at something nearer the truth.

During the evening before the murders, DeFeo had been visiting his estranged wife, Geraldine. At around 8.00pm, she received a telephone call from Mrs DeFeo, who was in a distressed state and crying. She asked to speak to her son who came to the telephone, and then informed everyone else present that there was trouble between Dawn and her father. 'The fuckin' bitch,' he said, 'she's started again.'

Dawn was not the neatest person in the world, and had often left food to spoil in her room, which subsequently attracted a plague of flies all over the house. Now aged 18, she was attending the Katherine Gibbs Secretarial School, at her parents' request. She was in love with her boyfriend, William Davidge, who was moving to Florida, and she wanted to join him. Her parents were strongly against this idea and, according to friends and relatives, she had started experimenting with drugs as an escape from her situation at home and, when aroused, she, like her father and eldest brother, had a terrifying temper that knew no bounds.

In his sworn affidavit before Theodore Yurak, Notary Public for the State of New York, dated 27 July 1990, William Davidge affirmed that he knew that Dawn wanted to follow him to Florida, that she was using drugs such as LSD and Mescaline, and that she had a 'bad temper that got out of hand at times'. Davidge also said that Dawn had a deep hatred for her parents and her eldest brother, whom she used for cash handouts.

Immediately after receiving the telephone call from his mother, DeFeo, and Geraldine's brother, Richard Romondoe, departed for 'High Hopes'. When they arrived, Butch gave Dawn the keys to his car and told her to take a long drive until she cooled off. Apparently, she followed his advice. Under the influence of drink and drugs, Butch and Richard went down to the basement, leaving the door open so that they could hear what was going on upstairs. They turned the television down low and began to play pool. Time seemed to pass very quickly for the two men, when, to their shock, they heard a 'loud roar'.

Rushing upstairs, they located the bodies of the DeFeos with the exception of Dawn, whom they found in her third-floor bedroom, dressed in a nightgown, and cradling the .35-calibre Marlin rifle. Butch made a grab for the gun and, in the struggle that followed, his sister was shot in the head. Butch and Richard disposed of the weapon and the other incriminating evidence in the manner later explained to the police.

Geraldine DeFeo recalled that during the early morning of the murders, Butch had woken her up and had told her what had happened. He then left the house and that was the last she saw of him until his trial. She also recalled that her brother had confirmed the story, saying, 'I have got to leave and get away otherwise I am going to get fitted up for something I didn't do.'

Richard, who now lives under an assumed name in Florida, has since got married and has a son. 'I know what I saw', he told the author,' and what Ronnie says is the truth. Problem is that my wife knows nothing about this, and I don't trust the police.'

Geraldine DeFeo has since been threatened, pushed to the ground, arrested and released by the police for conspiracy in the Amityville slayings. The officer involved was Detective Dennis Rafferty.

If DeFeo's claims of innocence were to stand up, it was vital that two forensic issues were resolved. First and foremost was the matter of DeFeo's clothing that was contaminated with a small trace of blood. Detective Rafferty claimed that this was Dawn's blood, an assumption he had arrived at solely because the suspect had said he had picked up a blood-covered cartridge case and wiped it on his shirt and jeans. For his part, DeFeo says, 'This was an outright lie by Rafferty. The blood on my clothes was mine from the several beatings given to me by the Suffolk County Police. DNA testing can easily prove this because they still have the clothing.'

For many years, DeFeo has argued that it was his sister who killed the family, and that he shot Dawn, during the struggle, when he tried to retrieve the weapon, so the second issue revolves around Dawn's nightgown and the traces it bore of unburned gunpowder, indicating that she must have fired the .35-calibre Marlin rifle at least once that fateful night.

At the autopsy, it was proved that the single bullet that had killed her had been fired at a distance of about three feet. This discounts any possibility that Dawn had shot herself, which leaves only one outstanding question: which member, or members, of the family did she shoot dead?

In June 1992, DeFeo's request for a motion for discovery and re-examination of the nightdress was heard before Judge Stark who said that if DeFeo could fund the tests, and if the clothing was still in existence, he would order further forensic examinations.

Gerald L Lotto, acting for DeFeo, had received $10,000 from his client's grandmother, Angela Brigante, for DNA and gunpowder analysis. This money was now in an escrow account and, therefore, satisfied the first part of the Judge's ruling. Lotto's task was now to ascertain the whereabouts of Dawn's nightdress. In reply, Assistant District Attorney Karen Petterson twice told the court, under the penalty of perjury, that the garments had been destroyed. Perhaps her deceit weighed heavily on her, for several days later, her colleague, Barbara Rose, wrote a letter to the Judge that significantly watered down Petterson's claim. Again, under penalty of perjury, Assistant DA Rose said, 'The clothing is no longer in the possession of the Suffolk County District Attorney's Office, nor the Suffolk County Police Department.'

On 21 August 1991, an investigator working on another case had reason to visit the Suffolk County Police Property Evidence Bureau at Yaphank. While rummaging around, and quite by accident, Dennis O'Doherty discovered two boxes marked 'DeFeo'. They contained Dawn's nightdress, a bag of bullets and DeFeo's clothing, comprising a pair of black and blue socks, construction boots, brown work uniform, pair of blue jeans, plaid shirt, three printed pillow cases and one blood-stained pillow case.

Several days after this discovery, Karen Petterson wrote to Judge Stark, apologising, and explaining, '… the clothing was found due to the ongoing efforts of the DA's office and the police department', which was yet another distortion of the truth. With the funding for tests in place, and the clothing re-discovered, Judge Stark was legally obliged to honour his ruling, except that he chose not to.

The evidence in question is still in existence today and, when interviewed during the research for this book, Dennis Rafferty said, 'Not a chance in Hell. This stuff [the clothing] will never be looked at again. We'll make sure of that.'

* * *

In reality, Ronald DeFeo Jr is a short, insignificant little man with a blood-drenched reputation. Ferret-faced, with a good physique, he angrily argued his case of innocence for two hours, during his interview as part of the research for this book, but doubts that he will ever be released from prison. So what do we understand about Ronald DeFeo?

We know that he was, and still is, an illiterate and bullying thug: characteristics which he shares with many individuals who are not criminals. We know that he was addicted to heroin: again, hardly an unusual occurrence in today's society. We know that telling lies was routine, commonplace behaviour for him. He manufactured countless versions of the crimes, in a manner so characteristic of serial killers and mass murderers. Yet none of these qualities necessarily makes a multiple murderer. The main problem is that DeFeo cried 'wolf' too many times, so who would believe a word he says today? He is a liar through and through.

More recently, Butch argued that he did not throw the rifle into the dock. 'I did not throw the .35 Marlin rifle in the water,' he wrote in a letter, 'nor did I realise that he [Richard] threw it there.' When shown the map of the dock and the drawings made by the police, which were initialled by him, I asked Butch how the police diver managed to locate the exact location of the rifle so quickly, when no one had told them where it was? He contradicted himself saying, 'I told them it was behind my house because I didn't want to be beat up any more.'

When pressed about the diagrams, he changed his story again: 'The Marlin rifle was found after I was in the Suffolk County Jail, so there is no way I told the police. I never knew where the gun was thrown and that's the truth. And I never signed any diagrams. I initialled blank pieces of yellow paper only.'

What do we know about the trial and surrounding circus? If we know nothing else, we know that many questions, possibly of grave importance, were both unasked and unanswered. Even today, the issues raised by the bloodstained clothing and unburned powder found on Dawn's nightdress, which could so easily be resolved, remain in the realms of mystery.

We know about the strange conversation between Butch's grandfather and another thug. This was recorded on tape by the police, and included references, among other unsavoury topics, to the murder of Butch in prison. We know that the police investigation and the resultant convictions were concluded in a very untidy manner, clearly just to get the job done. Yet none of these qualities necessarily makes a false conviction.

With the exception of any startling new evidence which might appear to dispel public anxieties about the behaviour of those in authority, it is clear that at least some of the police, lawyers and one judge involved in the case, acted unethically, if not illegally. To assume otherwise would blind oneself to the true nature of the American judicial system. Disturbing though this may be, it does not necessarily entail a false conviction. Nevertheless, William E Weber seemed to do very well for himself out of the DeFeo case.

Over a few bottles of wine, during the evening after Butch was sentenced on 4 December 1974, Weber and the new owners of 'High Hopes', George and Kathleen Lutz, cooked up a story that shocked the world. The house was haunted, they said, possessed by the evil spirit of a long-dead Shinnecock Indian chief and, of course, had been built on an ancient Indian burial ground. It was this story that subsequently became the movie, *The Amityville Horror*. Once the Lutz's realised now much money was involved, they decided to cut Weber out of the deal. In turn, he filed a lawsuit in the US District court in Brooklyn, presided over by Judge Jack B Weinstein.

In his decision, the Judge stated, '… the canons and ethics of law prevent Mr Weber from being involved in Mr DeFeo's criminal case and his appeals, while at the same time being involved in movie deals, books etc …'

As a result of this ruling, Weber had to settle for a small amount of money out of court but it did not prevent him taking $20,000 from DeFeo's relatives for appeals of the conviction. Nor did it stop him from finding other ways to profit from the Amityville tragedy. He teamed up with Professor Hans Holzer, a ghost-hunter from England. Together, they wrote a book called, *Murder in Amityville*, which, subsequently became the motion picture, *Amityville II – The Possession*.

Was one of Butch's stories true and, if so, which account can we believe? Did he stumble upon some kind of gangland execution in progress. This is feasible to the extent that the medical examiner was convinced that at least three people had been involved with the subduing and shooting of the victims. But if this was the case, is it not likely that Butch would have been shot along with the rest of his family? Who else, incidentally, knew about the .35-calibre Marlin lever-action rifle that belonged to him? Were there conspirators who wanted a pawn, someone trained to passivity and dependence, who would take the blame for them? Why, then, the long silence from Butch and his friends until 20 or so years after the crimes were committed?

An answer may lie in the fact that each and every one of Butch's close friends, including his estranged wife, were threatened, bullied and even assaulted by the police at the time. Many of these police officers, including Detective Lieutenant Robert Dunn and Detective Dennis Rafferty were still employed with the Suffolk County Police at the time this book was being researched. Perhaps these witnesses had every reason to fear reprisals from law officers who survived immense criticism, only to resurface, unscathed, many years later. Another factor is that DeFeo came from a family with strong links to organised crime and the Mafia. Is it any wonder that Richard Romondoe, for example, went into hiding and assumed a false identity?

* * *

George and Kathy Lutz moved into 112 Ocean Avenue on December 18. Twenty-eight days later, they fled in terror.

So begins Chapter One of Jay Anson's novel *The Amityville Horror*. Written as a work of non-fiction, the book purports to relate the day-to-day events that drove the new residents of 'High Hopes' from their home in terror. The book became a runaway bestseller and was made into a popular movie starring Rod Steiger, Margot Kidder and James Brolin.

Their fantastic story, never disclosed in full detail, makes for an unforgettable book with all the shocks and gripping suspense of The Exorcist, The Omen or Rosemary's Baby, but with one vital difference … the story is true … reads the trailer on the book's back cover. In truth, the entire book and subsequent movies were little more than fiction. Nevertheless, the Lutzes brief stay and claims of supernatural activity at High Hopes thrust Amityville and 112 Ocean Avenue into the world spotlight. For more than 30 years, the house has stood as an icon of terror, erasing the happier times that any family had enjoyed inside the charming Dutch colonial property. Eventually, the notoriety the Lutzes had heaped upon themselves paid them back. Pestered by sightseers, and turned into pariahs in their own decent community, they were forced to move out. On 30 August 1976, they returned their home to Columbia Savings and Loan, instead of returning to live in it, or selling it to another family in the normal way.

On 18 March 1977, Jim and Barbara Cromarty purchased the house for a mere $55,000, quite unaware of its infamous reputation. When they learned about its recent history, they were forced to change the address to 108, and add a fake window to the front of the building. Determined as they were to make their home part of the community again, the Cromartys were bombarded with hordes of tourists looking for ghosts and demons. Eventually, the fans proved unbearable and they put the house on the market and moved out.

The Cromartys left Frank Birch to tend to the property, and act as house-sitter while they were away. Neither Mr Birch, nor the Cromartys ever reported supernatural occurrences in the house. The family eventually moved back in and took the house off the market. They remained there until 1987, when David Roskin, Barbara's son from a previous marriage, passed away unexpectedly.

On 17 August 1987, Peter and Jeanne O'Neill bought 108 Ocean Avenue for an unspecified amount. They lived happily there until 1997, when they were forced to sell the place because of the high taxes associated with it, which amounted to $7,000 a year. According to friends, they chose to spend the money on their children's college education, rather than give it to the tax collector.

On 10 June 1997, Brian Wilson purchased the house for $310,000. At the time of writing, he resides there with his wife and two children, who attend college. Mr Wilson says that he is very happy with the house and has no complaints. In fact, he has invested in the property by restoring the boathouse and improving the accommodation. When I visited 'High Hopes' I asked Brian Wilson whether perhaps, he might consider at some time in the future to replacing the spooky quarter-moon windows on the third floor?

He smiled and said, 'Maybe'.

This chapter is based on an exclusive videotaped interview with Christopher Berry-Dee and Ronald Joseph 'Butch' DeFeo within the Greenhaven Correctional Facility, Stormville, New York, on Friday, 23 September 1974, and extensive correspondence.

Ronald DeFeo welcomes correspondence, and his address is: Inmate #75-A-4053, Drawer B, Greenhaven CF, Stormville, NY 12582-0010.

AILEEN CAROL WUORNOS

USA

'I've got respect for myself. Always

did have. Weird, right?'

AILEEN WUORNOS TO CHRISTOPHER
BERRY-DEE

Aileen (Lee) Carol Wuornos arrived at the Broward Correctional Institute, Pembroke Pines, Florida, on 31 January 1992. Lying mid-way between Fort Lauderdale and Miami, Broward is a prison for women at which Death Row is sited in a large grey building, trimmed in pink and bordered with tropical flowers. Here, Aileen Wuornos joined the State's five other women who live in cells that look like drum-tight submarine hatches, a shower room down the hall, a caged outdoor exercise yard with a basketball loop, and additional cells apiece for future residents. Also located on the 'row' is a room designed as the 'death-watch' cell where inmates are housed 24 hours prior to execution. Death is now delivered by lethal injection, at the Florida State Prison, Starke.

At the time of writing, there are currently 47 women condemned to die in the United States. Working alone or with a partner, they have been convicted of killing their husbands, children, boyfriends and strangers. A large percentage have well-documented histories of physical or sexual abuse, as well as drug and alcohol addictions. More than half are white. Many are mothers with school-age children. Few have murdered for monetary gain. The majority live in specially-designed cell-blocks separated from the main prison population, and where their movement is greatly restricted.

Compared to their male counterparts, numbered in the hundreds throughout the penal system, women comprise only about 2 per cent of the nation's felons who have been condemned to death. California, Florida and Oklahoma have the largest number of women on Death Row. A handful of other states, such as Idaho, have only one condemned woman and must grapple with a unique problem because most States are mandated by law to segregate women from the regular male prison population.

No woman has been put to death in the United States since the execution, in Texas, of Karla Faye Tucker on 3 February 1998. This was the first time the Lone Star State had executed a woman since the Civil War. Tucker was convicted of the murders of 27-year-old Jerry Lynn Dean and his companion, 32-year-old Deborah Thornton, at their apartment on Watonga Drive in north-east Houston, on 13 June 1983. Her weapon was a pick-axe.

* * *

Aileen (Lee) Carol Wuornos was born in a leap year on 29 February 1956, in Clinton Hospital Detroit, Michigan, to teenage parents, Diane Wuornos, just 16 years old, and 19-year-old handyman, Leo Dale Pittman.

The marriage, which proved to be tumultuous, ended a few months before Lee was born, leaving the young Diane to raise the new baby and her older brother, Keith. Lee never knew her father, who was jailed on charges of kidnapping, rape and child molestation. He fashioned a noose from a bed sheet and hanged himself in prison. Lee was 15 years old at the time.

Diane soon found the responsibilities of single motherhood unbearable and, when Lee was six months old, her mother left home and never returned. Diane did, however, call her parents, asking them to pick up the children.

Laurie Wuornos, a Ford factory worker, and his wife, Eileen Britta, subsequently adopted both children. Their home was an unprepossessing one-storey building. Its wood cladding was a sad yellow colour, sited amidst a cluster of trees, away from the roadside in suburban Troy, Michigan. Innocent looking and otherwise unremarkable, the house was nevertheless a place of secrets. Near neighbours who were never once invited to set foot inside, even for casual pleasantries, recall the curtains always being tightly drawn across the small windows of the Wuornos house. The outside world was held very much at arm's length.

Laurie and Britta raised Lee and Keith with their own

children, but they did not reveal that they were, in fact, the children's grandparents.

Behind those shaded windows, frequent clashes of will took place between young Lee and her adoptive father. The omnipresent third party was a wide, brown leather belt, with Western-style tooling, that he kept hanging on a peg behind his bedroom door. At his bidding, this strap was cleaned, almost ritualistically, by Aileen with saddle soap and conditioner which were kept in the dresser drawer.

Stripped naked and forced to bend over the kitchen table, the petrified child was beaten frequently with the doubled-over belt. Sometimes she lay face down, spread-eagled naked on her bed to receive her whippings, while all the while her father screamed that she was worthless and should never have been born. 'You ain't even worthy of the air you breathe,' he shouted, as the belt lashed down again and again.

During her ninth year, a chemical explosion, which Lee and a friend accidentally set off, resulted in her sustaining severe burns on the face and arms. She was hospitalised for several days and confined for months afterwards. The burns healed slowly, but Lee worried that she would be deformed and scarred for life. Today, faint scars on her forehead and her arms still bear grim testimony to the accident.

Around the age of 11, Lee learned that her parents were indeed her grandparents. She was already incorrigible, with a fearsome and socially unacceptable temper. Her volcanic explosions, which were unpredictable and seemingly unprovoked, inevitably drove a further wedge between her and her 'parents'.

When she was 14, she became pregnant and was sent to an unmarried mothers' home to await the birth of her child. The staff found her hostile, unco-operative and unable to get along with her peers. She gave birth to a baby boy, who was put up for adoption in January 1971.

In July of the same year, Britta Wuornos died. On hearing this news, Diane Wuornos invited Aileen and Keith to stay with her in Texas, but they declined. Lee then dropped out of school, left home, and took up hitch-hiking and prostitution.

* * *

In March 1976, Lee, now aged 20, married multi-millionaire Lewis Gratz Fell. By any measure, this was a curious match. Silver-haired Fell, with his reputable Philadelphia background, was 69 years old. He had picked up Lee when she was hitch-hiking. They married in Kingsley, Georgia, less than two months after the death of her grandfather, Laurie, who had committed suicide. Aged 65, he was younger than Lee's new husband.

Most of those who knew Lee viewed her marriage cynically, finding it impossible to judge it as anything other than a purely mercenary move. The unwitting Lewis Fell had no idea what he was letting himself in for, although some took the view that it was a mutually acceptable relationship. For his part, Fell had a pretty young woman on his arm, and Lee enjoyed the fruits of what his money could buy.

Early in July, she and Lewis rolled into Michigan in a brand-new, cream-coloured Cadillac and checked into a motel. Lee had sent a few friends newspaper clippings of their wedding announcement from the society pages of the *Daytona Press*, complete with a photograph of a man who looked old enough to be her grandfather, describing Fell as the president of a yacht club, with a private income derived from railroad stocks and shares.

On 13 July, Lee went out on the town and ended up at Bernie's Club in Mancelona where she flaunted her body and started to hustle at the pool table. Some time after midnight, the barman and manager, Danny Moore, decided he had seen enough of her.

She was drunk, rowdy, shouting obscenities, uttering threats to other patrons, and generally being objectionable. He casually walked over to the pool table and announced that the table was closing down. As he was gathering up the balls, he heard someone shout, 'Duck!' He turned just in time to see Lee aim a ball at his head. It missed him only by inches, but had been hurled with such force that the missile became lodged in the wall.

When Deputy Jimmie Patrick of the Antrim County Sheriff's Department arrived, Lee was arrested for assault and battery and hauled off to jail. She was also charged on fugitive warrants from the Troy Police Department, who had requested that she be picked up on charges for drinking alcohol in a car, unlawful use of a driver's licence, and for not having a Michigan driver's licence. She was bailed when a friend turned up with her purse containing $1,450. Three days later, her brother, Keith, aged 21, died of throat cancer.

As might be expected, the marriage between Lee and Fell was short-lived. From the outset, she had been torn between her desire to get drunk and hang out in bars and the boredom of sitting around with her older husband in his plush, beachside condominium. When he refused to give her more money, she beat him up. He obtained a restraining order and an annulment of the marriage. He claimed she had squandered his money and beaten him with a walking cane.

The divorce decree stated: 'Respondent has a violent and ungovernable temper and has threatened to do bodily harm to the Petitioner and from her past actions will injure Petitioner and his property ... unless the court enjoins and restrains said Respondent from assaulting ... or interfering with Petitioner or his property.'

Lee's marriage officially ended on 19 July, with a divorce issued at the Volusia County courthouse in Florida. She pawned the expensive diamond engagement ring. Two days later, Keith was cremated at the same funeral home as Britta and Laurie Wuornos. Lee arrived late for the service.

Having rejected her son in life, but acknowledging him in death, Diane flew in from Texas for Keith's funeral. Other mourners were surprised to see her, apparently too distraught to sit through the service for the son she had abandoned and who had not long joined the Army.

On 4 August, Aileen pleaded guilty to the assault and battery charge, paying a fine and costs of $105. Then Keith's army life insurance paid up and, as next of kin, she received $10,000. The money was immediately put down as a deposit on a shiny black Pontiac (which was soon repossessed). She also bought a mixed bag of antiques and a massive stereo system although she had no home in which to put them. The money was gone within three months.

Adrift in the world once again, she embarked on a series of failed relationships and small-time forgery, theft and a rather ridiculous armed robbery that put her in prison for a spell. From time to time she turned tricks, but even as a prostitute working exit-to-exit on the interstate highway, she was not exactly sought-after. When she met 24-year-old Tyria 'Ty' Jolene Moore at a Daytona gay bar in 1986, Lee was lonely and angry. She was ready for something new.

* * *

Getting to Daytona Beach was easy for Aileen Wuornos. She had run away from home, and run away from her marriage. She had crossed State line after State line, hitched south on Interstate 95, and found what she thought was paradise. There was sunshine, jobs and cheap living. You could even drive your car on the firm white beach at Daytona. Sea, sex, prosperity and exhaust fumes. An American illusion served up on a beach so exploited it was more like a sandy parking lot.

For a while, it was great. Ty loved Lee and stayed close to her. She even quit her job as a motel maid for a while and allowed her girlfriend to support her with earnings from prostitution. In due course, perhaps predictably, their ardour cooled and money began to run short. Yet, still Ty stayed with Lee, following her like a puppy, from cheap motel to cheap motel, with stints in old barns in between.

Lee's market value as a hooker, never spectacular, fell even further. Their existence, meagre though it was, became more difficult to maintain. Clearly something had to change, but getting out of Daytona was not easy. There was never enough money to get to Miami, and the two women now realised that jobs were scarcer than they had first thought. They had blown all of their money, and their dreams of good times had faded as quickly. Desperation crept in, and temptation was quick to follow. It was a formula that often leads to crime and, in Lee's case, it meant big-time crime.

People get murdered in Daytona, as in any city, for the usual reasons – money, revenge, sex and business – but Daytona Beach seems to provoke a unique end-of-the-line dementia. Looking at what the city has to offer, who is buying and what is the main product, it is always sex. The gritty beach town lies about 60 miles east of Orlando. A good bet for a cheap, working man's vacation. Redneck tourists from all over the south-east knew this, and so did 51-year-old Richard Mallory, from Clearwater, Florida, who disappeared on Thursday, 30 November 1989.

Richard Mallory was a private man, not very communicative, a mystery even to those who should have known him best. He lived alone in a multi-family apartment complex called 'The Oaks'. Few people came to know him on account of his erratic lifestyle and, at his television and video repair shop, Mallory Electronics, in the strip shopping mall in Palm Harbour, his absences were frequent and unexplained.

He was a good-looking man with a full head of dark hair combed back from a high forehead. Standing at just under 6ft tall, the neatly moustachioed Mallory surveyed the world through hazel eyes, behind wire-rimmed glasses. He cut a trim figure, tipping the scales at just less than 170 pounds, and he thought of himself as 51 years young.

A long-time divorcee, and recently separated from a girlfriend called Jackie Davis, he had always been drawn to the opposite sex. He loved to party in the carnal sense, a regular visitor to the kinds of establishment dedicated to catering to pleasures of the flesh. He liked the way women looked, the way they smelled and moved. He liked the way he felt when he was with them – powerful, controlling, sensuous. He was a sufficiently regular customer at the topless bars in the Tampa and Clearwater area that the strippers, go-go dancers and hookers mostly knew him by sight, if not by name, although no one knew that he had spent ten years in prison for sexual violence. But now, Richard Mallory's days, spent trawling for sex, were about to come to an abrupt end.

Mallory was also in dire financial straits. He owed $4,000 in rent arrears and his affairs were due to be audited by the Inland Revenue Service. He owned two vans, one white and the other maroon. But the night he disappeared, heading for a weekend in Daytona, he was driving his light beige, two-door, 1977 Cadillac Coupe de Ville, with its brown interior and tinted windows. It was a vehicle more suited to the pursuit of hard drinking and pleasure-seeking. In the early evening of Thursday, 30 November, he closed up his TV repair shop, drove home, threw a few bags into the back of his car and headed for Daytona.

A handful of northbound rides had deposited Lee Wuornos outside Tampa on Interstate Highway I-4, right at the point where it passes under I-17. It was raining heavily and she lingered under the overpass in order to avoid the downpour, until the weather improved. Mallory spotted her and slowed down, then reversed and offered her a lift. As they drove, they chatted amicably, and en route, stopped for a pack of beer. It was around 5.00am when Mallory broached the subject of sex. He pulled off the road and into nearby woods. Lee peeled off her clothes before he did, and they hugged and kissed for a while.

Suddenly, and apparently without being provoked, she produced a .22-calibre pistol and began firing at her companion. The first bullet struck his right arm and entered his body. Desperately, he tried to crawl out of the car when another bullet slammed into his torso, quickly followed by a third and a fourth. Mallory did not die immediately. The copper-coated, hollow-nose bullet, which struck him in the right side of his chest, had penetrated his left lung, passing through the organ before coming to rest in the chest cavity. During its passage, the bullet caused a massive and fatal haemorrhage. He struggled to cling on to life for a further 15 minutes as Lee Wuornos stood by and watched him die.

The following day, Mallory's car was found abandoned near John Anderson Drive in Ormond Beach. Deputy Bonnevier was out on a routine patrol when he stopped to examine the vehicle. He noticed bloodstains on the front backrest, behind the steering wheel, but there were no signs of either the driver or any passengers. The car ignition keys were not in the switch, but numerous items were found a short distance from the car. Partially buried in the sandy soil was a blue nylon wallet, containing Richard Mallory's Florida driving licence, miscellaneous papers, and two long-expired credit cards. There were also two plastic tumbler-type glasses and a half-empty bottle of vodka, along with several other items, suggesting that Mallory had not been alone. The driver's seat had been pulled as far forward as it would go, in a driving position which would have been extremely uncomfortable for a man of Mallory's size.

Two young men, out scavenging for scrap metal on Wednesday, 13 December, found Richard Mallory's corpse at a spot roughly five miles across the river from where his car had been found. Volusia County deputies, who answered the 911 call, saw a body which was skeletonised from the collarbone to the top of the head. It lay under a piece of cardboard with only the fingers showing. It was fully dressed in jeans and a pullover, the belt slightly askew. The pockets of the jeans had been turned inside out. The man's dentures lay on the ground next to the body.

Charles James Lau, an investigator with the Volusia County Sheriff's Department, oversaw an immediate autopsy of the unidentified body and recovered four bullets from its torso. The hands of the victim were removed and transported to the crime laboratory for latent print examination because, as Lau explained, 'When we have an unidentified body, you can't roll the fingerprints because of the decomposition.'

By the middle of May 1990, the murder of hapless Richard Mallory had been all but forgotten by the Volusia County Sheriff's Department. There was, seemingly, no reason to believe it was anything other than an isolated homicide.

* * *

As ex-husbands go, 47-year-old David Spears was a dream come true. Predictable, honest and hardworking, he was a man people counted on. He earned his living as a construction worker and lived in Winter Garden, near Orlando, travelling each day to Saratosa to work at Universal Concrete. A shy, soft-spoken giant of a man, 6ft 4in tall, bearded, greying and weather-lined from his outdoor lifestyle, he cared enough about his former wife, Dee, to give her a regular portion of his monthly pay cheque.

Just before lunchtime on Friday, 18 May 1990, David called Dee and told her to expect him to call in somewhere between

2–2.30pm the next day. On Saturday, he left work at about 2.10pm in his cream pickup and he was not seen alive again.

He spotted Lee Wuornos, somewhere near the point where Route 27 intersects with I-4, about 36 miles from Winter Garden, and offered her a ride. She explained that she needed to get to Homosassa Springs. This was right out of his way; nevertheless, he agreed to take her, and they ended up pulling off the road on US 19, close to Homosassa Springs, and then drove so deep into the woods that Spears was worried that his truck would get stuck.

David Spears' truck was found abandoned near County Road 318 and I-75 in Marion County on 20 May. A blonde hair was found on the steering wheel and a ripped condom packet was found on the floor of the vehicle. All his personal property, including tools, clothing and a one-of-a-kind ceramic statue of a panther, which he had bought as a present for Dee, was missing. The driver's seat was pulled too close to the steering wheel for a man of his height, indicating to the police that someone else had driven the truck after Spears had been killed.

On 1 June, a man found the body of an unidentified male lying in a clearing amidst pine trees and palmettos. Mathew Cocking had just walked past an illegal dumping site on Fling Lane, a dirt road south of Chassahowitzka and running adjacent to US 19.

When the police arrived, they found a badly decomposing body, naked except for a camouflage baseball cap which sat jauntily atop a ravaged head. On the ground near the body were a used Trojan condom, its torn black packet, and several empty cans of Busch and Budweiser beer. At first, because of the state of the body, the police were unable to determine the sex, age or likely cause of death. The corpse lay on its back, legs apart, arms outstretched, palms facing skywards. Lee Wuornos had stolen her victim's wages, his daughter's graduation money and a quantity of cash, which had been hidden in the truck for emergencies, amounting to about $600.

Dr Janet Pillow carried out the autopsy on Monday, 4 June. The man, who weighed around 195lb in life, had been reduced to 40lb by the time his body was discovered. Six .22-calibre bullets were recovered from the remains. Two days later, another body was found in Marion County.

* * *

Forty-year-old Charles Carskaddon, a sometime road digger and rodeo rider, was on his way from his mother's home in Prairie, Missouri, to Tampa to pick up Peggy, his fiancée. He never arrived. His naked body was found off State Route 52, and I-75 in Pascoe County, on Wednesday, 6 June. The corpse was covered with grass and foliage and a green, electric blanket. He had been shot nine times in the chest with a .22-calibre handgun.

Carskaddon's brown 1975 Cadillac, a car he had lovingly restored, was found the next day near I-75 and County Road 484 in Marion County. Although the licence plate had been ripped off, the vehicle identification number (VIN) was still intact and revealed the owner's name. Carskaddon's mother, Florence, told police that when her only son left home he was carrying a blue steel .45-calibre pistol with a pearl handle, a Mexican blanket, stun gun, flip-top lighter, watch, tan suitcase, black T-shirt, and grey snakeskin cowboy boots. 'He had removed the firing pin from the gun,' she said, 'because he was scared to use it.' None of these items were found in his car.

* * *

Peter Siems was a 65-year-old retired merchant seaman, living near Jupiter, Florida. Early in the morning of 7 June, neighbours saw the part-time missionary placing luggage and a stack of bibles into his 1988 silver-grey Pontiac Sunbird. They assumed, correctly, that the balding, bespectacled man, was off on another of his 'Word-spreading' trips as a member of the 'Christ Is the Answer' Crusade. On his travels, he intended to visit relatives in Arkansas.

On 4 July, a silver-grey Pontiac Sunbird careered off State Road 315 near Orange Springs, Florida. The car smashed through a steel gate and a barbed-wire fence, shattering the windscreen before coming to rest in the undergrowth. For a brief second, it appeared that it might roll over, but it righted itself, with steam hissing from the radiator.

Rhonda and Jim Bailey, who were sitting on their porch enjoying the sun, saw the spectacular accident happen. They observed two women clamber out of the car, noting that one was a short, heavy blonde (Lee Wuornos) and the other, a tall brunette (Tyria Moore). The blonde, whose arms were bleeding from the cuts sustained in the crash, started throwing beer cans into the woods and swearing at her fellow passenger, who said very little.

The bemused witnesses noted that the women grabbed a red-and-white beer cooler from the back seat and, still arguing, staggered off along the road. At the approach of other cars, they would dash into the woods and hide; only to reappear after the vehicles had passed. When the coast was clear, they returned to the car.

When Rhonda rushed over to offer what little assistance she could, the blonde begged her not to call the police, saying that her father lived just up the road. The two women climbed back into the car and, with some difficulty, managed to reverse it on to the road and drive off. Within minutes, a front tyre went flat and, with the car now disabled, Wuornos and Moore had no other option other than to abandon it. They pulled off the rear licence plate and threw it, together with the car keys, into the woods and walked away.

A motorist, thinking that the women might need help, pulled over and offered assistance. He noticed that the blonde was not only bleeding but also very drunk. When she asked him for a lift, he thought better of it and refused, whereupon Lee became angry and abusive. The man drove away, but contacted the Orange Springs Fire Department, and told them about the injured woman.

Two emergency vehicles were despatched to the scene, but when they arrived, Lee Wuornos denied that they had been in the car. 'I don't know anything about any accident,' she snarled. 'I want people to stop telling lies and leave us alone.'

At 9.44pm Trooper Rickey responded to the emergency call, and found the car. (It was not until almost two months later that detectives learned exactly where the Sunbird had first crashed, or heard the account given by Rhonda and Jim Bailey.) Marion County's Deputy Lawing was dispatched to investigate the abandoned, smashed-up vehicle. The VIN was checked, identifying the missing Peter Siems as the owner. Latent bloody prints were found in the vehicle and there were bloodstains on the fabric of the seats and on the door handles. Items removed from the car by the police included Busch and Budweiser beer cans, as well as Marlboro cigarettes and two beverage cosies. Underneath the front passenger seat lay a bottle of Windex window spray with an Eckerd Drugs price label attached to it. This ticket was easily traceable to a store on Gordon Street in Atlanta, Georgia.

By now, the police artist had drawn composites of the two women, based on descriptions given by witnesses of the incident with the Sunbird. Armed with these sketches and the bottle of Windex, the investigators travelled to Atlanta to question the manager of Eckerd Drugs. Viewing the pictures, he recalled the two women entering his store on a Friday night. 'We are in a bad part of town in a predominantly black area and white people do not venture into this area after dark,' he said. The manager remembered that the women purchased cosmetics and a black box of Trojan condoms, the same brand found near David Spear's body and inside the trunk of his car. A beverage cosy was also traceable to a Speedway store near to the entrance/exit ramps of I-75 in Wildwood.

Peter Siems and his wife were missionaries. They neither drank nor smoked, and relatives stated that the couple had never travelled to Atlanta. John Wisnieski of the Jupiter Police had been working on the case since Siems was reported missing. He sent out a nationwide Teletype containing descriptions of the two women, and he also sent a synopsis of the case, together with descriptions and sketches of the two women, to the Florida Criminal Activity Bulletin. Then he waited. He was not optimistic about finding Siems alive. The man's body had not been found, his credit cards had not been used, and money had not been withdraw from his bank account.

* * *

Ever-smiling Eugene 'Troy' Burress celebrated his fiftieth birthday in January 1990. With a natural gift of the gab, he was employed as a part-time salesman for the Gilchrist Sausage Company in Ocala, a resort town in northern Florida, where he also lived. He also ran his own company, Troy's Pools, in Boca Raton.

On 30 July 1988, Burress set out on Gilchrist business, travelling the company's Daytona route, which took him to several customers throughout central Florida. His last planned stop was to have been Salt Springs, in Marion County. This was 'Wuornos killing country', and he never arrived.

When he failed to report at his office after work, Gilchrist manager, Mrs Jonnie Mae Thompson, started calling around and discovered that Burress had failed to show up for his last delivery. She immediately went out in search of him and, at 2.00am, he was reported missing by his wife. The police recorded her description of a slightly-built man around 5ft 6in in height and weighing about 155lb, with blue eyes and blonde hair.

This time there was a fast response and a quick, though tragic, outcome. At 4.00am, Marion County deputies found the Gilchrist delivery van, distinctive with its black cab, white refrigerator back and company logo, on the shoulder of State Road 19, 20 miles east of Ocala. The vehicle was locked and the keys were missing, as was Troy Burress.

A family out for a picnic, in the Ocala National Forest, found his body five days later. They chanced upon his body in a clearing, just off Highway 19, and about eight miles from his abandoned delivery van. Florida's heat and humidity had hastened decomposition, precluding identification at the scene. Identification was confirmed later by his wife by means of the wedding ring he was wearing. He had been killed with two shots from a .22-calibre handgun, one to the chest and one to the back. A clipboard with delivery details and receipts, which had been removed from the van, was found near the body, but the company's takings were missing.

* * *

Dick Humphreys, of Crystal River, Florida, never made it home from his last day of work at the Sumterville office of the Florida's Department of Health and Rehabilitation Services. An investigator specialising in protecting abused and injured children, he was about to transfer to the department's office at Ocala. Aged 56 he was a man of some experience who had formerly served as a police chief in Alabama.

On 11 September 1990, he disappeared after picking up a blonde hitch-hiker. The following evening, his body was found off County Road 484 near I-75 in Marion County. He had been shot seven times. Six .22-calibre bullets were recovered from his body but the seventh copper-jacketed round had passed through his wrist and was never found. His money and wallet were missing.

Humphrey's Firenza car was found on 19 September, some 70 miles to the north. It had been backed into a space behind an abandoned Banner service station at the intersection of I-10 and State Route 90, near Live Oak, in Suwannee County. The licence plate, keys and a bright yellow Highway Patrol Association bumper sticker had been removed from the car. During an initial examination of the vehicle, it was noted that everything which told the world it had belonged to Dick Humphreys was gone or trashed, just like his life. Missing items incuded his ice-scrapers, his maps, his personal papers, business papers and warranties. His favourite pipe, in the newly-carved wooden tray up on the dashboard, was also gone. In return, Lee Wuornos left one can of Budweiser beer under the passenger seat.

Back at the police pound, a closer examination of the car's interior revealed a cash register receipt for beer or wine from EMRO store number 8237, a Speedway truck stop and convenience store located at State Route 44 and I-75 in Wildwood. The receipt was time-stamped 4.19pm on 11 September 1990, the day that Dick had disappeared. The clerk who had been on duty at the time could not identify the man but did recognise the composite police sketches of Wuornos and Moore. From their body language, the clerk formed the impression they were hookers. When they left the store, she believed they drove away and therefore did not call the police, as she was obliged to because prostitutes are banned from truck stops throughout Florida.

Most of the victim's personal effects, including his pipe, which was returned to his wife, were found a month later in a wooded field off Boggy Marsh Road in southern Lake County near US 27.

By now, a number of law enforcement officers, investigating the various murders, were starting to collate their evidence. Marion and Citrus detectives had compared notes on the Burress and Spears killings. Then they spoke to Tom Muck, in Pascoe County, after they read in the Florida Department Law Enforcement (FDLE) bulletin that Muck's victim might be linked to Spears. That made three, indicating that a serial killer was at large.

The crimes had a number of features in common, including the fact that the victims were all older men who had been robbed, and two of them had had their pockets turned inside out. All three killings had been carried out using a small calibre weapon. Bullets, recovered from the bodies, were .22-calibre, copper-coated, hollow-nosed, with rifling marks made by a 6-right twist firearm.

Another link emerged when the police exchanged the composite sketches made by their individual witnesses. They bore significant similarities, suggesting they were looking for the same short, blonde woman. If she was a sole killer, and not working with a man, the officers reasoned, then she might well use a small handgun as an 'equaliser'.

Captain Steve Binegar, commander of the Marion County Sheriff's Criminal Investigation Division, knew about the Citrus and Pascoe murders. Today, he is based at the County Jail in Tallahassee, where he recalled that he could not ignore the similarities between the murders, and had begun to formulate a theory. His first job was to form a multi-agency task force, with representatives from counties where the bodies were found.

'No one stopped to pick up hitch-hikers in those days,' Captain Binegar explained. 'So the perpetrator/s of those crimes had to be initially non-threatening to the victims. Specifically, when I learned that two women had walked away from Peter Siems's car, I looked at the Trojan brand of prophylactics. Then came the composites and the truck stop clerk who said that the two women looked like hookers. Then I said to the other guys, "We gotta be looking for a highway hooker, period." '

Binegar decided to turn to the press for help. In late November, Reuters ran a story about the killings, reporting that the police were looking for two women. Newspapers throughout Florida picked up the story and ran it, along with the sketches of the women in question.

* * *

Sixty-year-old Walter Antonio, from Cocoa, Florida, was driving to Alabama, in search of a job. Recently engaged, he wore a gold and silver diamond ring, a gift from his fiancée. On 18 November, a police officer, out hunting, found a man's body, naked except for a pair of tube socks, near the intersection of US 19 and US 27 in Dixie County. Walter Antonio had been shot four times, three times in the torso and once in the head, with a .22-calibre handgun.

His maroon Pontiac Grand Prix car was found on 24 November in a wooded area near I-95 and US 1, in northern Brevard County. The licence plate and keys were missing and, like Humphrey's car, a bumper sticker had been removed. A piece of paper had been crudely pasted over the VIN, and the doors were locked. Empty Budweiser cans were found on the ground near the vehicle, which had been wiped clean of fingerprints.

Detectives learnt that Antonio meticulously recorded every purchase he made of car fuel, retaining the filling station receipts on which he noted his mileage. From this methodical behaviour, they were able to deduce that, in the week since his disappearance, his car had been driven for over 1,000 miles.

His fiancée gave the police a list of possessions that had been in his car, including handcuffs, a reserve deputy badge, police billy club, flashlight, a Timex wristwatch, a suitcase, a toolbox and a baseball cap. All of these items were missing.

Walter Antonio's personal identification and clothing were discovered in a wooded area in Taylor County, approximately 38 miles north of the body's location. The rest was never found.

In just over a year, Lee Wuornos had scattered a trail of middle-aged male corpses across the highways of central Florida.

* * *

Following Captain Steve Binegar's appeal for information through the newspapers, calls began to pour in and, by mid-December 1990, detectives had a number of firm leads involving the two women suspects. A man in Homosassa Springs, where Wuornos asked David Spears to drop her off, said that two women, who fitted the composites, had rented an RV mobile home from him about a year earlier. After searching through his records, he came up with the names of 'Tyria Moore' and 'Lee'.

A witness in Tampa said two women had worked at her motel south of Ocala, close to where Troy Burress was murdered. Their names, she said, were Tyria Moore and Susan Blahovec and they let it be known they had bought an RV in Homosassa Springs. The informant remembered that the blonde, Blahovec, was the dominant of the duo and believed she was a truck stop prostitute. She also told the police that both were lesbians.

The information from these two callers rang immediate alarm bells with the task force – David Spears; Homosassa Springs; RV trailer; two women … Troy Burress; Ocala; RV trailer; the same two women. The investigation was starting to pay off as previously tenuous links started coming together.

Meanwhile, the composite sketches, published by the media, of the red-lipped blonde with the stringy hair and her dark-haired, moon-face companion in the baseball cap, began to haunt Moore day and night. This was her excuse to flee Daytona Beach and go home to Ohio for Thanksgiving. Tyria, who had never hurt anyone in her life, had a lot of serious thinking to do because, although she was emotionally attached to Lee, she could not believe that her lover was the serial killer for whom the State had launched a massive search operation.

The breakthrough for the investigators came from Port Orange near Daytona. Local police had picked up the trail of the two women and were able to provide a detailed account of the couple's movements from late September to mid-December. They had stayed, primarily, at the Fairview Motel, in Harbor Oaks, where Blahovec registered as Cammie Marsh Greene. They spent a short while living in a small apartment, behind a restaurant near the Fairview, but returned later to the motel. Then Wuornos – aka Blahovec, aka Greene – returned alone and stayed until 10 December.

A national police computer check gave driver's licence and criminal record information on Tyria Moore, Susan Blahovec and Cammie Marsh Greene. Moore had no record worth considering, having had breaking and entering charges against her, in 1983, dropped. Blahovec had one trespassing arrest, while Greene had no record at all. Additionally, the photograph on Blahovec's licence did not match the one for Greene.

The Greene ID was the one that finally paid off. Volusia officers checked area pawnshops and found that in Daytona, Cammie Marsh Greene had pawned a 35mm Minolta Freedom camera and a Micronta Road Patrol Radar Detector bought at Radio Shack (both of the type owned by Richard Mallory), at the OK Pawn Shop in Daytona Beach. Cammie got $30 for the trade, showed her driver's licence and duly left the obligatory thumbprint on the collection receipt. Few people even own a Radio Shack radar detector, let alone associated with a Minolta .35mm camera, so this combination sparked the detective's interest. In Ormond Beach, she had pawned a set of tools that matched the description of those taken from David Spear's truck, although the police failed to recover these.

The thumbprint proved to be the key. Jenny Ahearn of the FDLE's Automated Fingerprint Identification System found nothing on her initial computer search, but she visited Volusia County with colleagues where they began a hand-search of fingerprint records. Within an hour, she struck gold. The print showed up on a weapons charge and outstanding warrant against a Lori K Grody. Her fingerprints matched a bloody palm print found in Peter Siems's Sunbird. All of this information was sent to the National Crime Information Centre, and responses came from Michigan, Colorado and Florida, confirming that Lori K Grody, Susan Blahovec and Cammie Marsh Greene were all aliases for one Aileen Carol Wuornos.

Posing as leather-clad bikers, two undercover detectives, Mike Joyner and Dick Martin, finally spotted Lee Wuornos at 9.19pm on Tuesday, 8 January 1991, and kept her under surveillance. She was drinking at the Port Orange Pub, on Ridgewood Avenue, in Harbor Oaks, about half-a-mile north of her favourite bar, 'The Last Resort', one of the many bikers' bars that line Highway One. Suddenly, to the dismay of the undercover officers, two uniformed Port Orange police officers walked into the bar and took Wuornos outside. Joyner and Martin frantically telephoned their command post at the 'Pirate's Cove Motel' where authorities from six jurisdictions had gathered to bring the investigation to a head. They concluded that this development was not a leak but simply a case of alert police officers doing their jobs. Bob Kelly of the Volusia County Sheriff's Office called the Port Orange Police Station and told them not to arrest Wuornos under any circumstances. The word was relayed to the officers in the nick of time, and Lee was allowed to return to the bar.

The action shifted back to the two undercover detectives, who struck up a conversation with her and bought her a few beers. She left the bar at around 10.00pm, carrying a leather suitcase and declining the offer of a lift. Once again, the cautious arrest was almost ruined when two FDLE officers pulled up behind Wuornos, following her with their lights off as she walked down Ridgewood Avenue. Police at the command post radioed the FDLE officers to back off, allowing Lee to proceed to The Last Resort.

Joyner and Martin met her at The Last Resort, drinking and chatting until midnight, when she left. But she did not go far. Lee Wuornos spent her last night of freedom sleeping on an old yellow vinyl car seat, under the tin roof overhang of the bar.

Surveillance was planned to continue throughout the following day, but when the police learned that a large number of bikers was expected for a party at the bar that evening, they decided further surveillance would be impossible. By simply donning a crash helmet, Lee could quite easily disappear among the hundreds of motorcyclists milling around at the party, and vanish for good. The decision was made at that point to go ahead with the arrest. Joyner and Martin asked her if she would like to use their motel room to clean up before the party. At first she was reluctant, but then changed her mind and left the bar with them.

Outside, on the steps leading to the bar, Larry Horzepa of the Marion County Sheriff's Office approached Lee and told her that she was being arrested on an outstanding warrant for Lori Grody. This related to the illegal possession of a firearm and no mention was made of the murders. The arrest was kept low key and no announcement was made to the media that a suspected serial killer had been arrested. Their caution was well advised for, as yet, the police had no murder weapon and no Tyria Moore.

Lee's companion was located on 10 January, living with her sister in Pittston, Pennsylvania. Jerry Thompson of Citrus County and Bruce Munster of Marion County flew to Scranton to interview her. She was informed of her rights but not charged with any offence. Munster made sure she knew what perjury was, swore her in, and sat back as she gave her statement.

Tyria said she had known about the murders since Lee had arrived home with Richard Mallory's Cadillac. Lee had openly confessed that she had killed a man that day, but Moore had advised her not to say anything else. 'I told her I don't want to hear about it,' she told the detectives. 'And then any time she would come home after that and say certain things, telling me about where she got something, I'd say I don't want to hear it.' Tyria had her suspicions, she admitted, but wanted to know as little as possible about Lee's business. The more she knew, she reasoned, the more compelled she would feel to report Lee to the authorities. She did not want to do that. 'I was just scared,' she said. 'She always said she'd never hurt me, but then, you can't believe her, so I don't know what she would have done.'

The next day, Tyria Moore accompanied Munster and Thompson on their return to Florida to assist in the investigation. A confession would make the case against Wuornos virtually airtight, and Munster and Thompson explained their plan to her on the flight. They would register her in a Daytona motel and have her make contact with Lee in jail, explaining that she had received money from her mother and had returned to collect the rest of her things. Their conversations would be taped. She was to tell Lee that authorities had been questioning her family, and that she thought the Florida murders would be mistakenly pinned on her. Munster and Thompson hoped that, out of loyalty to Tyria, Lee would confess.

Still under the impression that she was only in jail for the Lori Grody weapons violation, the first call came from Lee on 14

January. When Tyria voiced her suspicions, Lee reassured her. 'I'm only here for that concealed weapons charge in '86 and a traffic ticket,' she said, 'and tell you what, man, I read the newspaper, and I wasn't one of those little suspects.' She was aware, though, that the jailhouse phone she was using was being monitored, and made efforts to speak of the crimes in code words and to construct alibis. 'I think somebody at work … where you worked at … said something that it looked like us,' she said. 'And it isn't us, see? It's a case of mistaken identity.'

The calls continued for three days. Tyria Moore became even more insistent that the police were after her, and it became clear that Lee knew what was expected of her. She even voiced suspicion that Moore was not alone, that someone was taping their conversations. But, as time passed, she became less careful about what she said. She would not let Moore go down with her. 'Just go ahead and let them know what you need to know … what they want to know or anything,' she said, 'and I will cover for you, because you are innocent. I'm not going to let you go to jail. Listen, if I have to confess, I will.' And, on the morning of 16 January, she did just that.

During her confession to Larry Horzepa and Bruce Munster, Lee returned again and again to two themes. First, she wanted to make it clear that Tyria Moore was not involved in any of the murders. Secondly, she was emphatic in her assertion that nothing was her fault, neither the murders nor the circumstances that had shaped her life as a criminal. She claimed that all the killings were acts of self-defence. Each victim had either assaulted, threatened or raped her. Her story seemed to evolve and take on a life of its own as she related it. When she thought she had said something that might be incriminating, she would back up and retell that part, revising the details to suit her own ends. Lee claimed to have been raped several times over the years and decided it was not going to happen again. In future, when a customer became aggressive, she killed out of fear. Several times, Michael O'Neill, an attorney from the Volusia County Public Defender's Office, advised her to stop talking, finally asking in exasperation, 'Do you realise these guys are cops?' Wuornos answered, 'I know. And they want to hang me. And that's cool, because maybe, man, I deserve it. I just want to get this over with.'

News that the police had secured a female serial killer's confession soon leaked out to the public domain and an avalanche of book and movie deals poured in to detectives, to Moore and Wuornos and to the victims' relatives. Lee seemed to think she would make millions of dollars from her story, not yet realising that Florida had a law against criminals profiting in such a manner. She commanded headlines in the local and national media. She felt famous, and continued to talk about the crimes with anyone who would listen, including Volusia County Jail employees. With each retelling, she refined her story a little further, seeking to cast herself in a better light each time.

On 28 January 1991, Lee Wuornos was indicted for the murder of Richard Mallory. The indictment read:

In that Aileen Carol Wuornos, a/k/a Susan Lynn Blahovec, a/k/a/ Lori Kristine Grody, a/k/a/ Cammie Marsh Greene, on or about the first day of December 1989, within Volusia County, did then and there unlawfully, from a premeditated design to effect the death of one Richard Mallory, a human being, while engaged in the perpetration of or attempt to perpetrate robbery, did kill and murder Richard Mallory by shooting him with a firearm, to wit: a handgun.

Counts two and three charged her with armed robbery and possession of a firearm and, by late February, she had been charged with the murders of David Spears, in Citrus County, and Charles Humphreys and Troy Burress in Marion County.

Lee's attorneys engineered a plea bargain, whereby she would plead guilty to six charges and receive six consecutive life terms. One State's attorney, however, thought she should receive the death penalty, so on 14 January 1992, she went to trial for the murder of Richard Mallory.

The evidence and testimony of witnesses were severely damaging. Dr Arthur Botting, the medical examiner, who had carried out the autopsy on Mallory's body, stated that he had taken between ten and twenty agonising minutes to die. Tyria Moore testified that Wuornos had not seemed overly upset, nervous or drunk when she told her about the Mallory killing. Twelve men went on to the witness stand to testify to their encounters with Lee along Florida's highways and byways over the years.

Florida has a law, known as the 'Williams Rule', that allows evidence relating to other crimes to be admitted if it serves to show a pattern. Because of the Williams Rule, information regarding other killings, alleged to have been committed by Wuornos, was presented to the jury. Her claim, of having killed in self-defence would have been a lot more believable had the jury only known of Mallory. Now, with the jury being made aware of all the murders, self-defence seemed the least plausible explanation. After the excerpts from her videotaped confession were played, the self-defence claim simply looked ridiculous. Wuornos appeared on the tape and seemed not the least upset by the story she was telling. She made easy conversation with her interrogators and repeatedly told her attorney to be quiet. Her image on the screen allowed her to condemn herself out of her own mouth. 'I took a life ... I am willing to give up my life because I killed people ... I deserve to die,' she said.

Tricia Jenkins, one of Lee's public defenders, did not want her client to testify and told her so. But Wuornos overrode this advice, insisting on telling her story. By now, her account of

Mallory's murder barely resembled the one she gave in her confession. Mallory had raped, sodomised and tortured her, she claimed.

On cross-examination, prosecutor John Tanner obliterated any shred of credibility she may have had. As he brought to light all her lies and inconsistencies, she became agitated and angry. Her attorneys repeatedly advised her not to answer questions, and she invoked her Fifth Amendment right, against self-incrimination, 25 times. She was the defence's only witness, and when she left the stand, there was not much doubt about how her trial would end.

Judge Uriel 'Bunky' Blount Jr charged the jury on 27 January. They returned their verdict 91 minutes later. Pamela Mills, a schoolteacher, had been elected Foreperson and she presented the verdict to the bailiff. He, in turn, handed it to the judge. The judge read it and passed it to the clerk who spoke the words that sealed Lee's fate. 'We, the jury, find Aileen Wuornos guilty of premeditated felony murder in the first degree,' she told an expectant assembly in the courtroom. As the jury filed out, their duty done, Lee exploded with rage, shouting, 'I'm innocent! I was raped! I hope you get raped! Scumbags of America.'

Her outburst was still fresh in the minds of jurors as the penalty phase of her trial began, the next day. Expert witnesses for the defence testified that Wuornos was mentally ill, that she suffered from a borderline personality disorder, and that her tumultuous upbringing had stunted and ruined her. Jenkins referred to her client as 'a damaged, primitive child', as she tearfully pleaded with the jury to spare Lee's life. But the jurors neither forgot, nor forgave, the woman they had come to know during the trial. With a unanimous verdict, they recommended that Judge Blount sentence her to die in the electric chair. He confirmed the sentence on 31 January, first quoting his duty from a printed text.

Aileen Carol Wuornos, being brought before the court by her attorneys William Miller, Tricia Jenkins and Billy Nolas, having been tried and found guilty of count one, first-degree premeditated murder and first-degree felony murder of Richard Mallory, a capital felony; and count two, armed robbery with a firearm … hereby judged and found guilty of said offences … and the court having given the defendant an opportunity to be heard and to offer matters in mitigation of sentence … It is the sentence of this court that you, Aileen Carol Wuornos, be delivered by the Sheriff of Volusia County to the proper officer of the Department of Corrections of the State of Florida and by him safely kept until by warrant of the Governor of the State of Florida, you, Aileen Wuornos, be electrocuted until you are dead.

'And may God have mercy on your corpse.'

A collective gasp arose from the courtroom, diminishing the solemnity of the occasion. The sense of shock was less to do with the judge's sentiment than his choice of words. May God have mercy on your corpse? Did Judge Blount really say that? *Corpse?* Members of the media stopped, with pencils poised in mid-air. He had got it wrong. Surely, he should have said, 'May God have mercy on your soul.' Could they quote him, they whispered among themselves?

Aileen Wuornos did not stand trial again. On 31 March 1992, she pleaded no contest to the murders of Dick Humphreys, Troy Burress and David Spears, saying that she wanted to 'get it right with God'. In a rambling statement to the court, she said, 'I wanted to confess to you that David Mallory did violently rape me as I've told you. But these others did not. [They] only began to start to.' She ended her monologue by turning to Assistant State Attorney Ric Ridgeway, and hissing, 'I hope your wife and children get raped in the ass!'

On 15 May, Judge Thomas Sawaya handed her three more death sentences. She made an obscene gesture and muttered 'Motherfucker'.

For a time, there was speculation that Wuornos might receive a new trial for the murder of Richard Mallory. New evidence showed that Mallory had spent ten years in prison for sexual violence, and attorneys felt that jurors would have seen the case differently had they been aware of this. No new trial was forthcoming though and, since then, the State Supreme Court of Florida has affirmed all six of her death sentences.

Today, Lee is in her second round of appeals, a process that will eventually wend its way to the United States Supreme Court. These many appeals advance haltingly, as Florida's efforts to streamline its appellate process create new delays. She was put to death on 9 October 2002.

* * *

Aileen Carol Wuornos has shared Death Row with several faces familiar to students of crime in the USA. Judias 'Judy' Buenonano, aged 48, and popularly known as 'The Black Widow', had been on Death Row since 1985. Convicted of poisoning her husband, drowning her quadraplegic son by pushing him out of a canoe, and planting a bomb in her boyfriend's car, she had the distinction of being the first woman to die in Florida's electric chair on 30 March 1998.

Deirdre Hunt was sent to Death Row in 1993 and her sentence has since been commuted to life.

Andrea Hicks Jackson was sentenced to death for shooting a police officer in 1983, and has also had her sentence reversed. Like Hunt, she no longer lives on 'The Row'.

Virginia Gail Larzelere, aged 49, has recently been given the death penalty for murdering her husband at Edgewater, near Daytona Beach, on 8 March 1991.

Ana M Cardona, aged 40, was sentenced to death for aggravated child abuse, and the first-degree murder of her three-year-old son, in Miami, on 2 November 1992.

At the time of writing, Aileen Wuornos is 46 years-old, but looks a decade older. The condemned woman, wearing an orange T-shirt and blue trousers, is 5ft 4in in height and weighs 133lb. The characteristic strawberry-blonde hair, described by witnesses, frames her face but her eyes are constantly bloodshot. Always looking washed-out, her once attractive looks have been replaced with a face that life has not treated kindly. She has a scar between the eyes and burn scars on her forehead. Her body is marked with a long cut along her lower left arm and a crude appendectomy scar across the middle of her abdomen.

The cell in which Lee is confined measures 8ft by10ft. It is painted a dull-looking pink, and the ceiling is quite high, maybe 15ft, which makes the room seem larger and more airy than it really is. She has a black-and-white television, placed above the stainless steel toilet, on a varnished brown shelf. The furniture consists of a grey metal footlocker that doubles as a desk, but no table and only a single chair. There is also a dirty, lime-green cupboard at the foot of a metal bed, which contains her clothes and personal possessions. Everything has to be locked away at bed inspection time, between 9.00am and 11.00am. The only view she has of the outside world is a parking lot and a high fence, festooned with glittering razor wire. There are no bars at her cell window but a metal door with a small hatch separates her from the rest of the cell block. It costs the State of Florida $72.39 a day to keep Lee Wuornos incarcerated.

Describing her routine, she said, 'The food ain't all bad. We're served three meals a day. At 5.00am, 10.30 to 11.00am, an' 4.00pm to 4.30. They cook it in here. We get plates and spoons; Nothing else. I can take a shower every other day, and we're counted at least once an hour. Everywhere we go, we wear cuffs except in the shower and exercise yard where I can talk to my cellmates. Lately, I like to be by myself. Apart from that, I am always locked up in my room. I can't even be with another inmate in the common room.'

She spends the long, solitary hours reading books on spiritual growth and writing lengthy letters to her mother. Lee's lifestyle is spartan and monotonous – and the days and years roll indistinguishably and uneventfully past her locked cell door. In the knowledge that 11.3 years is the average length of stay on Death Row, prior to execution, Lee knows that when her death comes, it will be a painful experience.

Yet, knowing this, Lee appears unfazed. 'Death does not scare me. God will be beside me, taking me up with him when I leave this shell; I am sure of it. I have been forgiven and am certainly sound in Jesus' name.'

On the highways and byways of Florida there are always crossroads, off and on-ramps, where two lives can meet, with destructive results. One comes to an end, and the other takes a permanent detour. Lee Wuornos haunted those places like a deadly spider sitting at the centre of its web. To all intents and purposes, she was a non-threatening woman hitching a ride. As she explained, 'What I'm sayin' … you want the truth. I want to tell it as it was. I'm telling you that I was always going somewhere, and most times I hitched a ride. There are thousands of guys and women out there who'll say they gave me a ride, and we got on just fine, ya know. They gave me no hassle. I'm a good person inside, but when I get drunk, I just don't know. It's just … when I'm drunk it's don't mess the fuck with me. Ya know. That's the truth. I've got nothing to lose. That's the truth.'

When asked who had initiated the subject of sex during the rides, Lee claimed, 'I was always short of money, so I guess sometimes I brought up sex. Mallory wanted to fuck straight off. He was a mean motherfucker with a dirty mouth. He got drunk and it was a physical situation, so I popped him and watched the man die. Spears was made out to be a nice, decent guy. That's shit. He wanted a quick fuck. He bought a few beers and wanted a free fuck ... an' you wanna know about the third one [Carskaddon]. How do think he got undressed? Wise up. He wanted sex ... got undressed. Ask yourself, what's that all about if he didn't want a cheap fuck? Cos the cops didn't say about the others ... never found the johnnies. Yeah, OK, man. Look, you gotta understand that guys don't get nude with some broad if they don't want sex. The last one ... I can't remember his name [Walter Antonio] was ... Jesus Christ ... he was fucking engaged. He bought a six-pack. The dirty motherfucker. And, I do have one thing, though ... their families must know that no matter how they loved the people that I killed, they were bad 'cause they were going to hurt me. I suppose you think I really suck, right?'

Most killers are able to describe their crimes, and Lee Wuornos is more adept than some, telling and retelling her story with added layers of gloss to suit her own ends. But one aspect of her story remains constant. She says that each of her victims wanted sex, and either raped her against her will, or intended to. For that very reason, she shot them dead, eliminating them with no more compassion than swatting a fly.

'You've gotta understand ... I ain't so bad. I've been with hundreds and hundreds of men. I just ain't killed them all. I would make money but they wouldn't abuse me or nothin'. I'd just make my money out in the boonies, stick it in my wallet and go. Never hurt them, right? Then you get a few dirty old men who go radical on me. So you see what I'm sayin' ... I kinda had to do what I had to do. What am I supposed to do? It was all their fault, and that's the God's honest truth.'

Because the body of Peter Siems has never been found, Lee was asked where she had left the corpse. 'Look. I can't remember their faces or their names, so don't shit me. How the fuck am I going to recall where he is? But I'm tellin' you that he's got to be seriously dead by now.'

Asked if her grandfather had sexually abused her, Lee said, 'Ya know. I have said different things about this over the years, but, the truth is, yeah. I was. He'd do stuff to me and give me pocket money to shut up. He'd finger me. I lost my virginity to his fuckin' finger when I was about seven. He'd beat the shit outa me, ya know. But he'd strip me naked beforehand ... that's fuckin wrong ... you understand? He made me what I am. He made me hate men like him. Dirty, cheap, no-good motherfuckers like him. Look at me ... I'm shaking all over even thinking about it. For fuck's sake, let's leave it. OK, Christopher? I'm sort of getting freaked out and I don't need this right now.'

* * *

Knowing the enormity of the crimes committed by Lee Wuornos, it is easy just to follow the general line of thinking and dismiss her simply as another one in a long line of serial killers. While there have been many female mass murderers, there have been few female serial killers. Lee Wuornos stands out because of her gender and her dismissal of the compassionate, life-giving qualities of her sex, not in response to a single act of murderous impulse but, time after time, in a series of violent deaths. By making a man suffer, she transformed herself from a victim to the victimiser, eagerly grabbing power for herself with both hands and with the aid of a handgun. She made herself unique in a gross kind of way.

Lee Wuornos has an anti-social personality disorder. Although one-in-twenty males suffer from such a disorder, meaning that their actions are not inhibited by guilt or moral boundaries, very few kill, and even fewer women kill. Even fewer in numbers are hookers who kill for money when selling their bodies; indeed, prostitutes are the all-too-familiar victims of male serial killers.

Lee Wuornos may fairly be described as unique and, as such, she merits more than a passing study. She perhaps represents a reason why society should not, out of revenge, use the ultimate penalty of execution, which is usually carried out more for the sake of political expediency, than for the sake of deterrence. If her life serves no other purpose, Lee Wuornos might just provide some valuable insights into a rare breed of killer.

Her life was a tangled thread of alcohol and loneliness, spent for the most part, rootless and penniless, roaming the highways of Florida. She hung around the haunts of bikers, but sought love from her female companion, Tyria Moore, hating men as the source of all her troubles and luring at least six of them to their deaths. But the question remains – what preceded Lee's dance of death? What finally made the bough break?

To answer the first question, it would be fair to say that she did not enjoy a healthy childhood. Her true father, a man she never met, was a sexual pervert who later hanged himself in prison. Her mother abandoned her when she was six months old, and she was adopted by an authoritarian grandfather and grandmother.

Throughout her entire formative years, the young girl was humiliated, sexually abused, beaten and rejected, and her world was filled with pain, rage and alcoholism, all suffered behind the closed curtains of a house of secrets.

In order to survive, she rebelled in the only way she knew. As she grew older, and mentally stronger, she learned how to fight fire with fire. No longer was she the easy pushover and handy repository for her grandfather's frustrations which stemmed from his own hatred of his weak daughter who had dumped her children on his doorstep. When this rebellious behaviour showed signs of success, and about the same time as she learned that Lauri and Eileen were not her real parents, Lee knew that she had won the upper hand. In a calculated way of exacting revenge for all of the suffering she had endured, she turned to childhood prostitution, became pregnant, left school and took to the road.

She had one tragic lesson in the forefront of her mind. Her grandfather and her true father, like so many older men, married or otherwise, have money, are attracted to young females and will willingly pay for illicit sex when the opportunity arises. She also knew that she was a law unto herself. No one could tame Lee Wuornos. But, she was not born a serial killer. She had been brought up in an environment where her innocence was mismanaged and abused. The foundations of her antisocial behaviour were implanted by the family surroundings in which she was reared. In that respect, her true parents and grandparents have much to answer for.

When her grandmother died, Lee was not upset. Understandably, when her grandfather committed suicide, she was elated, and when her brother died of throat cancer she was stunned, but the $10,000 she received from his army insurance soon compensated for the grief she endured at his passing.

When that money was exhausted, she hitch-hiked south and, after a series of one-night stands, met the wealthy Louis Gratz Fell, a well-connected man who should have known better. The 69-year old, with a grand ego, obscenely flaunted the 20-year-old as his fiancée. He paid for his mistake when a streetwise Lee Wuornos took advantage of the old man's sexual predilections. 'The bottom line,' said Lee, 'is that he was a cheap, flashy, dirty old man who had money. Basically, he bought my sex. Wanted to keep me at home with him. Give me a break … what else do you want to hear?'

After splitting with Fell, and like many millions of Americans, Lee went in search of a dream. She ended up in Daytona with all its sun-kissed mirages and promises and it was there, while drinking in a gay bar, that she met another lonely young woman. Tyria Moore would become the only true love of her life. Lee discovered that Tyria, unlike everyone else she had met, did not want anything from her. On the contrary, Tyria was not a materialistic person and demonstrated her love and respect by devoting most of her free time to be in Lee's company.

In an interview, Tyria said, 'Lee was very pretty in those days. She dressed very provocatively and I considered her a real catch. We had some great times. She was a great lover. Very gentle and caring as if she needed my love in return. She was my best friend. But what I admired the most was her strength. She was very … er, over-protective of me. No one messed with me when Lee was around. I truly loved her, but I don't think anyone will understand this. Even when she was drunk, she was funny. It was a ball of laughs, you know. They won't kill her, will they?'

So, why did the bough break, and why did Lee turn to serial homicidal violence? There are those who subscribe to the view that *all* serial killers enjoy using, abusing and controlling fellow human beings. This is why some observers have stated that Wuornos is a new type of breed of killer, leaping on the notion that she is a pioneer, a predatory hitchhiker, stalking the highways, from whom no man is safe. Conversely, it seems to be generally agreed that women rarely kill just for kicks.

Lee has always said that she was short of cash. That was a problem which could always be resolved with a trick here and there; besides, there is the undeniable fact that she hitched hundreds of rides from men, and only murdered six. There is no doubt that she had sex with many of those who offered her lifts and who were probably blissfully unaware that she always carried a gun.

So what was the murderous impulse that led her to homicidal violence? Captain Steve Binegar argued that 'when she was picked up by men they usually lived, but when they went into the woods with her, they never came out alive'. This is a simplification, as Captain Binegar later agreed. 'Maybe I was generalising,' he said. 'No guy is going to strip on the highway … risk police seeing a parked car … windows steamed up … rocking up an' down.

Perhaps I was wrong. I'm damned sure I wouldn't mess around like that on the highway.'

In trying to understand what triggered Lee's impulse to kill, it is plausible and, indeed, likely that her 'killing days', like those of Michael Ross, were precipitated by personal crisis or extra stresses in her life. As her feelings of powerlessness heightened, her mind tried to compensate by converting those feelings into a desire to exert control over another human being. Many serial killers, including most of those featured in this book, commonly admit that an argument with the opposite sex, a close partner or a parent, preceded the act of murder.

A study carried out, by the FBI, on male subjects, showed that 59 per cent specifically mentioned conflict with a woman. Lee had conflicts with Tyria Moore, her only love, at the time of the murders of Mallory, Spears, Carskaddon, Siems, Humphreys and Antonio. Either Tyria was threatening to leave, or the presence of a competing force for Tyria's affections had made Lee fear she might lose her.

Another attractive lesbian, called Sandy Russell, had entered Tyria's life, just a few days before Lee murdered Richard Mallory. When another woman, Tracey, visited Tyria, Lee killed David Spears, Charles Carskaddon and Peter Siems. When Tyria was dismissed from employment at the Casa Del Mar restaurant, she talked about leaving Florida and, by implication, deserting Lee. This happened in the week before Richard Humphreys was murdered. Tyria had left for Ohio, for Thanksgiving, amid talk about making a break from Lee, when Walter Antonio was shot dead. There seems to be a pattern here and it takes no great stretch of the imagination to envisage a crisis in their relationship, at the end of July, which preceded the murder of Troy Burress.

If this line of reasoning is valid, the idea that Lee took the lives of her victims in the image of her abusive grandfather is erroneous. Despite the monstrous picture she has painted for herself, she has always been – and will continue to be – a lonely, scared woman who shares the fundamental human desire for love, respect, and attention. She was denied such fulfilment from the beginning of her life and when she found the one person she could really love, and whom she imagined, unequivocally, loved her, she cherished this relationship in her own particular way.

Alone, out on the wet highways, with her domestic problems in the forefront of her mind, Lee found 'Murder Crossroads'. Older men with sex on their minds, maybe in the image of her grandfather, crossed her path. Seemingly respectable men with money, wives and lovers, who were only too keen to buy six-packs of beer and booze in exchange for cheap sex in the sordid confines of a car on a lonely track.

'I was really OK with these guys. That is the God's honest truth,' said Lee Wuornos during an interview, 'A few drinks, they thought I was cheap …started talking rough an' dirty like I'm shit, man. I've had that all my life … didn't need the shit … I'm a reasonable person. They wanted to fuck my ass … couldn't get that with their wives an' stuff. They wanted to abuse and humiliate me. Ya know, despite what you think, I've got respect for myself. Always did have. Weird, right!

Giving a ride to Lee Wuornos, buying her a few cheap drinks, pulling off the highway and talking her down was a murderous cocktail, indeed.

This chapter is based on an interview between Lee Wuornos and Christopher Berry-Dee on Death Row, Pembroke Pines Correctional Institute, Florida, in 1996, and other research.

KENNETH ALLEN McDUFF

USA

'Killing a woman's like killing a chicken. They both squawk.'

KENNETH MCDUFF'S CHILLING APPRAISAL TO HIS ACCOMPLICE ROY DALE GREEN

'He was out on parole when McDuff killed our kids. We got three death sentences, and now he is out on parole again. They are going to have blood on their hands, those people who turned him loose.'

BILL BRAND, FATHER OF ROBERT BRAND, ONE OF MCDUFF'S 1966 VICTIMS

H e didn't just kill his victims; he savaged them in unspeakable ways. He raped them with a sadism that made veteran police officers cringe. This killer blew off his victims' faces at point-blank range, he slashed and stabbed with knives, and bludgeoned with clubs. He crushed one victim's neck with a broomstick.

* * *

Tall, dour and icy-eyed, McDuff had scattered corpses around Central Texas – estimates have ranged upward of 15 – since he was a teenager, so who is this ogre who terrorised a whole State?

There is little recorded information on the early life of Kenneth McDuff. What we do know is that he was born on Sunday, 3 March 1946, at 201 Linden Street, in the small, central Texas hamlet of Rosebud, Falls County. The saying, 'All is Rosy in Rosebud', suggests a cosy place untroubled by violence.

The earliest settlers arrived in Falls County from Mexico at the time of the War of Independence, in 1836. The economy depended on cotton, slavery was rife and, between 1866 and 1890, the Chisholm Trail and Kansas railroads passed close by.

During the Wild West days, Rosebud's 11 saloons were filled with drunken cowboys. Saturday night shootouts were commonplace and, today, the original calaboose remains intact, as does 'open-range law', meaning that cows have the right of way.

On the eastern edge of Rosebud, Linden Street heads south from Main Street toward a baseball field, carved out of surrounding farmland. Small wooden houses, old but well kept, and shaded by large pecan trees, line the streets. On the east side of Linden, only the second building from Main, stands a premises that was once the Rosebud Laundromat. A small living area is connected to the rear of the laundromat, where the family of John Allen 'JA' McDuff lived. At least some of the McDuff's children, including two boys named Lonzo (Lonnie) and Kenneth, were born in far-off Paris, Texas, and no one seems to know why the McDuffs, who lived in the Blackland Prairie before moving to Rosebud, ended up in the area.

Kenneth was one of four children born to Addie L McDuff and John Allen 'JA' McDuff. 'JA' did farm, masonry and concrete work. His wife was a hefty, domineering woman named Addie. Addie ruled the roost and she was known locally as 'The Pistol Packin' Momma', on account of her violent temper and her habit of toting a sidearm in her handbag. Ken was in trouble from the moment he could walk.

He grew up to be a bully, a sadistic child who roamed the neighbourhood with a .22 calibre rifle, shooting any animal or bird that fell into his sights. The town's residents called him 'the bad boy of Rosebud'. People feared him even as a teenager and he beat up any youth who upset him, whether they were older or not.

Mrs Martha Royal, McDuff's fifth-grade teacher, remembers him as an intelligent youngster, but something of a loner. 'Kenneth was the son of a mild-mannered, hard-working father who was in the building trade, and a permissive mother who was quick to excuse his misdeeds. His troubles began in junior high, and never stopped. He did not get on with the other children very well. He seemed to live in a world of his own. On several occasions, I tried to speak with him in private, to ask if he had any problems at home, and things like that. But he wouldn't say a word to me. He just stared straight into my face. From the age of five, he had murder in his eyes. It was quite disturbing, I can tell you that.'

McDuff was always in trouble. In his teens, he was involved in robberies with his brother and, more than once, Sheriff Larry Pamplin said he tried to shoot their car tyres out, but they always got clean away.

McDuff's documented criminal career began in 1964, when, aged 18, he was convicted of 12 counts of burglary and attempted burglary in Bell, Milam, and Falls County. He received 12 concurrent four-year sentences for these crimes but achieved parole in Falls County in December 1965. Several months later, he got into a fracas and his parole was revoked. In 1966, he was released and, a short time later, he committed capital murder with an accomplice, a somewhat weak-willed 18-year-old, called Roy Dale Green.

Green was employed as a carpenter's helper. He had previously lived with his mother but, after she remarried, he moved in with a friend called Richard Boyd. It was Boyd who introduced Green to McDuff and, at the time of the triple homicide, the two men had known each other only a month.

The two men seemed to hit it off well. McDuff was a well-built, good-looking 20-year-old, who was proud of his criminal record. He was a tough, no-nonsense young man. He spoke his mind and he bragged about his sexual conquests, to the point that he said that he had raped two young women, and killed them. Green, on the other hand, was a weedy individual with a speech impediment who looked up to his stronger companion. But, secretly, he put McDuff's murderous claims down to hogwash.

The two men spent Saturday, 6 August, pouring concrete for McDuff's father and, after completing their labours, decided to drive into Fort Worth for a few drinks. At around 5.00pm, they climbed into McDuff's brand new Dodge Coronet, and rode around before buying a pack of beer from a 7-11 store. At 7.00pm, they visited Edith Turner, a mutual friend, and later they bought a hamburger.

Meanwhile, three teenagers – Robert Brand of Alvarado, aged 18; his cousin, 16-year-old Mark Dunman from Tarzana, California; and Robert's girlfriend, vivacious 16-year-old Edna Louise Sullivan, from Everman – spent the evening at a drive-in movie. When the show finished, they drove to a spot near a baseball field in Guadalupe County where they parked their 1957

Ford. At around 10.00pm, McDuff and Green came on the scene and the trio of teenagers became their randomly-selected quarry.

What took place is graphically described in the statement Green gave to Detective Grady Hight. This is dated Monday 8 August 1966, the day Green gave himself up:

We rode around the baseball park and wound up on a gravel road. He [McDuff] saw a car parked there, and we stopped about 150 yards in front of it. He got his gun and told me to get out. I thought it was all a joke. I just didn't believe what he said was going to happen. I went halfway to the car with him, and he went on. He told the kids in the car to get out or he would shoot them. I went on up there and he had put them in the trunk of their car. He drove his car back to their car, and he told me to get in his car and follow him. I did, and we drove for a while across the highway we had come in on, and he pulled into a field. I followed, and he said that the field wouldn't do, so we backed up and went to another field. He got out and told the girl to get out. He told me to put her in the trunk of his car. I opened the trunk and she climbed in. It was then that he said that we couldn't leave any witnesses, or something like that. He said, 'I'm gonna have to knock 'em off,' or something like that.

I got really scared. I still thought he was joking, but I wasn't sure. They were on their knees, begging him not to shoot them. They said, 'We're not going to tell anybody.' I turned towards him and he stuck the gun into the trunk of where the boys were and started shooting. I saw the fire come out of the gun on the first shot, and I covered my ears and looked away. He shot six times. He shot one twice in the head, and he shot the other boy four times in the head. A bullet went through a boy's arm as he tried to stop the fire. He tried to close the trunk, but it wouldn't close. He then told me to back up his car. By that time I was almost dying of fright, and I did what he said. He got in the boy's car and backed it into a fence, and he got out and told me to help him wipe off the fingerprints. I wasn't going to argue with him. I was expecting to be next so I helped him.

After a break in the interview, Detective Hight asked Green about the murder of Edna Sullivan, and what follows is again taken verbatim from Green's statement:

We wiped out the tyre tracks and got into his car and drove off another mile and turned off on another road and he stopped, and he got the girl out of the trunk and put her in the back seat. He told me to get out of the car, and I waited until he told her to get undressed. He took off his clothes and then he screwed her. He asked me if I wanted to do it, and I told him no. He asked me why not, and I told him I just didn't want to. He leaned over, and I didn't see the gun but thought he would shoot me if I didn't, so I pulled my pants and shirt off and got in the back seat and screwed the girl. She didn't struggle or anything, and if she ever said anything I didn't hear her. All the time I was on top of the girl I kept my eye on him. After that he screwed her again.

After Edna Sullivan had been raped several times, the two men drove her a short distance then stopped. McDuff ordered Green out of the car and asked him if he had anything with which to strangle the girl. He offered McDuff his belt. Green then described the most brutal murder, which followed.

He told the girl to get out of the car. He made her sit down on the gravel road, and he took about a three-foot piece of broomstick from his car and forced her head back with it until it was on the ground. He started choking her with the piece of broomstick. He mashed down hard, and she started waving her arms and kicking her legs. He told me to grab her legs and I didn't want to, and he said, 'It's gotta be done,' and I grabbed her legs, and held them for a second or so, then let them go. He said, 'Do it again,' and I did, and this time was when she stopped struggling. He had me grab her hands and he grabbed her feet and we heaved her over a fence. We crossed the fence ourselves, then he dragged her a short ways and then he choked her some more. We put her in some kind of bushes there.

That night, the two men stopped at a Hillsboro gas station, for Coca-Colas, before returning to Green's house, where they slept in the same bed. The following morning, McDuff buried the revolver by the side of his accomplice's garage and they drove to a friend's house where Richard Boyd allowed McDuff to wash his car.

Later in the day, Green was so overcome with fear and remorse that he had to confide in Boyd whose parents called Green's mother, and she convinced her son to give himself up to the police.

In 1968, McDuff received three death sentences, while Roy Dale Green was sent to prison for 25 years. He served 13 years before being released on parole. In a damning indictment of the judicial process, McDuff's death sentence was commuted to life and, on 11 October 1989, he was set free and paroled to Milam County.

* * *

During his time behind bars, McDuff walked to the electric chair on two occasions and, each time, received last-minute stays of execution. Then, in 1992, the Death Statute was ruled 'unconstitutional' by the United States Supreme Court, so McDuff's death sentence was commuted to life. He would serve just a handful of years, before his mother bribed a parole board official to rubber-stamp his release. The result was that he was turned loose to murder again ... and again ... and again.

In the final outcome, McDuff's case revealed to the public what Texas politicians had known for years; that the State parole system was rife with bad judgement and the potential for corruption. His case provided just the latest twist in the old story that goes back at least to the early 1920s, when first the colourful governors – Pa Ferguson, and then Ma Ferguson – used their power of clemency to free thousands of highly dangerous convicts by bribing officials. According to one apocryphal account, the way to get out of prison in those days was to buy a mule from Pa for $200. And why would a convict need a mule? 'To ride home from jail,' was Pa's suggestion.

The McDuff scandal was not simply limited to a corrupt parole board official. The seeds were sewn in 1972, when a federal court ruled that the Texas Department of Corrections was overcrowded. The State was faced with two choices: either build more prisons, or lock up fewer prisoners in the existing ones.

Three successive governors – Dolph Briscoe, Bill Clements – and Mark White – talked tough about crime, but did nothing to encourage the construction of new facilities because they were too expensive to build. By the end of Clement's second term in office, the system had just about broken down. With public pressure mounting by the day, the Governor was forced to reconsider, and plans were drawn up for several new jails. In addition, in order to reduce the overcrowding problems, parole considerations were relaxed. The order was to parole 750 of the lowest-risk inmates a week. Before long, there were not even 750 inmates left in the entire system of some 60,000 who met eligibility standards. At that point, the parole system cracked under the strain. In its haste to meet the quota, the board began rubber-stamping the applications almost as soon as it received them. Applications were rushed through without being read properly and, with McDuff being just another number amongst thousands, he became one of the 20 former death row inmates and 127 murderers to be released.

This shambles resulted from the fundamental problems with the system as it then operated, and Jim Parker, the Legislative Director for Governor Ann Richards, later made this point: 'Some people put in prison were less dangerous than the people being released. We're jailing hot cheque writers and DWI's (driving without insurance), and letting out the Kenneth McDuffs. In our panic to make our streets safe again, we're imprisoning non-violent offenders; we're filling up the available space with people who belong in drug rehabilitation centres, or whose debt to society could be paid by doing community service.'

Because the Board of Pardons and Paroles was not empowered to set policy about who achieved parole, they relied on a few assumptions and wild, speculative theories in determining who was safe to release and who was not. As one distinguished attorney put it: 'This was as random as throwing darts in the dark.'

Among the assumptions was the belief that, as most murders are committed in moments of rage or passion, such offenders are good parole risks because they are unlikely to kill for a second time. The weakness of this concept was that it did not take into account those criminals who kill for pure enjoyment: one of whom was Kenneth McDuff.

Another ill-conceived theory was that a long time in prison breaks an inmate and 'burns out' their meanness. This was certainly a parole consideration for McDuff when he was released after having served 23 years in jail. But, in the lottery of number crunching to which the parole system had been reduced, McDuff and his ilk were inevitably lumped together with the more benign killers who fitted the so-called category of 'unlikely to kill again'. The strange consequence of this, as Jim Parker explained, 'isn't that we have just the one McDuff, it's that we don't have hundreds of McDuffs back on the streets'.

* * *

Within days of being released in October 1989, McDuff murdered 31-year-old Sarafia Parker, whose body was found on 14 October by a pedestrian strolling the 1500 block of East Avenue, Temple, a small city 48 miles due south of Waco. She was black, in her twenties, about 5ft 6in tall and weighing about 150 pounds. She had been beaten and strangled no more than 24 hours before her body was found.

She was quickly identified and Texas Ranger John Aycock later located and interviewed a witness who thought he could place Parker in a pick-up truck, driven by McDuff, on or around 12 October. On that day, Kenneth McDuff had reported to his parole officer, who happened to work in Temple. No other connection between the murder of Sarafia Parker and McDuff has been established or made public.

McDuff was returned to prison for breaking his parole conditions after he made death threats against a black youth in Rosebud, and it was at this point that Addie McDuff stepped into the picture. She paid $1,500 to Huntsville attorney Bill Habern and his consulting partner, Helen Copitka, of Austin, plus a further $700 for her 'expenses', to evaluate her son's new parole prospects.

Habern next spoke to James Granberry, the chairman of the parole board, a man known for his tendency to release convicted murderers from prison. It came as no surprise to learn that McDuff was back on the streets within a year, walking out of the prison gates on Tuesday, 18 December 1990. Subsequently, Granberry resigned, after coming under fire from a House Investigation Committee. He had the gall to set up his own parole consultancy firm which he was forced to close amid a storm of public protest.

* * *

Sometime during the evening of 10 October 1991, Brenda Thompson, a prostitute and drug addict, climbed into McDuff's red pick-up truck in Waco. They drove south on Miller Street and encountered a Waco Police Department vehicle checkpoint on Faulkner Lane. McDuff stopped about 50ft from the barrier and one of the officers walked to the pick-up. As he did so, he shone his torch on himself so that the driver could see clearly he was a police officer.

Suddenly, Brenda began screaming and kicking. To the officer, it appeared as if her arms were tied behind her back and she was desperately trying to get out of the truck. She lay back and began kicking at the windshield with such force that it shattered on the passenger's side. She continued to kick vigorously, with her legs clad in a pair of red polyester pants, cracking the windshield more and more with each kick. McDuff immediately floored the accelerator and drove straight at the officers. According to the police report filed that day, three officers had to move quickly to avoid being hit. As the vehicle sped off, the patrolmen scrambled to their cars to give chase. McDuff raced south on Miller Street toward Waco Drive, turned off his lights and disappeared into the darkness, taking Brenda Thompson with him. He eluded police by going the wrong way on one-way streets. Eventually, he turned west on US 84, and then north on Gholson Road for about eight miles until he arrived at a wooded area where, furious at the damage done to his prized pick-up, he inflicted an excruciatingly torturous death on Brenda. Her body was discovered near Gholson Road on 3 October 1998, just a month before McDuff's eventual execution.

* * *

On 15 October 1991, McDuff dated a 17-year-old hooker called Regenia DeAnne Moore. At around 11.30pm, the couple were seen arguing, outside a Waco motel, and a witness said they then drove away in a pick-up truck. McDuff took Regenia to a remote area along Highway 6, north and east of Waco. At the site of a bridge traversing the Tehuacana Creek, McDuff pulled off the road on to a very steep embankment down to the edge of the creek, where he drove under the bridge. Passing motorists could not have seen his car. The road there is a freeway, and cars rushing over the bridge easily made enough noise to drown out any screams Regenia may have made.

A forensics team recovered Regenia's body, on Wednesday, 29 September, from a sinkhole near Tehuacana Creek. Her hands had been tied behind her back and her ankles were bound with stockings tied together in such a way as to allow her sufficient movement to hobble along. McDuff had apparently 'marched' her to the spot where she was killed. The remains of her dress were wrapped around her pelvic area. She was found lying on her back with her legs bent. After being missing for seven years, Regenia was finally going home to her mother.

* * *

During the late afternoon of Sunday 29 December 1991, 28-year-old Colleen Reed, a native of Ville Platte, Louisiana, drove into the Texas State capital of Austin where she deposited $200 at an ATM. She then went shopping, for a gallon of milk and a bottle of vitamins, at Whole Foods Market on North Lamar Boulevard and, afterwards, drove to the carwash at West Fifth Street. Witnesses recalled seeing a light-coloured, late-model Ford Thunderbird, which was heading towards the carwash. They heard a short scream before the car's doors slammed shut and watched in amazement as the vehicle screeched away along Powell Street leaving a cloud of exhaust smoke in its wake.

Standing at 5ft 3in, weighing 115lb, with dark-brown hair and brown eyes, Colleen was wearing gold-rimmed glasses, blue jeans, a T-shirt, and a black-and-white Nike jacket. Her body was found on 6 October 1998, after McDuff gave police the location of the grave. It was in a grassy area that had been a popular fishing and partying spot for McDuff when he was growing up.

By now, police suspected that he was a serial murderer, although he remained extremely elusive and almost impossible to track down. The best hope was that he would make a mistake. The pursuers' luck changed when Investigator Tim Steglich, of the Bell County Sheriff's Department, pulled in one of McDuff's known associates for questioning. What follows is the April 1992 statement of 34-year-old Alva Hank Worley, who was an accomplice of McDuff's in the abduction, rape and murder of Colleen Reed.

McDuff picked me up at 6 or 7 that night. We went to Love's Truck Stop near Temple, and he got gas. I don't know if he used a credit card or paid cash. We started to go towards Austin, and it was just kind of understood we were going to get some speed or coke, whatever we could find. We stopped at a Conoco truck stop on Interstate 35, on the northbound side of the highway, past Jarrell. I bought a six-pack of Budweiser Longnecks. We had already drunk a six-pack or better before that.

McDuff drove on to Austin, and I thought we were going down to the UT (University of Texas) campus to get the dope. But Mac drove downtown, and drove around because we had beer left. He would not let me get any more beer after the second six-pack. I don't know why. I know we went down Sixth Street and in that area. I remember we got a hamburger at Dairy Queen, I think on Congress. I remember the streets were real lit up at that time. We rode around and ate. Mac was just driving, and he pulled into a car wash, right into a bay, and I thought he was going to wash his car. I need to explain that we were in Mac's cream Ford Thunderbird. It was about 8.30, or 9 pm when we pulled into this wash.

Worley went on to explain that McDuff spotted the young woman, and within seconds he had her by the throat and was dragging her towards his car. 'She was shouting like hell,' Worley added, 'She was screaming, "Not me, not me. Please let me go." '

'He took her to the driver's side and shoved her in the back seat. Her hands were tied behind her. I think she was saying, "Please let me go, please don't let this happen to me." I was stunned. I didn't know what to say. He got in the driver's seat and drove off, just fast enough to get away in a hurry.'

Begging for her life, Colleen Reed was subjected to what can only be described as a ride of terror as the threesome headed north along Interstate 35 towards Round Rock, where McDuff pulled over and stopped the car. Climbing into the back with Colleen, McDuff ordered Worley to drive, and then the raping started.

I remember he told her to take her clothes off, so I don't know if he untied her. He was telling her, 'All you have to do is fuck.' He was trying to put it in her head that if she would just fuck, she would be turned loose. She was saying she would do what she was told. She was trying to buy time. That's what she was trying to do. Mac had his shirt off, and I believe he had his pants down. I do not know if the kid was facing up or down when he raped her. I remember he made her give him a head job. I remember that because he almost choked her. Mac had hit her several times in the head when he first got in the back with her. He was forcing her head down on him, and she was choking.

I was just driving, and when I got to the Stillhouse Hollow exit, I decided to get out there to go to my sister's house. Mac was just sitting there at Stillhouse. I pulled over near the spillway, near the trailer houses there. I moved over to the passenger seat, and Mac got the keys out and popped the trunk. He pulled her out of the back seat, and put her in the trunk. She was quiet at that time and he had to force her into the trunk. That was the last time I saw that girl or heard anything about her. Mac drove to my sister's house.

After further questioning, Worley admitted that McDuff had asked to borrow his penknife and a shovel. He also said that McDuff had burned the woman, with a cigarette, on the vagina, but insisted that he did not know what happened to Colleen Reed after that. He said that he had not seen McDuff since.

The next day, Tim Steglich interviewed Worley for the second time. Under pressure from the intensive interrogation, he admitted that they had driven along a deserted track, just a mile from McDuff's parent's home at Temple.

'I did rape her,' Worley finally conceded, 'but Mac broke her neck after he tortured some more with the lighted cigarettes. He snapped her neck, and it sounded like a tree limb breaking, then he threw her, like a sack of potatoes, into the trunk of his car.'

Frank Worley was charged with rape and murder, and he was held in the Travis County Jail, in lieu of $350,000 bail, while a manhunt for McDuff was launched. The body of Colleen Reed was recovered, shortly before McDuff's execution.

* * *

On Sunday, 24 February 1992, McDuff strangled a part-time black prostitute and student called Valencia Joshua, while he was attending the Texas State Technical College in Waco. At the time, he was studying to become a machinist, and shared a campus dormitory with students who were half his age. He used his seniority to good effect, selling marijuana, methamphetamine, LSD and 'crack' cocaine to his fellow students as a means of augmenting his student grant.

It is thought that Valencia had only been in Waco a week or two before being killed. 'The public doesn't get as outraged when someone like Valencia turns up dead. But it's still a homicide and just as important as any other,' said Richard Stroup, McLennan County Deputy Sheriff. The police described her as a 'street person, but a sweet woman who loved children'. She had no local address, no suitcase and no belongings. In fact, no one had a clue why she was in Waco at all. 'She had no relatives there,' said her father, Tommy, who lived in Bryan, and it was her mother, Roma, from Fort Worth, who finally reported her missing.

Twenty-two-year-old Valencia had last been seen alive on the day she died, knocking on McDuff's dormitory door, number 118. The skinny woman was wearing a dark windbreaker, tight, blue jeans, and an ornate barrette in her hair. When she received no answer, she went to the window and called out, 'Are you ready yet?' She was not seen alive again.

On Sunday, 15 March 1992, walkers found a human skull, that had been exposed by animals, behind the James Connally Municipal Golf Course and close to the college. An unclothed body was buried in soft, moist clay close by, and the deputies initially had just one lead to help them identify the corpse – a cloisonné hair comb lying near the body. The inlaid pattern depicted an orange butterfly among green leaves and red flowers – it was Valencia's proudest possession. Dallas medical examiners eventually identified the body by means of fingerprints. Cause of death was recorded as strangulation.

McDuff was seen pushing a Ford Thunderbird car, a short distance from the Quik-Pak No 8 convenience store in the 4200 block of La Salle Avenue, off Interstate 35, south of Waco, on Monday, 1 March 1992. Richard Bannister said he noticed the incident at about 3.45pm.

A little later that afternoon, 22-year-old Melissa Northrup went missing from her place of work, at the Quik-Pak store. Described as 4ft 11in tall and weighing 110lb, with shoulder-length brown hair and blue eyes, Melissa was two-and-a-half months pregnant. She lived with her accountant husband, Aaron, at 3014 Pioneer Circle, Waco. The diminutive young woman would have proved no match for a man of McDuff's height and bulk. He stood at over 6ft and weighed in at 245 lb.

At around 4.15am, a local man, who knew Melissa, saw her car heading north on Interstate 35. She was in the front passenger seat and looked frightened.

When she did not return home, Aaron phoned her, and when he received no reply, he drove to the store, which was closed. The cash register drawer was open and the contents were missing. 'A customer was in the store,' Aaron later told police, 'and when he saw me, he got real scared and threw his hands up in the air. I threw him the bathroom keys, and told him to please go look for my wife.' Then he dialled 911. Police soon determined that $250 had been stolen from the cash register and, despite the fact that several people were sleeping in their cars close to the store, there were no witnesses to Melissa's abduction, although McDuff's Thunderbird was found close by.

At approximately 9.00pm the same day, Shari Robinson said that McDuff arrived at her Dallas County home and he asked for some food.

Within hours of Melissa's abduction, McDuff's details were placed on the US 'Most Wanted List', and appeals were placed in the newspapers, and on television, asking for information regarding his whereabouts. As the police intensified their manhunt, Mark Davis, a former college student friend of

McDuff's, came forward to say that, on an earlier occasion, McDuff had tried to enlist him to rob the Quik-Pak store.

Another student, Lewis Bray, reported that McDuff had once boasted that the easiest way to get rid of a body was to slit the abdomen and throw it into water. It was also determined that McDuff had once worked at the Quik-Pak store and, ironically, he had been trained by Melissa's husband, Aaron.

A fisherman discovered Melissa's corpse, floating in a water-filled gravel pit in South-East Dallas County, at 6.00pm on Sunday, 26 April. The body was partially dressed, in a purple suit and a dark coloured jacket. Part of her lower torso was missing. Her car, a burnt-orange 1977 Buick Regal with a white vinyl top, licence plate TX LP287 XHV, was found, parked, just a mile away and close to Shari Robinson's home. After forensic tests had been completed, human hairs, identical in every respect to those taken from McDuff, were found on the car's upholstery.

* * *

McDuff was committing his murders throughout Texas, thereby creating jurisdictional problems which brought a dozen law enforcement agencies to the conference table to co-ordinate their enquiries. What was needed was to combine the organisational capabilities of the FBI, US Marshal's Service and the Texas Rangers, but rape and murder are State rather than federal offences.

Two US Marshals from Waco, Mike and Parnell McNamara, had an idea which offered a way out of the bureaucratic impasse. They had been told that during the time McDuff was at the technical college, he had been supplying LSD and was known to be in possession of a firearm, both of which are federal offences. Consequently, on Friday, 6 March 1992, the local State Attorney issued warrant No 9280-0310-0506-Z for McDuff's arrest. Two months later, they had the break they were waiting for.

Thirty-six-year-old Gary Smithee worked for a Kansas City refuse collection company. After arriving home on Friday, 1 May 1992, he tuned his television set to the *America's Most Wanted* show and, as was his usual practice, videotaped the programme. Smithee was taken by the $5,000 reward for information leading to the arrest of Kenneth McDuff and thought he saw a striking resemblance between the face on the screen and a new co-worker called Richard Fowler. The new man had created an impression with his constant boasting about his sexual prowess, particularly with very young women.

Smithee thought very carefully about the implications of reporting his suspicions. He did not want to upset Fowler, but the chance of a fast $5,000 was too good an opportunity to miss. He discussed the tape he had made of the TV programme with a work colleague before phoning the Kansas City Police. Sergeant JD Johnson took the call, and immediately ran a search through their computer for the name, Richard Fowler. Information came on the screen reporting that a man, answering a description that fitted both Fowler and McDuff, had been arrested during a prostitution sting and been charged with soliciting. The detective then carried out a fingerprint comparison between the two names with the result that Fowler's record card matched that of McDuff.

The next morning, Johnson ascertained which truck McDuff was due to join as a crew member and determined the route that the trash-collection truck would take on Monday, 4 May. He learned that it would be going to a landfill site, south of Kansas City, between 1.0.0pm and 2.0.0pm. The police set up a six-man surveillance team working under the guise of a commercial vehicle stop detail. 'We wanted to make sure the location we picked was isolated in the event of trouble,' Johnson explained. 'McDuff was reported to be armed and dangerous. The site we picked was the type where some vehicles were routinely stopped, and there were no people around.'

To lend further authenticity to their plans, the police borrowed a car that Kansas City Engineers used for their routine truck inspections. When the vehicle in which McDuff was riding approached, a lone officer waved it to the checkpoint. Instantly smelling danger, McDuff made an attempt to get out and make a run for it, but he was stopped in his tracks at gunpoint and made no further attempt to escape.

McDuff was indicted in the Fifty-fourth Judicial District Court of McLennan County, Texas, on 26 June 1992, for the capital murder of Melissa Northrup while in the course of committing and attempting to commit kidnapping, robbery, or the murder of another pursuant to the same scheme and course of conduct. He was found guilty as charged.

On 18 February 1993, following a separate punishment hearing, the jury affirmatively answered the first special issue submitted to Article 37. 071(b) (1) of the Texas Code of Criminal Procedure, and answered negatively to the second special issue submitted pursuant to Article 37. 071(e). In accordance with the State law, the trial court imposed the death sentence.

McDuff's conviction and sentence were automatically appealed to the Texas Court of Criminal Appeals, which affirmed the conviction on 28 April 1997.

Then, McDuff filed a petition for a writ of *certiorari* to the US Supreme Court, a legal technicality requesting that proceedings be moved to a higher court. This was denied on 12 January 1998.

Next, McDuff filed a petition for a State writ of *habeas corpus* which was denied, on 15 April 1998, by the Texas Court of Criminal Appeals.

On 29 April 1998, the Fifty-fourth Judicial Court of McLennan County, Texas, set McDuff's execution date for 21 October 1998.

Counsel was appointed on 30 April 1998, to represent McDuff in the US District Court for the Western District of Texas, Waco Division.

On 8 July 1998, McDuff filed a petition for a Federal Writ of *habeas corpus*. The State responded with an answer and motion for summary judgment on McDuff's claims.

The Western District Court denied *habeas corpus* relief on 15 October 1998, granting summary judgment for the State, and lifting the stay of execution. The court also rescheduled McDuff's execution for 17 November 1998.

McDuff filed a Notice of Appeal on 23 October and, three days later, the Western District Court denied McDuff's request for a certificate of appealability. His appeal to the Fifth US Circuit Court of Appeals was denied, and the Supreme Court denied his last appeal for a stay of execution on 16 November 1998.

* * *

A man familiar with the routine of carrying out executions by lethal injection is Assistant Warden-in-Charge of Executions in Texas, Neil Hodges. Speaking about the reality of this method of judicial death, he said, 'People think this is all painless and stuff like that. It ain't! Basically, they [the condemned] suffer a lot. They are sort of paralysed, but they can hear. They drown in their own fluid and suffocate to death really.

'Yeah, we get problems. Sometimes the guy doesn't want to get on to the table. But we have the largest guard in Texas here. He gets them on that table, no problem. They are strapped down in seconds. No problem. They go on that mean old table and get the goodnight juice, whether they like it or not.'

On 17 November 1998, a large group of reporters stood outside the Walls Prison in Huntsville, Texas, in an area reserved for the press. The Walls is the oldest of all the prison units in Texas; it also houses the death chamber. Perfectly suiting the occasion, a single, heavy, dark cloud hovered over the prison. Near a concrete picnic table, a jungle of photographers' tripods looked like a flock of ostriches. Mercifully, a gentle breeze flapped at the cautionary yellow 'DO NOT CROSS' police tapes. No one in the press saw a single anti-death penalty protester.

Earlier in the day, inmate number 999055, Kenneth McDuff had been taken from his cell at Ellis Unit, and driven 15 miles to the Walls. Even for a stone-cold killer like McDuff, his first sight of the death house was a sobering one. The truck that had brought him to his final destination, pulled to a stop in front of a set of wire gates topped with razor wire, glinting and sparkling in the Texas sunlight. Shackled and cuffed, he was led through two steel doors. On his left was a row of cells; he was allocated the second one, furnished simply with a bunk, a small table and a chair. The bed linen was spotless, as were the cream-painted walls. Next to McDuff's cell was a 'strictly no contact' cell. The door was covered with a fine steel mesh screen, painted black. It was used by inmates, should they wish to give instructions to an attorney.

In the corridor, and to his right, was another wooden table with two chairs. On it, McDuff noticed a bible and a telephone. There was no ashtray as smoking was forbidden.

Lethal injection was first legally introduced as a method of execution in 1977 in the States of Oklahoma and Texas. The first prisoner to die by this means was 43-year-old Charlie Brooks, who had been sentenced to death for his part in the murder of a used car dealer, in Fort Worth, in 1971. Brooks finally gave up his appeals against the death sentence and died in Huntsville Prison on 7 December 1982.

The practice of giving hospital patients a pre-med injection to sedate them before going into the operating theatre, prior to general anaesthesia, is a common procedure. It relaxes the patient and takes away the tension. This concept offered a number of advantages to those responsible for despatching condemned inmates to perdition. The drugs were certainly available and cheap to use. There was also the added humane dimension inasmuch as lethal injection was a clinical procedure carried out in appropriate surroundings. Gone were the dreaded gallows, the ominous electric chair with all its wiring and leather helmet and death mask. Gone, too, was the evil-looking gas chamber, with its sickly green-coloured walls and mass of rods, tubes and linkages. When using a lethal cocktail of drugs, the condemned inmate would be led from a holding cell to a hospital gurney to be strapped down and injected intravenously.

There were benefits as well for the state authorities. The whole idea would appeal to the media and public alike, for execution could not possibly be made more merciful. A team of paramedics would attend to the inserting of a needle into the victim's right or left arm, and a doctor would be, as with all executions, in attendance to pronounce death.

Addie McDuff had arrived too late to see her son on his last day and he was allowed no special privileges other than a choice of menu for his final meal, which consisted of two T-bone steaks, five fried eggs, vegetables, French fries, coconut pie and a single Coca-Cola. As he completed his meal, he contemplated the end, which he thought would be painless, but he didn't know that he was going to be injected with a combination of three drugs, all acidic, with a pH value higher than 6, which would burn so terribly that he would feel as if he was being injected with fire.

At 5.58pm, the warden received word that the Supreme Court had turned down McDuff's final request for a stay of execution, and the witnesses started to arrive through the main prison gate to be escorted to the Death House. They might have noticed the sheeting, now draped over the steel gates, hiding the hearse that was waiting to receive the body. After being given a body search to check for hidden weapons or concealed cameras, they were led to the viewing room, which was separated from the gurney by a window and closed curtains.

At 5.44pm the killer was given a pre-injection of 8cc 2 per cent sodium pentothal. Waiting silently, in an adjacent room, was the cell extraction team, wearing protective clothing and armed with Mace gas to subdue McDuff if he caused trouble. Their particular skills have never been called upon at an execution in Texas.

At 6.08pm, McDuff was invited to leave his cell. He agreed and no guard touched him as he walked the few steps to the chamber door, which opened before him. He paused, momentarily, when he saw the gurney with its white padding and cover sheet. Two arm supports were pulled out and he saw the brown hide straps dangling loose with an officer by each one.

At 7.08pm, McDuff was strapped down, and the paramedics inserted two 16-gauge needles and catheters into both of his arms. These were connected by flexible tubes to the executioner's position which was hidden from view. The doctor also attached a cardiac monitor and stethoscope to the prostrate man's chest.

The curtains were drawn back and Warden Jim Willett asked McDuff if he had any last words to say into the microphone above his head. McDuff replied simply, 'I'm ready to be released. Release me.' Inside the witness area, Parnell McNamara gently placed his hand on the shoulder of 74-year-old Jack Brand.

'I've been waiting for this for 32 years,' said the father of Robert Brand, who was murdered by McDuff in 1966.

'Are you all right?' Parnell asked quietly.

'I feel like 32 years have been lifted from my life,' the old man said.

McDuff looked scared as, over the next ten seconds, he was given an injection of sodium thiopental, a fast-acting anaesthetic which takes effect within about ten seconds. He would have felt a slight pressure, and his arm start to ache. Then he would feel light-headed.

After a one-minute interval, this was followed by 15cc of normal saline, to ease the passage of 50mg/50cc Pancuronium bromide. Pavulon is a curare-derived muscle relaxant which paralyses respiratory function and brings unconsciousness in about ten seconds.

McDuff felt pressure in his chest. It was a suffocating feeling that caused him to gasp several times for air. He was dizzy and hyperventilating; his heart beat faster and faster as his entire nervous system came under attack. This is called the 'stress syndrome', a common feature during the first stages of dying.

As the poison permeated through his body, McDuff entered the second stage of death. He was unable to breathe or move, but he could still see and hear. He was paralysed and not able to swallow at this stage: a condition which leads many witnesses to believe that death has intervened. McDuff was still alive, but his central nervous system was beginning to shut down. His eyes dilated and the hairs on his skin stood erect as he was injected with another 15cc of saline and, finally, a massive dose of Potassium Chloride (1.50–2.70mEq/kg). When injected intravenously in large doses, this drug burns and hurts, because it is a naturally occurring salt and instantly disrupts the chemical balance of the blood. It causes the muscles to tighten up in extreme contraction and the instant it reaches the heart muscle, it causes the heart to stop beating. While McDuff was sedated by the thiopental and couldn't draw breath because of the Pavulon, he was physically unable to scream in pain when the potassium was injected, sending his heart into a crunching, excruciating cramp.

There was a two-minute wait while the doctors examined McDuff and pronounced him dead. The curtains were opened for the witnesses to view the body. Mrs Brenda Soloman, mother of one of McDuff's victims, was moved to say, 'He looked like the Devil. He's going where he needs to go. I feel happy … I feel wonderful.'

The cost of the drugs administered to take McDuff's life was $86.08.

* * *

'The sad thing about this particular case is that if Colleen had screamed and someone had heard her, it would have been McDuff's mother. She would have been in earshot because she lives just a few hundred yards away,' commented Investigator Tim Steglich.

Enquiries into the life and crimes of Kenneth Allen McDuff included interviews with his mother, Addie, his schoolteachers and several residents of Rosebud who knew the McDuffs well. I spoke to Falls County Sheriff, Larry Pamplin; McDuff's accomplice, Roy Dale Green, who now lives in a flea-ridden shack in Marlin; US Marshals, Mike and Parnell McNamara; the State prosecutor, Bill Johnston; and Tim Steglich. Background research included a visit, accompanied by Tim Steglich, to the lonely track where McDuff murdered Colleen Reed. 'In the dead of night, that would be a terrible place to die,' said States Attorney William 'Bill' Johnston, with just a hint of tears in his eyes.

The McDuff family are a tough lot, with a reputation to match. The 'Pistol Packin' Momma', Addie McDuff, has never given an interview, and even refused to speak to the police, but she made a rare exception by speaking to me. Such is her reputation for pulling a gun that the Waco police offered to keep watch, outside her isolated ranch at Belton, and waited until I emerged unscathed. Although I was expecting immediate hostility, a frail, confused old lady appeared at the door offering a traditionally cautious Texas welcome.

Addie is a protective mother, despite her son's evil deeds. Over coffee – and she apologised that she didn't have tea – she explained that one of her sons had been shot dead, while sleeping with another man's wife, and that a daughter had died in a road crash. Mr. McDuff had been buried way back, and now she had no one except a niece. Addie was about to sell up and move in with her.

Asked how she had acquired the name 'Pistol Packin' Momma', she smiled. 'Rosebud was a tough place to live in the early days,' she said in a cracked voice. 'The driver of a school bus threatened to throw Ken off as he had spent the fare. It was dark, and no boy of mine was gonna walk a long ways home. So, I just visited the bus depot the next morning, and pulled out my .22. Told him that next time he did it, it would be his last.' Then she chuckled, 'No one never did talk down to my family again.'

She rooted through cardboard boxes of mementoes, looking for documents or any picture of Ken in his early days, but there was precious little to find. She had destroyed everything years ago.

The next port of call was Rosebud itself. A dusty, one-horse town, and, with just over 1,000 inhabitants, it has the pretension to call itself a city. Main Street is nearly always deserted, even on weekends. During a 'Texas Barbeque', a mid-afternoon indoor feast, the town manager, a reporter, several residents, and the 70-old Chief of Police, recalled the young Ken McDuff. Clearly, they had been terrorised by the youth in those days, a feeling supported by Falls County Sheriff Larry Pamplin, whose father was the sheriff before him. Driving me around in his beat-up, unmarked police cruiser, which was stocked full of shotguns and pistols, Larry explained that McDuff and his older brother, John, were among the roughest hooligans he had ever met. Larry Pamplin has since been dismissed from office, after committing aggravated assault, official misconduct and racketeering. It was proved that he had misspent funds to feed his prisoners, keeping a tidy sum back for himself.

Interviewing Regenia Moore's mother in a Waco motel proved a harrowing experience. She is now a mental wreck who, for several years, drove the dirt roads of Waco, with a spade, in search of her missing daughter's body. 'I don't wish ill on McDuff,' she sobbed, 'I just want to give her a Christian burial, just as Addie McDuff will want for her son.' Her wish has now been granted.

Finally, there was the much-anticipated meeting with Kenneth McDuff, on Death Row, Ellis Unit, Texas. In life, he was a tall man, well built, with greasy, black hair. Wearing a constant sneer, he whinged on for an hour about the injustices committed by the judicial and prison system. He argued about the merest technicalities of his case yet, ever the hypocrite, he admitted all of the crimes attributed to him, while refusing to say where his victims were buried, unless he was paid a handsome fee.

'I don't think that the State of Texas will let me live, unless they want me to have a long drawn-out, slow life. I have sugar diabetes, so at some point I am going to have some serious problems. But the bottom line is – I want to be the one to decide when I'm to die. And I will do this by deciding when I'm going to drop my appeals. I've never been one to run, and I won't grant them the satisfaction of running me all the way to the ground. I believe there is a good possibility that both my convictions may be reversed.'

Asked why he had not settled down and started some form of meaningful relationship with a woman, he replied, 'I feel very old and tired. Once I wanted a wife and family just like other people do. Right now I'm like a man in the desert that is thousands of miles from the nearest water, with no possibility of reaching water, but keeps walking anyway. I don't know why I keep walking. Is it some inter-instinct [sic] to strive on?

Now, let's talk about money. Well, on this one, I'm like the man in the desert that struck gold, and can only carry out what he can carry. I only have need for a few thousand dollars, like for burial expenses, and to maintain myself while I live. I will charge whomever, $700 per body. Use an international money order or postal orders will do. Have it sent to my inmate's trust fund in my name. When the first amount clears, I'll give you and the law a body. That way I don't get shafted, you know.'

Now, that is an expression of true evil.

This chapter is based on exclusive, videotaped Death Row interviews between Christopher Berry-Dee and Kenneth Allen McDuff within Ellis Unit, Huntsville, Texas in 1995, and extensive correspondence.

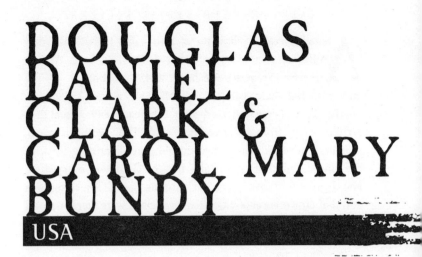

DOUGLAS DANIEL CLARK & CAROL MARY BUNDY

USA

'I used to be a good-looking guy, ya know. But, see what they done to me in here. My hair is falling out, my teeth are rotten and still they want to kill me. Still we all gotta fuckin' die some time. I've outlived the judge, and the prosecutor; it's just they're killing an innocent man.'

DOUGLAS CLARK TO THE AUTHOR AT SAN QUENTIN STATE PRISON 1995

A small piece of yellow metal, found in a North California millstream in 1894, precipitated the Gold Rush. At that time, San Francisco was home to 459 inhabitants – by the end of the following year, the population was almost 25,000.

The 'Forty-Niners', named after the year, 1849, when they arrived, came from all over the world. They were dreamers, schemers, adventurers, young and old, but all turning up with the single ambition of striking it rich. Gold was everywhere and the streets of towns such as Columbia, Sierra City, Hangtown and that crown jewel of cities, San Francisco, were literally paved with gold.

While life was fast and hard, so was justice. The miners, whores, and saloonkeepers were a rough bunch. There were fights over mining claims, and fights over women. Stealing was an easier way to obtain the much-sought-after, precious gold than labouring all day, panning in a muddy streambed. Participants in the Gold Rush drank heavily and gambled unwisely; they also killed each other.

By the time California became a State, in 1850, it needed a State prison, so they built San Quentin. Driving north on US Highway 101, from the Golden Gate Bridge to Interstate 580, San Quentin comes into view as a massive white concrete construction on a 30-acre site.

Originally called Point Quentin, the isolated area was named after a minor Indian chief who lost a battle against Mexican soldiers in 1824. Squat, buttressed walls with a red roof, this is a correctional cathedral, set in green flatland that tips into the north San Francisco Bay area.

The California Department of Corrections has an annual operating budget in excess of $3.4 billion, with around 124,000 inmates being confined at any one time. San Quentin – also known as 'SQ' – is not only the most notorious prison in the State; it is arguably the toughest in the country. It houses the

State's Death Row where, at any one time, up to 500 men may be awaiting execution. These days, in a gesture towards more humane methods, death is administered by lethal injection. Douglas Daniel Clark is one of these Death Row inmates. He costs about 50 dollars a day to keep fit and well for his execution.

It is a 500-yard walk from the gate of 'SQ' to the menacing front portico. Once through this entry, and just 30ft down a corridor, is an interview room. Opposite, there is a secure holding area and a tirade of foul language is issued by Clark, who is chained to a strong point on the wall. He is also shackled; handcuffed to a body belt, and his ankles are bound with steel chain.

Forget Doctor Hannibal Lecter, because Clark looks the epitome of evil and he is not acting. His blue eyes are wild and demonic. His hair is unkempt and prematurely grey. But, it is mouth that is so foul, in every way. The teeth in it are rotten and he spouts an incessant stream of venomous filth. Assisted by guards, he shuffles forward to meet his visitor, with intimidating hatred emanating from every inch of his powerfully built, 6ft frame. He is wearing a grey prison sweater and loosely fitting slacks, and a baseball cap is perched, cock-eyed, on his head. He is also sweating profusely.

However repulsive they may be, looks and foul language don't make a killer and, as Clark's story unfolded, it would prove to become an enthralling whodunit. Moreover, his life may even be a monument to the frustrated protestations of an innocent man.

During the summer months of 1980, a string of horrifying murders rocked Hollywood. All of the victims were hookers, trading sex for dollars along the notorious Sunset Boulevard. This prompted the press to dub the, as-yet-unknown, serial killer 'The Sunset Slayer'. The principal players in this dance of death were Carol Mary Bundy, Douglas Daniel Clark, and John 'Jack' Robert Murray.

Carol Bundy (no relation to the serial killer, Ted Bundy) is short and unattractive. Her mother, Gladys, was part-Algonquin Indian, and her father, Charles Peters, was a French-Canadian with a build that might be described as roly-poly. Carol once remarked that, 'He was a male version of me with a bald head. He had blue eyes, a pleasant appearance, and a dynamite personality. He was a good father. He worshipped me because I was bright.'

Born in 1943, Carol was the second of three children and the family lived in various cities across the USA. She claims to have attended 23 different schools before the ninth grade. By the age of 11, she had already started shoplifting, and stealing money from her parents and neighbours.

Gladys Peters died of a heart-attack on Sunday, 10 June 1957. The following night Carol says she was in bed with her father who 'performed oral sex on me and sexually abused my 11-year-old sister'. One night, just after her sixteenth birthday, she was sent out to a local store, by her father, to buy provisions. When she arrived home, she claims, she found 'globs of blood everywhere and a rifle on a chair'. She explained that her father, who was remarried by then, couldn't take life any more and had planned to commit murder. 'That's why he sent me to the store,' she said. 'He was going to kill his new wife while I was gone, then kill me when I got home.' Apparently, the plan literally backfired when he and his wife wrestled with the rifle, which discharged, blowing off his thumb.

After this incident, Carol's stepmother arranged for the children to be taken to a foster home. This was a temporary arrangement, for then they were packed off to Indiana to live with an uncle. Two years later, Charles Peters hanged himself. He was 52.

Carol was married in 1960, to a 33-year-old pimp whom she had known for two weeks. The marriage had lasted only six days when Carol left because her husband apparently wanted her to have sex with his friends. She was not prepared to tolerate that sort of treatment, although she later told psychiatrists that she had been involved in sex for gain before marrying, and also claimed to have been a prostitute in Portland, Oregon, in the mid-60s.

Following her divorce from the pimp, Carol says she tried to pull her life together by attending the Santa Monica City College, where she studied to become a vocational nurse. Unfortunately, the college is unable to support her claim that she graduated class in 1968.

The following year, she married a hospital orderly, called Grant Bundy. This marriage lasted 11 years and the couple had two boys. But Grant was a women beater, and court records show that, in January 1979, Carol sought refuge, in a battered-women's shelter, before leaving him and going on welfare. She attempted suicide on two occasions. After taking a job as a licensed vocational nurse at the Valley Medical Centre in Los Angeles, Carol, now overweight, moved with her two children to Valerio Gardens, an apartment block in Van Nuys, which was managed by Jack Murray.

John 'Jack' Murray – full name John Robert Murray – was a 41-year-old Australian who lived with his wife and two children. He had a reputation as a ladies' man and, in no time at all, he and Carol were in the throes of an affair. Recently divorced from her second husband, whom she called a 'homosexual screaming faggot', Bundy received half the sale proceeds of her previous home. This was a substantial amount and randy Murray, to give him a more appropriate name, soon got wind of Carol's good fortune. Lavishing love, care and attention over her, Murray encouraged her to have her eyesight examined. She had appalling vision, to the extent that she was subsequently declared blind and therefore eligible for monthly disability payments from the Social Security.

Murray was not known for being a philanthropist, or even charitable, for he conned money out of his friends and frequently cheated on his wife. On one occasion, he was caught pocketing wads of notes from a Telethon charity collection with which he had been involved, and there is no doubt that Bundy's disability payments found their way to Murray's pocket, too.

When he eventually learned of Carol's sizeable bank account, the relationship changed direction, becoming one of prostitute and punter in reverse. Now completely infatuated with Murray, she started paying him for sex and, by the end of that year, he had wheedled $18,000 out of her on the grounds that he needed the money for his wife's non-existent cancer operation. In reality, he used half to pay off the outstanding debt on his Chevrolet van, a vehicle that he frequently used as his mobile sex den. The balance was used to refurbish the vehicle's interior.

By Christmas 1979, Bundy was so obsessed with Murray's sado-sexual performances on her, that she approached his unsuspecting wife, offering her $1500 in exchange for her husband. The woman was so furious that she insisted that Bundy vacate the apartment complex, while Jack timidly agreed to keep the peace. For him, it was a matter of selfish economics, as his wife cooked his meals and laundered his clothes, services he could not afford to lose. Also, from a purely cynical viewpoint, Carol was simply his subservient sex partner. Now that he had acquired most of her money, she was of no further use to him. Nevertheless, he did arrange for her to move into an apartment on Lemona Avenue, Van Nuys, and some three miles from his home.

On arriving at Lemona Avenue, in May 1980, Carol was immediately attracted to a neighbour's 11-year-old daughter, called Shannon. The girl was mentally and physically well-developed, and the unlikely pair established a relationship by trading adult jokes. Inevitably, this arrangement took on a sexual dimension and Bundy encouraged the minor to cross the bridge from gentle petting and cuddling to full-blown lesbianism.

Despite their apparent split, Jack and Carol continued their clandestine affair, but in a less evident manner. Progressively, the sex turned increasingly deviant, and the couple tried to encourage other young girls to indulge in three-way sex with them. Fortunately, they were all put off by Bundy's unsavoury looks and, now totally dejected, she took her two sons out of school and sent them to the Midwest to live with their father's parents.

* * *

'Carol Bundy, that half-blind bitch? She shit-canned her kids and sent them in a hand basket to Hell.'
DOUGLAS CLARK DURING HIS INTERVIEW AT SAN QUENTIN STATE PRISON

Douglas Clark had been born Daniel Clark, in 1948, in Pennsylvania, where his father, Franklyn, was stationed in the Navy. He was the third son of five children. In the third grade, he decided that he wanted to be called Doug instead of Daniel. The family moved regularly, from Pennsylvania to Seattle, to Berkley and Japan. By 1958, Franklyn had retired from the Navy as a Lieutenant Commander. In 1959, he moved, with his wife Blanch and their children, Frank Jr, Carol Anne, Doug and Jon Ronlyn, to Kwajalein, an atoll in the Marshall Islands, where he took up a civilian position running the supply department for the Transport Company of Texas. Blanch worked as a radio controller.

They spent two years in Kwajalein, living a life of colonial privilege, in a housing complex that was built specifically for the many American families who lived on the atoll. When they returned to America, they lived in Berkley for a short time before moving to India. The Clarks lived in a manner reserved for only the very wealthy back in the States, with a number of servants who would wait dutifully on the children and parents alike.

Other Americans living in the area described the Clark family as pleasant people who kept themselves to themselves. As for Doug, none could remember any startling behaviour problems, although they had found that if Doug was ever in trouble for any of the usual childhood pranks, his father would defend him aggressively, refusing to acknowledge his son's responsibility for his behaviour.

Later, both Walter and Doug were sent to Ecolat, the International School in Geneva attended by the children of UN diplomats, international celebrities and European and Middle Eastern royalty. Unlike his brother, Walt, who was popular and outgoing, Doug was considered sullen and arrogant and made few friends. He did not do well with his studies, as he couldn't be bothered to do the work or complete assignments. Doug Clark claimed that he had developed his preferences for kinky sex while living in Geneva. He was expelled from Ecolat for this reason.

After he left Geneva, 16-year-old Doug was sent to Culver Military Academy in Indiana. Frank Jr and Carol Ann had already left home by this time and Walt was sent to a boarding school in Arizona; Jon Ronlyn joined him there later. Doug's parents continued to move around the world: first to Venezuela, then Perth, Western Australia.

Although intelligent, Doug Clark was happy to scrape through his schooling with minimal effort. He was involved in a number of sports and played saxophone in the dance band. In the three years that he attended the Academy, he did not have any close friends. Instead, he hung around with a group of kids who shared Doug's distain for authority and had a distinct 'don't give a fuck' attitude. He would boast of his family's wealth and sexual exploits, oblivious to his friends' annoyance and boredom. The fact that most of his classmates refused to mix with him, and would often avoid contact with him altogether, did not seem to bother him at all.

Doug's behaviour and attitude led to many meetings with the school therapist, Colonel Gleeson. Despite the fact that Gleeson had written many letters informing the Clarks of their son's bad conduct, they showed no concern. In the time he was there, he only received one visit from his mother. The only visit his father made occurred while the lad was on holiday.

Like most teenage boys, Doug and his classmates were obsessed with teenage girls and the fantasy of sex, but for Doug it was much more than fantasy. He would often bring a girl to his room where he would record their moans and groans as he had sex with them. He would then replay the tapes to his classmates, revelling in the obvious jealousy.

Aged 17, Doug claimed to meet the love of his life at a Culver dance, where he took her away from another boy. Despite his claims to have been in love with Bobbi, he would take photographs of them having sex and pass them around the school, enjoying the notoriety that they brought him.

In 1967, at the age of 19, Clark graduated from Culver and went to live with his parents, who were now retired and living in Yosemite. When he was drafted, he enlisted in the Air Force in radio intelligence to ensure that he would not end up in the front line in the Vietnam War. He went first to Texas, and then Anchorage, Alaska, where he was given the job of decoding Russian messages.

The military discipline in Anchorage reminded him of Culver and he resented his senior officers' corrections: but the city life made up for it. He spent most of his time in the many dancer bars where he would nurture his ego as he left each night with one of the dancers hanging on his arm. Before his term was up, Douglas Clark left the Air Force with an honourable discharge, a National Defence Service Medal and his benefits intact. What the events were that led up to this are unknown as his story is different every time he tells it, and the Air Force will not reveal anything. Doug claims that he had been witness to the murder of a black man by a white man, and that he had fled when he was called in for questioning.

With over $5,000, Doug planned to drive from Alaska to the Mexican border, but stopped when he got to Van Nuys, in Los Angeles, where he moved in with his sister, Carol Ann, who was living with her abusive husband.

At 24 he met, and later married, 27-year-old Beverley in a North Hollywood bar. Blonde and heavy, the woman saw herself as fat and ugly, but felt that Doug, with his big dreams and ambitions, would always try to build her up.

They bought a car upholstery business, which Doug ran, while Beverley had a job and did the books at weekends. He insisted that he was the one with the intelligence, not she, and refused to listen to any advice she gave about the business. Whenever they began to get ahead financially, Doug would quickly blow it. During the Seventies, the business began to falter, so they sold it. To pay off their debts, Doug worked in a gas station and as a security guard before he started buying goods at auctions to resell at swap meets. Beverley had the job of loading and unloading the truck because, in his opinion, he was a better salesperson than she was.

Although Beverley could not exactly say what went wrong in the marriage, she did say that Doug was lazy. She would not consider the fact that he liked to wear her underwear as any more unusual than his desire to try wife-swapping, or three-way sex.

As Beverley gained more weight during their marriage, Doug spent less and less time at home, preferring to go to bars. According to Carol Ann, her brother drank heavily and would become over anxious and angry when drunk. Beverley would deny this, even though she had persuaded him to join Alcoholic's

Anonymous as a condition of them staying together. He kept off the booze for two years.

Doug was ambitious but could not commit himself to the work that was required to achieve the success he longed for. It had been Beverley's suggestion that he apply to work for the city as a steam-plant trainee. He agreed and actually completed the training course.

In 1976, four years after they were married, Doug and Beverley separated and later divorced, although they remained close friends.

Douglas Clark began work at the Jergen's soap factory in 1979. His duties as an engineer required him to tend the large boiler. While not befitting his level of education, he enjoyed the sense of power that controlling the three-storey structure gave him.

In February 1980, Clark set fire to his car outside the factory, while he was working the night shift, in order to claim the insurance. He later bragged to Carol Bundy that the real reason was to destroy evidence.

By the time he met Bundy, Clark had developed quite a talent for insinuating himself into the lives of fat, unattractive women who would willingly give him free rent, food and money in return for the attention he gave them. When the women demanded more in return, he would quickly leave them and move on to the next lonely soul.

Just after the Christmas of 1979, Carol Bundy, then aged 37, met Doug Clark at the 'Little Nashville Country Club where Murray sang Tom Jones hits. Douglas Daniel Clark was a boiler engineer by trade but he was a tradesman with his incredibly smooth manner. He was also well read and liked to sprinkle his conversation with quotations from Shakespeare and French phrases. Thirty-one-year-old Clark was a handsome man with a soft, slightly European speaking voice, a gift which enabled him to have the pick of any woman he chose. He was a leech and a sexual hedonist who enjoyed nothing more than a varied choice of eager girlfriends who were willing to share their home with him. Indeed, at times he was so much in demand he would even forget where he was actually living himself.

On the evening of their first meeting, Carol Bundy and Douglas Clark spent the night together. On learning of Doug's rent problems with his landlady, Carol offered him lodgings in her apartment. For a short period, the arrangement was mutually satisfactory. Put simply, Clark traded his body and sex for a roof over his head. Eventually, he came to the view that cash for sex would be more agreeable to him. During his brief stay at Lemona Avenue, Bundy introduced Clark to her sexual playmate, Shannon.

The tempting proximity of the sexually advanced youngster, and prompted by Carol's encouragement for three-way sex, proved irresistible to Clark. Bundy photographed him simulating sex with the made-up child, an exposure which would later prove to be his undoing. During an interview at San Quentin State Prison, Clark ranted on about the subject, saying, 'I had sex with Bundy about three times in all our relationship, although Carol will say otherwise. Murray was her intense S&M lover. She and Jack had sex with the 11-year-old. He tried to orally and vaginally rape the kid. They repeatedly tried to engage my room-mate, Nancy, in three-way sex. Carol even tried to get Nancy to join her and Shannon in three-way female sex. She told Nancy and Shannon not to let me know she was busy with Jack, trying to have sex with them, since I would not like her and her lover fuckin' around with one of my girlfriends.'

* * *

The first confirmed murders committed by The Sunset Slayer were the double killing of 15-year-old Gina Marano and 16-year-old Cynthia Chandler. The naked bodies of the two attractive teenagers were found, on an incline off the Ventura Freeway, by a Caltrans street cleaner on Thursday, 12 June 1980. The medical examiner established that they had died the previous day. Cynthia was killed by a single .25 calibre gunshot wound to the back of her head, which had left the bullet lodged in her brain, and a second shot had penetrated her lung bursting open her heart. It was also determined that both shots had been fired at point-blank range. Gina had also been shot twice. One round entered behind her left ear, exiting near her right eyebrow, and the second bullet blasted through the back of her head, also exiting behind the left ear.

At around 8.00pm, on Saturday, 14 June, a woman called the LAPD Northeast Division at Van Nuys. She told a detective that she thought her lover was a murderer. 'What I'm trying to do,' she said, while officers recorded the call, 'is to ascertain whether or not the individual I know, who happens to be my lover, did in fact do this. He said he did. My name is Betsy.'

Later in the same call, she changed her name to Claudia. The police were anxious to learn the full name of the alleged killer. The informant refused to give out this vital information, but when pressed, she did give a brief description. 'He has curly brown hair and blue eyes. His Christian name is John, and he's 41 years old,' she added. 'I've found a duffel bag in his car, full of bloody blankets, paper towels, and his clothes.'

This description matched Jack Murray perfectly, and not Clark, who was only 37 at the time. Warming now to her theme, the woman added, 'He tells me he fired four shots. Two in one girl's head and virtually blew her head away. One shot in the head and one shot in the chest of the other girl. He used a .25-calibre pistol. Does that jibe with what you've got?' When the caller hung up, a detective wrote on the tape cassette: 'Either the killer, or one who knows the killer!'

Over the following days, investigators compiled a list of people who had purchased .25-calibre pistols in recent months. Carol Mary Bundy's name came up for she had purchased two .22-calibre Raven automatics in Van Nuys on Friday, 25 April. In fact, she was the only female on the register. The gun shop provided the police with her address, vehicle registration and social security number. Amazingly, the police chose to ignore this crucial information, despite the previous telephone call from a woman, indicating a connection with two of the murders. Quite why the police chose to act this way would remain a mystery for some time to come.

Meanwhile, on Saturday, 22 June, Bundy moved from her apartment to Verdugo Avenue in Burbank. Clark, among others, helped her by taking her furniture and other possessions across town to her new home, which was a stone's throw from his place of employment at the Jergens soap factory.

At 3.05am the next day, a Burbank police officer found the fully-clothed body of prostitute Karen Jones, lying in the gutter of a residential street near the NBC studios in Hollywood. She had been shot in the temple, with a .25-calibre pistol, and there were indications were that she had been thrown from a moving vehicle. Ballistic tests on a bullet retrieved from her head at autopsy proved that it matched, in every respect, the same bullets that had killed both Chandler and Marano.

Later that same morning and, just a few miles away in a Sizzler Diner parking lot, police found the headless corpse of Exxie Wilson, another hooker. The body, which had been dragged behind a trash dumpster, was naked and lying in a pool of congealing blood. Wilson and Jones both shared the same pimp, and he reported that he had last seen them, both alive, shortly before midnight. They had been together.

During the late hours of Thursday, 26 June, a resident drove into the driveway of his home in Studio City and found an ornate wooden chest obstructing his access. 'I'd thought I'd found some treasure,' he later told police, but upon opening the chest, the man was horrified to find a severed head which had been wrapped up in a T-shirt and jeans. At autopsy, it was determined that Exxie had been shot with a .22-calibre bullet, the head had been washed and make-up roughly applied. It had also been refrigerated after decapitation, which had taken place while she was still alive. There were traces of what appeared to be semen in her throat. The recovered bullet matched, in every respect, the bullets that had been used to kill Marano, Chandler and Wilson.

* * *

Snake hunters were out looking for trophies in a ravine in the hillside country near Foothill Boulevard in Sylmar, on Sunday, 29 June, when they found the body of 17-year-old prostitute, Marnette Comer. Partially naked and covered with scrub, the corpse, which had been dehydrated and mummified in the summer heat, was lying on its stomach. It was determined, at autopsy, that she had been shot three times in the chest with a .25-calibre pistol and her belly had been slit open. Marnette had last been seen alive on 31 May. The bullets recovered matched, in every respect, the rounds that had killed all of the other previous victims.

By now the police had traced the ornate chest to a Newberry's store, in Reseda, where a clerk remembered the customer being an overweight woman who wore glasses with thick lenses and short, black gloves. The sales assistant especially remembered the gloves because it had been a very hot day. 'She was dumpy, and kinda ugly,' the clerk told police.

By now, the clues floating around as to the identity of the mystery informant called 'Claudia' were adding up. Five hookers had been shot with the same .25-calibre pistol, and the description of the buyer of the chest matched that of Carol Bundy, the only woman in the whole of California who owned two Raven pistols. Yet still the police couldn't match up these leads.

On 29 July, Bundy started to deteriorate mentally. She begged Clark to shoot her. When he refused, she attempted suicide. She sat in her Datsun car and injected herself with insulin and librium. Then she swallowed a handful of sleeping pills. Despite her knowledge of drugs, gained from her nursing experience, the suicide attempt failed, and she was found and taken to hospital.

The next day, her first action was to telephone Jack Murray, from her hospital bed, and ask him to pick her up in his van. When they met, she saw that he was accompanied by a woman called Nancy Smith. Carol was so furious she refused to get in the Chevy and, seething with rage, walked home. Yet none of this prevented her and Murray from having three-in-a-bed sex with young Shannon four days later.

On Sunday, 3 August, Bundy made arrangements to meet her lover again in the parking lot of the Little Nashville Country Club. Her timing let her down, though, for when she turned up at the rendezvous as planned, she found Murray was already in his van and having sex with a woman called Avril Roy-Smith. Carol banged on the door and Avril left.

This chance encounter with yet another woman was to be the straw that finally broke the camel's back. Bundy and Murray drove away from the club together and parked a few blocks away where they prepared for sex in the back of the van. Now undressed, Murray lay on his stomach while, crouching behind him, Bundy parted his buttocks and pushed her tongue into his anus. As Murray groaned with delight, she reached into her over-extended waistband and drew out one of her Raven automatics. With her tongue still in place, she touched the muzzle of the gun to the back of Murray's head. He felt the cold steel, and froze for an instant before she fired a single shot into his brain. She checked for a pulse and ascertained that he was still alive, so she fired again. Still his heart kept on beating. Throwing the gun to one side, Bundy pulled out a heavy boning knife from her bag, which she repeatedly drove into his back. After a dozen stabs he finally died. To complete her gruesome work, Bundy then slit open her victim's buttocks and mutilated his anus before hacking off his head. After rummaging through the van's cupboards, she scattered pornographic videotapes and magazines around the body. Emptying Murray's briefcase, she removed several Polaroid sex snapshots, and took his keys and his gun, before placing his head in a plastic bag. She then returned to her own car which was still parked in the club's parking lot. Now, in the early hours of Monday, 4 August, she drove to a call box and telephoned her own apartment where Clark was sleeping.

Doug Clark was in bed with Nancy Smith when the shrill ring dragged him out of a heavy sleep. 'Carol was whispering and giggling on the phone', he explained, and as the call continued, Nancy, who suffered from epilepsy, started a seizure. Doug told Bundy to shut up and get back home, and then he called for an ambulance. When Bundy arrived five minutes later, paramedics were already on the scene. After the ambulance left, Bundy took Clark to her car where, in the well of the front passenger seat, was Murray's head in the plastic bag. The ragged and bloody stump was exposed and Clark fell back and vomited. What with Nancy's fit and now this, it was all too much, but then Bundy coolly asked him if he would help her dispose of the mess. Like a complete fool he agreed, despite the fact that he was about to start his shift at the Jergens soap factory within the hour.

They drove off in the direction of the factory, with Bundy cradling the plastic-wrapped head in her lap. As they passed a pile of rubbish, she wound down the window and tossed the grisly article out. Murray's head was never seen again.

Three days later on Tuesday, 7 August, the sexually insatiable Bundy invited Tammy Spangler, one of Murray's former girlfriends, over for dinner. Clark knew that Carol was trying to initiate another three-way sex session and declined to take part. In any case, he fancied the attractive woman himself, and he also feared for Bundy's state of mind. 'If she could do that to Jack,' he said, 'what the fuck could she do to someone else? What about my fuckin' head?'

After the meal, Tammy left to go to work, and Bundy and Clark were now alone. Her sexual expectations had been disappointed, so she convinced Doug that they should drive into Hollywood and find another girl who would treat him to a hooker's blow-job. This was to be his birthday present from Bundy and, reluctantly, he agreed.

They drove to Highland Avenue where they saw a suitable whore. The prostitute was called over and a deal was agreed. The girl's name was Cathy, but before she took payment, she said, 'I don't do nothing with no woman.' Her concerns were allayed, and she climbed into the back seat followed by Clark, who left the driver's seat tilted forward against the steering wheel. This enabled Carol, who sat in the front passenger seat, to have a grandstand view. She gloated at the unedifying sight through her inch-thick spectacles. Clark described what happened next.

'I was on the left an' Cathy was on my right, and twisted around with only her left buttock on the edge of the seat. She was working me up with her mouth, an' stuff like that. Then I noticed Carol fidgeting in her seat. She began heaving herself up and down, craning her neck to view the area around the car, like she was looking to see if there was anyone around. I saw Carol's hand reach around the seat, like she was gonna grope Cathy. Then I saw the fuckin' gun. For an instant, I thought she was going to shoot me, like she did Murray. But Carol placed the pistol to the back of the hooker's head and pulled the trigger.'

The bullet passed clean through the prostitute's head and struck Clark in the lower side of his stomach. Fortunately, it was only a flesh wound but blood flowed on to his work shirt. 'I was shocked and freaking out,' he explained. 'Carol told me to drive the fuckin' car while she climbed in the back, tore the clothes off the dead girl and sexually assaulted her, all the while ranting that she was sure the dead girl would have liked it.'

When the body had been dumped, the two drove back to Bundy's apartment where he changed his soiled clothes. He wouldn't see them again until the police arrested him.

On Saturday, 9 August, the Van Nuys police received a complaint about a Chevrolet van that had been left unattended on Barbara Ann Street. The caller also mentioned a foul smell emanating from the vehicle. Within minutes, a squad car arrived to investigate and a police officer, looking through one of the vehicle's windows, saw a body in the rear. As the scene was being cordoned off, Detective Roger Pida climbed in to conduct a preliminary investigation and, among the documents scattered about, he found a wallet, which identified the male victim as John Robert Murray. Checking through their computer, the police learned that Murray's wife had reported him missing several days earlier, and officers were able to ascertain that he spent a lot of time with a woman called Carol Mary Bundy.

The following morning, two detectives called at Bundy's apartment in Burbank. She invited them in and they were introduced to Clark and Tammy Spangler. Clark and Bundy were taken downtown for further questioning while Spangler followed in her car to bring them home after the interview.

At the police station, the couple offered different alibis for the time of Murray's murder. Clark told the truth and said that Bundy had come home later that night. In a separate interview room, Bundy lied, claiming to have been at home all evening. She was adamant that she had not ventured out. Asked if she owned any firearms, Bundy said that she had recently sold a pair of pistols to a tall guy with red hair and a scar. The only name she could conjure up at short notice was Mike Hammer, which provided the officers with a moment's amusement. Then Tammy Spangler piped up. She told the detectives that she had seen Murray with a woman called Avril Roy-Smith on the night of the murder. 'Perhaps you'd better go talk with her,' she suggested.

With no solid evidence with which to hold Bundy, they allowed her and Clark to leave while they went in search of Avril who subsequently gave a verifiable alibi to account for the time encompassing Murray's death. She said that when she left the Chevy van, Jack Murray was very much alive. As Avril departed, heading for the club where she spent the next three hours drinking with friends, she saw Carol Bundy climb into Murray's van.

The homicide cops were now very interested in Bundy. The next day, while they were completing their paperwork for the arrest warrant, Bundy walked off her job at the hospital after confessing to colleagues that she was responsible for murdering and decapitating her lover. She told them that she was going back to her apartment to 'clean out the evidence before Doug gets home'. As soon as she left, a senior official at the hospital reported Bundy's bizarre allegation in a frantic call to the police.

On her way home, Bundy called in to see Clark at the soap factory during his shift. She asked the gatehouse security officer to summon him. When he came out, she told him that she had told the police everything. Clark was livid. 'You crazy cunt', he snapped, 'get the fuck away from me.'

With Bundy now off the premises, Doug stormed back into the factory where he tried repeatedly to phone detective Pida who was not in his office. 'Bundy was trying to fit me up with murder,' he has said many times while protesting his innocence for the Sunset Slayings, 'an' who the fuck is gonna believe a woman is doing all this murder stuff? An' she had incriminating photos of me and Shannon hidden away. Blackmail. Yeah. That's what it fuckin' is.'

Just after 11.00am that morning, there was call to the Northeast Division of the LAPD, and a woman – Carol Bundy – asked to speak to homicide detectives. When Officer James Kilgore picked up the phone, the woman said, 'Sometime, way back, you were having a string of murders involving prostitutes in Hollywood.'

'We still are,' replied Kilgore, totally unaware that the caller was recording their conversation.

'Do you still have a code name on the girl by the name of Betsy/Claudia?'

Kilgore said he wasn't sure.

'All right, never mind,' said the caller. 'Would you like your man today?'

She talked about the murders, and said that the weapon was a .22-calibre automatic. She said her man had told her he had 'hit over 50 people'. Then she said that she had killed a man named Jack Murray, and admitted her involvement with several of the other murders. 'The one he cut her head off. Well, I played around with that one … and the fat girl [Karen Jones] that he dumped off near the NBC studios, I was involved with that.'

Kilgore asked how many murders there had been. 'Probably 12 or 14 total,' came the reply. 'But I can't verify all of them. I can only verify about eight or nine.'

'And you helped him on some of them?'

'Yes, I did,' said Bundy. 'Specifically how I got involved with it was a case of being scared to death because I knew that he had done these things. I felt I had to get involved. If I was involved he'd have no reason to kill me.'

She then said she was calling to give herself in, and that her real name was Carol Bundy. Finally, referring to the killer, she blurted out, 'He's my boyfriend and his name is Douglas Daniel Clark.'

'Doesn't it make you feel bad that you killed somebody?' asked the detective. Bundy replied, amazingly, 'The honest truth is, it's fun to kill people, and if I was allowed to run loose, I'd probably do it again. I have to say, I know it's going to sound sick … it's like going to sound psycho, and I don't really think I'm psycho, but it's kinda fun. It's like riding a roller-coaster. Not the killing, not the action that somebody died, because we didn't kill them in any way that they'd suffer. It was just killing them straight out.'

* * *

After making her telephone call, Bundy started rearranging her apartment, in the belief that she had a few hours to get things in order. She was bent on doing everything she could to incriminate Clark, but she had just minutes, because detectives were about to arrive on her doorstep and arrest her. When they did, they conducted a careful search of the place.

Almost immediately, Bundy held up a cardboard box that contained a pair of panties and assorted clothing. These items later proved to belong to an, as yet, undiscovered murder victim who would later be tagged 'Jane Doe 28'. The box also contained a purse belonging to another unidentified victim, 'Jane Doe 18'.

'This box belongs to Clark,' she said, 'And, do you want to see what kind of guy Doug Clark is?' she asked, as she reached for her handbag on a table. An officer stopped her because he suspected that the bag might contain a gun but, inside, was Bundy's key ring. She selected a key and offered it to one of the police officers, to open the cabinet in Clark's bedroom. The cupboard contained a photo album of Clark with his numerous lovers, including photos of his poses with the 11-year-old Shannon. Also, hidden among various papers was a firearm sales receipt, made out to a Juan Gomez, which later proved to be false.

Meanwhile, Detective Pida had taken Clark in for questioning to Van Nuys Police Station where he was held for hours, without water or food and denied the use of the toilet. This treatment was illegal, especially when Clark had not even been told of the reason for his arrest. Indeed, at the time, he actually believed the arrest was all about Murray. When he was finally asked what he knew about this murder, to his credit, he admitted everything he knew. When he was asked why he hadn't gone straight to the police, Clark truthfully answered that Bundy had dozens of incriminating pictures, of himself and Shannon, which she had used as a threat.

When Pida produced the photograph album, taken from his bedroom cabinet, Clark started to feel decidedly uneasy. The detective showed him a mugshot of the dead Cynthia Chandler, and Doug explained that he knew her personally. They talked about the prostitute murders, to which Clark retorted, 'Someone is tryin' to lynch my ass, and I have hunch I know who it is.'

With little else to book him with, the police initially detained Clark on a holding charge of child molestation. This was a stop-gap measure, for they had wider ambitions as far as Clark was concerned. There was certainly no evidence to say that he had been involved with the Sunset Slayings, other than Carol Bundy's wild accusations. Nevertheless, Clark was held, without his legal rights read to him, for a further eight hours because he demanded to see an attorney.

It was now late at night and, when the police finally acceded to his request for legal representation, they informed him that all the lawyers had gone home, and it would take hours before one could be recalled. Then he was illegally moved to another police station 30 miles away. When an attorney did turn up, at Van Nuys Police Station, Clark was no longer there and no one seemed to know where he had been transferred.

If the police were being 'unco-operative', then Clark was quite the opposite. He gave them permission to search his apartment, his motorcycle, and his place of work. 'I gave them everything,' Clark railed on. 'I gave them my fuckin' boots, my fuckin' saliva, my fuckin' blood. I offered to take a polygraph, but changed my fuckin' mind 'cos I ain't never trusted the cops. I could see a fit-up coming from a mile off.'

While he was being grilled, Bundy was unloading her story on the detectives interviewing her. She corroborated Doug's denial of guilt for Murray's murder, saying that while she had shot Murray, another man, 'a psycho', had hacked the head off to remove the evidence of traceable bullets. Questioned as to why she had left the cartridge casings in the Chevy, she gave conflicting answers. At first, she stated that she didn't realise that the weapon automatically ejected the cases. Then, in a complete reversal, she said that she did realise that the cases had ejected from the weapon but, had simply forgotten to pick them up.

During the initial, and extremely thorough, search of Murray's van, there was no record of any shell casings being found. Some time later, however, a detective said that he had found a single shell casing in the van, and that it had been fired from Bundy's chrome-plated Raven pistol. This discovery took on a more sinister aspect when it transpired that a police evidence envelope, sealed and marked '2 x shell casings found at unspecified sources' had been torn open and one of the shell cases was missing.

When she was asked why she had shot Murray, Bundy gave four vague reasons in rapid succession. The first was that he had stolen money from her; second, because he had jilted her; then, she had shot him as he had planned to rape and kill Shannon;

and finally, that he was going to report Doug to the police, accusing him of being the deadly Sunset Slayer. None of this made any sense whatsoever but, incredibly, the police seemed inclined to believe her. Regarding which of the four stories, they didn't seem to know.

With an attentive audience of good-looking police officers surrounding her, Bundy went on to say that she had been involved with the Cathy murder. The hooker had been shot while sitting in her Datsun. When the police told her that there was no forensic evidence of a shooting in the car, let alone a murder, she changed her account, saying that the crime had taken place in her Buick, which she had loaned to Clark. For his part, Doug says it was most certainly the Datsun because the car only had two doors, and he had to push the driver's seat forward to let the hooker in.

Bundy went on to say that she had paid the hooker to give Clark a blow-job as a birthday present, but claimed that it was agreed that he would give her a signal as to when to shoot the prostitute in the head. Douglas Clark vehemently denies this, arguing, 'No, man, I don't care who he is. Who would let a half-blind bitch reach over, shoot at the head of a hooker suckin' his cock and hope like hell she didn't blow a hole in his knee or chest? I mean, what if her jaw locked shut?' Perhaps Clark has a valid point!

When questioned about the Marano and Chandler murders, Bundy claimed that she had not been involved. She had merely learned of the crimes through Clark. It was Doug, she said, who had told her that he had shot both women in the head while they were giving him oral sex. During his interview at San Quentin, Clark was asked to comment on Bundy's claim.

'You are pulling my pecker,' he declared. 'Do you think I'm fuckin' crazy, man? Some broad is blowin' me off an' I stick a gun to her head and blast them away. What about the fuckin' blood, man? What about my dick, man? I'd have been covered with the shit and it would have been painted all over the inside of the fuckin' car.'

Bundy told the police that Doug 'dragged the bodies from the Buick and into his lock-up garage where he had sex with them'. She added, 'And it was because of this bloody mess in the car that Doug put it through a car wash.' Clark has never denied washing the Buick and, indeed, he even volunteered this information to the detectives who confirmed that he had been to the carwash on 21 June, exactly a week after Bundy made her Betsy/Claudia call to the police.

Clark asserted, 'Everyone who saw or rode in the Buick from 14 June to 21 June – and there will be many who testify to this – will say that the car was dry, and right after the car wash on 21 June it was soaked and damp with steamy air for a full week. The point is, what fucking vehicle was she washing out, just before the taped call to the police on 14 June? The Datsun was broken down, the Buick was dry, and only the Murray's Chevy van fits the details she made in that call.'

It later proved to be the case that, indeed, Murray's van had been washed out after the first three murders, although the police chose to ignore this vital evidence, that would prove beyond any doubt that Bundy was lying once again to save her own skin. Yet all of this begs the question as to why Clark washed the Buick in the first place. The answer lies in supporting evidence, given by four other people, who confirm that he is telling the truth.

During the evening of 20 June, Clark visited Joey Lamphier, one of his many girlfriends and, when he left the woman's apartment, he accidentally reversed over an alley cat, crushing its hindquarters. He lifted the badly injured animal into the Buick where it crawled under the front passenger seat. Douglas Clark is known for his love of cats and, in the past, had taken in several strays. He rescued many more from animal pounds and found new homes for them. Any cat-lover will confirm, therefore, that it would have been in his nature to have been very concerned about this particular cat's welfare following the accident. Unfortunately, the cat died before he could reach a vet, so he placed the dead creature in a cardboard box and left it by garbage skip.

After work on the 21 June, Clark drove Timmy, the young son of his current landlady, and Bundy, in the Buick, to the carwash. Carol was pressing for the return of the car, in preparation for her move to Burbank. Doug hosed the cat's blood, urine and excrement from under the seat and vacuumed the excess water away. Later, Timmy told police that the small amount of blood was still wet when he got into the car, which totally contradicted Bundy's claim that the blood had been there for some ten days. And, Clark explained, 'If this car wash had a sinister motive, why would I have taken a mouthy kid along?'

Police evidence technicians did find a small amount of what appeared to be blood, under and around the front seat of the Buick, yet in no way was the back seat contaminated in the manner which would have been consistent with Bundy's claim that three brutal and bloody murders had been committed in this vehicle.

Around mid-1991, Carol Bundy changed her story yet again. This time for the benefit of a journalist who was writing a book about the Sunset Slayings. She now said that the car wash on 21 June followed the murder of Cathy (Jane Doe 28), which had been committed the night before. Now, according to her latest claim, the blood was no longer that of Chandler and Marano, neither was the Cathy murder committed in the Datsun. This time it was someone else but, once again, the police seemed to ignore these contradictions.

When questioned about the murders of Karen Jones and Exxie Wilson, Bundy denied any involvement in these crimes, and merely related an account allegedly given to her by Clark. 'There were three hookers working together,' she said. 'Clark picked up Exxie and shot her in the head before decapitating her behind the Sizzler' Diner.' (Witnesses heard a vehicle racing away from this precise location at about 1.15am.) Bundy went on to say that Doug returned to pick up Karen Jones and he shot her while she was giving him oral sex in the car. 'He killed her and dumped the body,' she said. Witnesses heard a scream around 2.40am, and Karen's corpse was discovered at this location less than an hour later.

Following these two murders, Bundy alleged that Clark brought Exxie's head back to her new apartment, in Burbank, where he placed it in the freezer before phoning her at her old apartment at Lemona, where she was still living. Telephone records show that this call was made at precisely 3.08am. But is Bundy's story true? She claims that it was Clark who called her to explain what he had done. Doug says that it was Bundy phoning him. The difference is that his account can be verified, for he had an alibi that night.

Tammy Spangler confirmed that Bundy had called Doug at around 3.00am at the Lemona where they were sleeping on an old mattress. 'Doug was in a lot of pain because he had hurt his back while moving Carol's stuff,' she said. 'He was in agony and pretty wild that Carol had got him out of bed.' Once again, the detectives ignored Clark's story and chose to believe Bundy, who, at best, was a pathological liar. But was there any other evidence to support Clark and Tammy Spangler's claim, that they had spent the night at Bundy's old apartment? There was.

Douglas Clark said, 'I argued with Cissy Buster on the Sunday. She said, "Leave me if you don't want to live with me." I said, "Fuck it," and lugged my stuff down to the Buick. Carol had complained about the dampness and lingering smell of the cat faeces from the previous day's car wash. I had offered to dry it out 'cos I needed the car. I promised to dry it out and return it in time for Carol's move to Burbank. I then drove to Lemona, at about 1.30pm, to 2.30pm. The movers came about 3.00pm, to 4.00pm and moved her into Burbank in two trailers and pick-up loads. I rode with them and Carol had a slew of kids to help her put the kitchen shit in the Buick.

At the other end, the movers moved it all up. I helped and strained my back and ended up nearly unable to move. I left early and rode my bike to Van Nuys. I called Al Joines, my assistant at Jergens, around 6.00pm. I told him that I'd hurt my back, and asked him if he would start up the boiler, the following morning. I then drank several beers.

Tammy came over and we crashed on a mattress in the now empty Lemona apartment. I was woken from my sleep by a call from Carol at a time I know to be 3.08am, because the police confirmed that such a call was made.'

Every detail of this statement was later shown to be true.

Most prostitutes are reluctant to trick alone, preferring to work in pairs, for safety. Contrary to this practice, Bundy claims that Exxie Wilson allowed herself to be picked up by Clark, who killed her and then returned to the red-light district on his own with the intention of enticing the now dead girl's colleague into the Buick. Furthermore, as was later shown at autopsy, Exxie Wilson was still very much alive during her decapitation, and that it would have been impossible to accomplish this act of mutilation without Clark being sprayed with arterial blood, which was not the case. Even more startling, was the coroner's statement, which claimed that both Murray's head, which Bundy had admitted cutting off, and Exxie Wilson's headless body, had been decapitated by the same hand, using knives which had been found in Bundy's apartment.

The time interval which elapsed, between the murders of Exxie Wilson and Karen Jones, is also of interest for it has the Bundy/Murray *modus operandi* written all over it. Bundy revealed her MO when she offered Clark his birthday present and shot the hooker into the bargain. That Exxie had been decapitated by the same skilled hand that had cut off Murray's head, and that it had been Murray's van that had been washed out several times, just after the murders, all points to Murray and Bundy as being the real murderers of Exxie Wilson and Karen Jones.

Then there is Bundy's telephone call to the police on Saturday, 14 June when she described the killer as a man called 'John' and gave a description that matched that of John 'Jack' Murray down to his correct age.

During her tape-recorded interrogation, on Monday, 11 August, Carol Bundy made reference to Clark murdering another hooker (Jane Doe 18) 'two weekends ago', and she was adamant about the date. Somewhat curiously, she was allowed to change this all-important date when the police ascertained that Clark was 380 miles away, attending his brother's wedding, on the weekend pinpointed by Bundy. Eventually, Bundy could only say 'some time in July'. But if this female killer was allowed to change a specific date to any one of her choosing in a given month, it paled into significance when she added that the crime committed on that date had been 'Doug's last murder'.

'He told me nothing about it,' she explained to the detectives. 'Absolutely nothing at all, and if he won't tell me, then he won't tell you, so you might as well forget it.'

But, within minutes, she changed her tune yet again, by giving a full description of the crime, including the nickname Clark had supposedly assigned to the victim – 'Water Tower' – and then offered up the location of the body. She even described Doug placing the girl's body on the bonnet of her Datsun, and having intercourse while the motor ticked over and he simulated 'coital movements'.

With Bundy lying, and changing her story at every twist and turn, it may come as no surprise to learn that she told police that the handbag they found in her apartment belonged to the Water Tower victim, too. But the bag actually belonged to someone else, and it contained a woman's business cards, telephone numbers and a driving licence; yet, no effort was made by the police to check out these vital details, or to try to find the rightful owner.

Quite rightly, Clark believes that if Jane Doe 18 had been identified, that information could have established a date when she was last seen alive and probably murdered, thereby giving him the opportunity to confirm an alibi. More recently, he has also commented on the nickname he allegedly gave to this victim.

'I have never named anyone by that name, dead or alive,' Clark says. 'The police say the body was found by an oil tank. I am a four-year educated engineer, and tanks are not towers, and oil is not water. This location was probably in the oil pumping area of those hills, and I would never nickname a girl 'Water Tower'. Only a layman who didn't know the difference might do that.'

Even when confronted with her lies, which the police anxiously accepted as 'truths', to suit their case against Clark, Bundy continued to lie and lie again. She further confused the already vexed situation by claiming that the cosmetics she had used, to transform Exxie's head into a 'Barbie Doll', had been taken from the purse belonging to Jane Doe 18. She insisted on this, despite the obvious fact that Wilson had been killed a month earlier than Jane Doe 18, ruling out Bundy's possession of her purse.

During her trading of accusatory testimony to escape execution, Carol Bundy insisted that Clark was a necrophile. She said that he shot the prostitutes through the head as they performed oral sex on him. In such a bizarre case, anything is possible, but common sense suggests that even the most deviant sexual psychopath would be deterred from such perverse activity. Not only was there the real danger of exiting and ricocheting bullets, as in the case with Cathy, but also the very real peril of reflexive, death-spasm bites on the penis, and Doug was very proud of his manhood.

While there was no evidence to support Bundy's claim that Clark was a necrophile, there was strong evidence to say that she was. She had admitted to having her tongue in the anus of Jack Murray when she fired the bullets into his head. Furthermore, when her Datsun car was stored after it had been released from the police pound, a letter was discovered which seemed to have been missed during the first police search of the vehicle. In Carol's handwriting, and signed 'Betsy' – the pseudonym she had used in her first call to the police – the letter contained sexually explicit details of 'vaginal death spasms'. She continued by describing, in sexually graphic detail, how Doug had taken the severed head of Exxie Wilson from the freezer and into the shower, where he performed oral sex with the icy remnant.

Yet again, her account is a pack of lies and testimony to her powers of grisly imagination. Now, this is not about a 'chilled head'. The alleged object of Clark's sexual outrage was not simply 'chilled', it was frozen solid. The severed head had become a solid block of ice, as both Bundy and the police confirmed, when it was discovered, and it took several days to thaw out. When interviewed, Clark said, 'The cops said it was froze solid, and Bundy says the same fuckin' thing. The jaw was locked shut. So how do you get a penis into that mouth? Give me a fuckin' break, will ya?'

This argument, nevertheless, could be missing the obvious. There was nothing to say that the head had not been used as a sexual receptacle before it had been frozen.

Despite Bundy's claim that Clark ejaculated into the mouths of both Marano and Chandler, internal swabs taken from the bodies showed no traces of semen. Traces of blood and sperm were found, though, on Exxie Wilson's body and Chandler's external vulva area. When tested, this was shown to be blood type

'A', the same grouping as Murray's, and distinct from Clark, who is type 'O'. Traces of acid phosphates were found in Exxie's throat, but this probably came from her spinal fluid, although the prosecution later insisted it was Clark's sperm, even though it did not match his blood group.

Shortly after her arrest for murder, detectives took Bundy for a meal. During this break in proceedings, she was given the freedom to empty her bank safety deposit box, while the police stood by, making no record of the contents. She also took officers to Clark's private post box, where, without a search warrant, they unlawfully ordered the clerk to hand over the mail it contained. Then, Bundy was allowed to return to her apartment so that she could arrange the sale of furniture, despite the fact that much of it belonged to Doug Clark. He stated quite correctly that 'they [the police] then let her have her car back before it was tested by the defence team,' emphasising, 'They never let murder cars back, never'.

Someone who was storing the Datsun for Bundy after her arrest, found the death spasm letter and a bloodstained jacket, which has never forensically tested, or blood-grouped. The garment did not belong to either Clark or Bundy, or to any of the known victims. Subsequent research identified the true owner as Jack Murray. When his wife was shown a photograph of the jacket, she unequivocally identified it as belonging to her late husband.

Incredibly, the generosity shown by the police to their star witness knew no bounds, even though Bundy was shown to be a pathological liar. On 29 August, and only 18 days after her arrest, they allowed her access to Jack Murray's bank deposit box and allowed her to remove $3,000. This was cash to which Mrs Murray had lawful title. The money simply vanished into thin air. For many years, the police adamantly denied that this incident took place. It was only when Clark finally proved the lie in court that the police agreed that the deposit box was opened in their presence.

'Oh, yeah. That day. Sure, but what money are we talkin' about?' asked a detective. 'Money, we ain't seen no money.'

At the time of writing, the police deny that any back-handed deal was done with Bundy. If they did admit that favours-for-cash deals had been conducted, three attorneys and a dozen police officers would be facing court proceedings. For her part, Carol Bundy insists she gave the $3,000 to the police for safekeeping and says that the money hasn't been seen since.

* * *

If mystery after mystery surrounds the lies and accusations of Carol Bundy, then the firearms involved in this case create a veritable minefield of problems and enigmas. It was established that she had purchased two .25-calibre Raven automatic pistols on 16 May 1980. These guns were similar, but not identical, in their appearance. They were distinguishable insofar as one was chrome-plated, while the other was nickel-plated. Ballistic tests identified the nickel-plated firearm as the weapon used in all of the murders, with the exception of those of Cathy (Jane Doe 18), and Jack Murray. In the latter case, no ballistic evidence was possible, for the very good reason that his head was never found. By now, both of the two cartridge cases, allegedly found in his truck, had mysteriously gone missing, in much the same manner as Mrs Murray's cash. Not to be beaten, Bundy now came up with the explanation that the nickel-plated gun actually belonged to Clark. He denied it, and other people, whom the police chose not to believe, corroborated his denial.

During the Memorial Holiday weekend, which began on 24 May, Clark and a girlfriend, Toni, had made arrangements to travel north, to Yosemite, with the intention of visiting his parents. He planned to make the journey on his motorcycle and, just in case Toni was too nervous to travel by this means of transport, he telephoned Bundy to see if he could use her Buick, should the need arise. It was during this phone call that Bundy told him that she had recently bought the Raven pistols, and she asked him if he could check them over because one kept jamming. When Clark took possession of these guns, they were unloaded but they came with a two-thirds-full box of shells.

On his return from Yosemite, Clark told Bundy that the chrome-plated gun was still jamming. She retained the nickel-plated pistol, which was later proved to be the murder weapon, and gave the malfunctioning chrome-plated pistol to Clark as a gift. She confirmed as much to the police.

On 16 June, Clark gave the gun to Joey Lamphier, showing her how to clear it if it jammed again. Early in July, Bundy demanded the return of this gun. There was an argument, following which, Clark returned the Raven to Bundy. The next time he saw it was on the night of 7 August, when Carol used it to shoot Cathy through the head.

The two pistols surfaced again, on 9 August, after the police discovered Murray's headless corpse. Bundy handed the firearms to Clark, saying, 'Get rid of these where they'll never be found.' He took them to the soap factory, where they were eventually discovered by police, still in Bundy's make-up bag, which was hidden on the top of a boiler.

Police investigators had had a field day, combing through Bundy's apartment and, in her bedside cabinet, they found 29 rounds of .25-calibre ammunition. An officer flicked through the pages of *Hustler* and *Playboy* magazines, while another detective amused himself by studying a particular bondage and domination magazine. Also in the living room, investigators found several film reels of 'Super' pornography, and a book that contained an illustration of a severed head. All of this material was owned by Bundy, but at Clark's trial it was all attributed to him.

During her lengthy interviews with the police, Bundy told them that Clark had had sex with the dead bodies of Marano and Chandler in his garage where he stored wood, along with his motorcycle and several boxes of his personal belongings. The detectives' ears pricked up and they obtained a search warrant for the place. No sooner had this accusation poured from Bundy's mouth than she frantically insisted that they wouldn't find any evidence there. 'We scrubbed the place out,' she confided. Nevertheless, police found Clark's boot print on the floor and they were keen to ascertain if the stain was blood.

Forensic experts carried out a 'presumptive' blood test, which gave a positive indication that the stain was organic in origin. Further tests were required, to authenticate the true nature of the stain. This was never done, and the reason, according to the police, was to 'preserve the boot print for identification and comparison'. This was a relatively lame excuse, as the print was recorded photographically, and there was no reason why a positive blood test could not have been completed after photographs had been taken. Another possible explanation lies in the concerns that the stain might fail the test, thus proving, for the umpteenth time, that Carol Bundy was a liar.

Police also claimed to have found a further bloodstain, measuring 2ft by 8ft in size, on the floor of Clark's garage. They concluded from this that heavily bleeding bodies had been dragged across the floor. Hence, they reasoned, this corroborated Bundy's testimony about the necrophile orgy that had supposedly occurred in the garage with the bodies of Marano and Chandler. As with the boot print, only a presumptive test was carried out and, again, the test proved inconclusive. Furthermore, when examined, the girls' bodies showed no signs of blood smears or streaks, as would have been the case if they had been dragged in such a manner. Post mortem abrasions on Chandler's back were attributed, by investigators, to the act of dragging the body across a rough surface. On the other hand, the medical examiner argued, these marks could have been the result of the body being dumped down the ravine.

Clark was astonished that the police should be so surprised to find his boot print in his garage, and with his usual droll sense of humour, he commented, 'What the fuck am I supposed to do? Levitate around my garage?' He also provided an explanation for the long drag marks which had been discovered on the floor.

'There was a track where the bike went in and out over a period of six months right down the middle of the garage. I stored raw wood, ply and particleboards there. There were four woodworking shops within a 50ft radius that directly dusted the area. The door allowed leaves and dust to blow in, round and under it.' This would certainly explain why the drag marks were organic in origin.

After careful investigation of Clark's garage, the police could only say that there 'might have been blood on the floor'. There was certainly not a shred of evidence to support Bundy's allegation that Clark had had sex with two dead and heavily-bloodstained bodies there. Moreover, Bundy's other statement, that they had scrubbed the place clean, proved to be another of her lies, for it was patently obvious, even to the police, that the place had not been cleaned out for years.

If anything could save Clark from the death sentence, it lay in establishing solid alibis for at least a few of the murders. But alibis seemed to be lacking, especially for 11 June, the date of the Marano and Chandler killings. Doug argues that he could not even remember where he was living on that day, let alone what he did after work, when, Bundy says, the crimes were committed. It soon became apparent that he was lodging with Cissy Buster, one of his many on-and-off again girlfriends. She told detectives that he arrived home around 8.00pm that evening, but time-keeping records from the soap factory suggest that he finished much earlier, at 1.00pm. Cissy Buster added that Clark had phoned her to say he would be home late, and she remembers this because it was her son's graduation party. It was subsequently shown that these events actually took place on Friday, 13 June, and not on the day of the murders.

One thing that could seal the case against Doug Clark would be a survivor who could identify him. While he and Bundy were under lock and key, a regular jailbird named Charlene Anderman, a mentally-unhinged woman who had been frequently arrested on drug and prostitution charges, was also behind bars. Around the same time as the 'Sunset Slayings' occurred, a series of savage knife attacks and robberies were committed against hookers. In April, Charlene had fallen victim to one such assault. She had joined a punter in his car when the man pulled out a knife and stabbed her several times in the back before kicking her out of his vehicle on to the street.

Police arrested Jerome Van Houten, whom Charlene Anderman identified in a line-up, but her recollection of the attack was hazy because she was high on cocaine at the time. She told the police that the attack had taken place in a motel room, then she changed her story to say that she had been stabbed in a car, the colour and make of which constantly changed. Understandably, the police deemed her identification to be unreliable, but they had enough on Van Houten to secure his conviction based on positive identification provided from other victims.

Now locked up in jail, Anderman started bragging about Clark being her assailant, so the police decided to interview her again. They showed her a photograph of Doug and, suddenly, she decided that he was the knifeman, adding that she was willing to testify to this in court providing that the police would free her from custody after the case was over with. Fortunately for Doug Clark, the court thought that she was totally unreliable and her evidence was thrown out. The police had to honour their part of the deal, and Charlene, whom her sister said was 'a liar who would say or do anything to get out of trouble', was released almost immediately.

Doug Clark has always maintained that Bundy and Murray killed most of the victims while driving around in Murray's Chevy van. During the forensic investigation of this vehicle, a vital piece of evidence was found, hanging from the roof vent hatch. It was a sliver of human scalp with strands of blonde hair attached to it. This gruesome artefact was approximately two inches in length, dehydrated, and probably detached from a head as the result of a gunshot blast. As most of the victims had been blonde, and Murray was dark-haired, it would seem evident that at least one of the prostitutes had been killed in the van, which would support Clark's claim. The State, however, desperately needed to convict Clark. After all, Murray was dead, and if he had been The Sunset Slayer, then the crimes had been allowed to run their bloody course. None of this would have gone down well with the police departments involved, especially as they had now gone out of their way to implicate Clark. The skin tissue, with hair attached, was taken away and no investigation was carried out to determine its origin. Clark was also refused the right to have it submitted as evidence at his trial.

With all the cards stacked against him, what luck Clark had remaining totally evaporated when an attorney was appointed to defend him who was inexperienced and ill-equipped to handle such a serious case of serial homicide. Clark's counsel had recently been declared bankrupt, and had appeared in court to answer matters against him of legal malpractice and theft of a client's funds. As a result of this, the lawyer had turned to drink and, when he appeared for Clark, he was an out-of-control drunk. He addressed the court claiming that he was an alcoholic and, throughout the trial, he was so distracted by his own bankruptcy that he paid scant attention to Clark's case. Family, friends, witnesses for the District Attorney and court officials all saw him drinking, usually doubles, before the court convened. The Bailiff even complained to the judge about the lawyer's alcoholic smell, which pervaded the air during his appearance at morning sessions.

On the first day of the trial, the attorney simply opened the proceedings by saying that Clark was guilty as charged, but that he was insane and should, therefore, be given a lenient sentence. Quite rightly, the judge was shocked by such an admission and, as the attorney staggered back to his seat, the judge was forced to remind him what the proceedings were all about. This was just the first phase of the trial in which an attempt was made to discover who had committed the crimes, and any suggestion of sentence would be dealt with at the later penalty phase.

Muttering under his breath, the lawyer sat down, only to rise, momentarily, an hour later, to say that he was ill prepared because he had not seen Clark for weeks. This was not so, for jail records of visitors, and the attorney's own financial records, proved he had been taking instructions from his client almost every day, right up to the first day of the case.

As the trial progressed, Clark became increasingly aware that his lawyer was a major liability. In a desperate effort to do something to save his own skin, he requested that he be allowed to represent himself. Several times, while he was being cross-examined by the prosecutor, he noted that his attorney was asleep, and had to wake him up. On other occasions, he had to interject the legal objections to lines of questions the court had ruled inadmissible. The prosecutor saw the defence attorney nodding off and, taking advantage of the situation, tried to slide contentious problems past him, an underhand tactic that worked on several occasions. The court ruled that Clark could not object on his own behalf; only his lawyer could do this, whether he was in dreamland or not.

From the outset, it became patently obvious that the State was determined to get a conviction at any cost. Faced with a defence in the hands of a totally incompetent attorney, who was either asleep or drunk, the prosecution was likely to have its wish granted.

Occasionally, Clark burst out with angry rants and accusations. One afternoon, he was manacled and tied to a chair in which he was gagged with a leather strap and a sanitary towel. At other times, he was escorted from the courtroom and locked up in a small holding-room, equipped with speakers, so that he could listen to his right to live being eroded away.

Eventually, with the trial having reached its midpoint, Judge Torres acceded to Clark's insistence that he should be allowed to represent himself. Despite this being exactly what Doug had wanted from day one, nothing improved. Indeed, if it were possible, things became far worse. He was denied co-counsel, advisory counsel and the services of a law clerk, and the judge, illegally, told him to 'go it alone'. At one point, Clark gave the court a list of items he required as evidence, including the items found in Murray's van. Some of these were sex toys and home-made pornographic videos. (Bundy had bought Murray a video camera, and it has always been suspected that they may have been recording their murders as snuff movies.) Needless to say, the judge blocked Clark's request. The accused man was astounded, screaming, 'If I had a colour movie, with the sound of Carol and Jack committing these murders, you would not let me bring it in?'

The judge smirked and said, 'You are right, Mr Clark. I would not.'

At another stage of the trial, it became evident that Clark did indeed have an alibi for the night that Exxie Wilson's head was deposited in the ornate chest. Several people recalled that he had been partying with a go-go dancer who was about to return home to New Zealand. Clark had also written her a cheque that night, and he was able to provide banking documents to support the fact that it had been cashed the following day. Not even the most adept serial killer can be in two places at the same time, and Bundy had told police that it had been Clark who had dumped Exxie's severed head, so this provided a problem for the prosecutor. The dancer even offered to return to the USA to give her evidence if her airfare was paid.

In vain, Clark asked for this dispensation, rightly arguing that the District Attorney had flown in scores of witnesses, one of whom had been an FBI agent from Virginia, to confirm that the boot print found in Clark's garage was indeed Clark's, something that he had admitted from the outset. Indeed, the prosecution spent over $10,000 on travel for their witnesses, and Clark was allowed just $20 – which amounted to his entire defence funding – in dimes, for a single telephone call.

In a last-ditch effort to get the dancer to testify, he begged that she be allowed to give her evidence over the telephone. This is a legally accepted procedure, if the witness is positively identified and sworn in at a local court. But, once again, his request was denied.

Meanwhile, another problem surfaced, when the court began hearing about the discovery of Exxie's head, and the clothing it was wrapped up in. The police had made efforts to identify the jeans and T-shirt, and detectives Stallcup and Jaques of the LAPD, who were working the Marnette Comer murder, telephoned the Sacramento PD. Stallcup required contact with known associates of Comer, such as co-hookers and pimps, and also wanted to interview Marnette's sister, Sabra, who was also a prostitute.

Sabra categorically told the two investigators that the T-shirt and jeans had belonged to a hooker called Toni Wilson, a

Caucasian, aged 19, with natural blonde hair and, blue eyes; she was slim, 5ft 7in tall, and had freckles. This was a positive identification and one which was supported by numerous other characters, including a pimp named Mark. These witnesses even told Stallcup that the last time they saw Toni Wilson, she had been wearing the very same clothing described.

In his handwritten report, timed and dated 1600 hrs, 9 August 1980, Stallcup made a careful note of this information. Then, later in the evening, he inexplicably reproduced an 'official' version in typewritten form, the substance of which somewhat changed the testimony of Sabra Comer, to read that she had identified the T-shirt and jeans as belonging to her deceased sister, which was not the case. During the trial, the prosecution called Sabra Comer as a witness, to identify the clothing, and she did identify the items as belonging to her sister, Marnette. Somewhere, there was a major discrepancy and Clark picked it up. He called Detective Stallcup to give evidence.

He asked the detective about the handwritten notes he made from replies given by Sabra, and enquired whether it was his usual practice, when typing them up, to turn the details around 180 degrees. Stallcup answered, 'No. I would put myself in a very bad spot of jeopardy there. The crime for doing such … something like that, if it ended up to be a capital case, I would be under the same problem that you have got sitting there.'

Stallcup knew that for a police officer to falsify evidence and to commit perjury in a capital case left that officer open to a capital charge himself. After being pressed on this issue by Clark, the detective agreed that he made the handwritten notes. Stallcup 'thought' the typed version was his, too, but only after his signature was pointed out to him on the page. This incident was allowed to pass, without a stain on Stallcup's character.

A similar situation to the one Clark found himself in occurred in the more recent case of Roger Coleman, who continually protested his innocence of murder. When Coleman's defence submitted solid proof of innocence for a retrial, it was deemed too late, but he was given the benefit of doubt and offered a polygraph test, which took place just a few hours before his execution. This test, which simply detects any slight heartbeat increase, or sweat secretion, when the vital questions are asked, was unsurprisingly failed by Coleman, who was about to die an agonising death, and he was escorted to the electric chair on 21 May 1992.

Like Clark, Coleman had solid alibis, witnesses and forensic evidence, suggesting he had not committed murder. Furthermore, a woman claimed that another man, who was a known killer, had confessed to her that he had carried out the murder attributed to Coleman. This witness was found dead on the day following her statement. Also, in the Coleman case, the State offered a fellow inmate freedom if he would say that Coleman had told him that he had committed the crime. He talked and walked, while Coleman died. On his subsequent release, the jailhouse snitch retracted his admission.

Douglas Daniel Clark was found guilty on six counts of first-degree murder and sentenced to death. For her part, Carol Bundy was found guilty on two counts of first-degree murder, those of Jack Murray and Cathy (Jane Doe 28), and she was sentenced to two life terms of imprisonment. But is Clark really a serial murderer?

He had alibis and witnesses for all the murders except one. The police obtained statements from many of these witnesses and allowed them to be altered in order to circumvent the alibis and thereby incriminate Clark.

The weapons and vehicles, associated with all the murders, belonged either to Carol Bundy or Jack Murray.

Bundy lied at every twist and turn. Money went missing and she says she gave it to police officers who, in turn, granted her extraordinary indulgences.

Most of the prosecution witnesses had criminal records representing leverage, by means of which, the police could coerce the 'required' testimony from them. Indeed, Sabra Comer has recently said that she was forced to change her evidence because the police officers had threatened to put her 'out of business' if she didn't co-operate with them.

The judge refused to allow the jury to hear tape recorded evidence of Bundy confessing her involvement and pleasure in the murders.

Murray's van was returned to his wife before the trial began, thus denying Clark any opportunity to have the interior independently examined.

Vital trace and ballistic evidence was either mislaid or 'lost' by the police.

The State's Attorney General admitted that Bundy had been given a deal to testify against Clark in return for her life. She is already eligible for parole.

* * *

Today, Clark awaits his appointment with San Quentin's executioner. As his time is just about to run out, it is perhaps unfair to criticise him for being a very angry man who is full of contempt for the police and the US system of justice.

Without any doubt, Doug Clark was a fool. He most certainly was an accessory after the fact, in the case of Jack Murray, for he has admitted he was with Bundy when she threw her former lover's head out of the car. And Clark was certainly present when Bundy shot a hooker through the head as she gave him oral sex in a car. He did not report this murder either, which would have bought at least a life sentence when he was arrested.

Clark's early years still remain something of a mystery, and he is loath to discuss this part of his life when he has far more pressing matters on his mind. Unlike Bundy, it is known that Doug came from good stock, enjoyed a healthy childhood, and a first-class education.

Doug Clark used to be a handsome man, well read, and he spoke, as most would agree, beautifully. He was a philanderer who wooed different women on an almost weekly basis and he was a Don Juan of almost epic proportions, too. But all of his lady friends say he treated them well and he has never been accused of using violence against them, even though his sexual interests were hardly conservative. Clark also used women to provide him with lodgings, often in return for sexual favours, a practice, which ultimately proved to be his undoing when he fell in with Bundy. Therefore, in every respect, and even by the FBI's own reckoning, he does not fit the psychological profile of a serial killer.

Like so many serial killers, Carol Bundy had had a troubled upbringing. She is an ugly, duck-shaped woman who could hardly see 2ft in front of her. She paid men to have sex with her and Murray was a willing partner who satisfied all of her perverse sexual needs. By her own admission, she was a necrophile, and a hedonist killer.

Hedonist killers may be divided into sub-types. Lust murderers kill for sexual enjoyment. Thrill killers kill for the excitement of a novel experience. Both of these sub-types may show evidence of sadistic methods, mutilation, dismemberment and pre- and post-mortem sexual activity. Bundy fits both categories extremely well.

There is little evidence to contest the view that it was Bundy and Murray who killed at least five of the Sunset prostitutes, following which, Bundy, spurned and inducted by her lover and accomplice in serial sexual homicide, killed and decapitated him in a fit of jealous rage. Indeed, the Betsy/Claudia telephone call to the police, when she pointed an accusatory finger in Murray's direction, proved beyond any doubt that the seeds of anger and resentment had already been planted well before she shot him.

Doug Clark distanced himself from Bundy at this time and, in an act of spite, she turned him in. Casting herself in the role of the State's only – and totally untruthful – witness, she engineered a life sentence for herself and a death sentence for Clark. Good luck, Doug Clark.

This chapter is based on exclusive videotaped Death Row interviews between Christopher Berry-Dee and Douglas Daniel Clark within the San Quentin State Prison, California, 1995, and extensive correspondence.

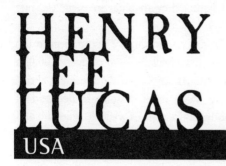

HENRY LEE LUCAS

USA

'Just as the living tree retains its early core, within the core of each of us is the Child that we once were. This Child constitutes the foundation of what we have become, who we are, and what we will be.'

DR R JOSEPH, PSYCHOTHERAPIST, NEUROPSYCHOLOGIST AND NEUROSCIENTIST

'Texas is a state of mind,' wrote John Steinbeck. 'Everything seems oversized and unreal, be it oil production, the cattle, or the size of the hats which everyone seems to wear whether they are a garage owner, a shoe salesman, or a Texas Ranger.'

Texas has the second-largest prison inmate population in the USA, and some time during their lives, 560 out of every 100,000 Texans will spend time in jail. At any one time, there are about 100,000 inmates within the Texas penal system, 46 per cent of whom have killed somebody. At the time of writing, there are 453 inmates on Death Row at Ellis Unit. Henry Lee Lucas used to be one of them until his sentence was commuted, a year ago, to life without parole. On Monday, 12 March 2001, he died of a heart-attack aged 64.

* * *

FBI statistics say that the majority of serial killers have come from broken homes, or they have suffered from some form of extreme abuse as children. Henry Lucas was no exception. His father, Anderson 'No Legs' Lucas, had been a habitual drunken hobo who had fallen from a freight train and lost both of his legs as the result. 'My pa,' Henry once said, 'well, he hopped around on his ass all his life. Done sold pencils, an' skinned mink for a living.'

Henry's mother, Viola Dison Wall Lucas, was a prostitute who had been previously married. She dumped her first four children in foster homes prior to marrying Anderson. At the age of 35, she bore a son, Andrew, and five years later, during the early hours of 23 August 1938, Henry Lee entered this world.

Viola was of mixed race; somewhere in her genes was part Chippewa Indian, and those who knew her claimed that she could be as mean as an overheated rattlesnake. 'She was a dirty old woman you would not want to be around,' was how her granddaughter described her.

Henry described his mother as having just two teeth. She was prone to outbursts of extreme violence and she chewed tobacco. 'Some people say they gonna give a whipping with a switch or something,' Lucas said to me. 'When she went and got a switch, she done went and got a broomstick, an' she'd wear it out.'

Henry was born in a four-roomed, run-down cabin, nine miles from the hick town of Blacksburg, Montgomery County, Virginia. The place, with no plumbing or electricity, was tucked into a steep cleft between the rolling slopes of the Get and Brushy Mountains, which form part of the Appalachian Mountain system of East North America, extending from Quebec province in Canada to central Alabama. The cabin is still in existence today and, several miles from the nearest neighbour, the Lucas smallholding was fit only for raising a scrubby cereal crop and equally lean livestock, which included a few scrawny chickens and a cow. The outbuildings, of which there were two, were in the same state of disrepair as the cabin, and everything, including the family, looked like something that had been sucked out of an earlier century by a twister and dumped unceremoniously into nowhere land. Through neglect, the house has been left to the ravages of time and weather. Most of the windows were broken, or simply non-existent, their sun-bleached, peeling frames, hanging limply from rusty hinges, and primed for firewood and nothing else. The roof was rotten, as was the stoop, where Anderson Lucas washed away his days.

The Lucases inhabited the property with Viola's pimp, Bernie, who was a scrawny low-life and always on the make. Henry, Andrew, Anderson, Viola and Bernie all shared the same filthy bedroom, and Lucas says that he was forced to watch his mother and Bernie, or her many clients, have sex.

In the tradition of the local people, the Lucases distilled a particularly volatile moonshine. With the kick of a southern mule, the making of this spirit was a profitable venture for Anderson who was, in every sense of the word, continually legless and literally out of his mind on drink. Any surplus hooch was sold, to supplement the family income. Therefore, it is not surprising to learn that, by the age of ten, Henry, who tended his father's still, was hooked on the illegal corn liquor. For this work, Henry and his brother were paid the occasional nickel, a quarter on a good day, as wages. With a few cents in their pockets, they would scoot into Blacksburg and watch a movie. The Lucases usually ate food that was stolen, or scavenged from trash dumpsters. It was eaten off the dirty floor because Viola wouldn't wash the plates. She cooked only for herself and Bernie, while the rest of the family were left to their own devices.

Forced to wear a girl's dress by his mother on his first day at school, Henry turned up as a scrawny, undernourished child with long, blonde hair. His teacher took pity on him. Annie Hall found him a pair of trousers and, before the day was out, she had even cut his hair. In return for this act of Christian goodwill, Ms Hall was severely reprimanded by Viola Lucas. Henry had fond memories of his teacher, who bought him his first pair of new shoes. She also made him sandwiches, and occasionally took him home with her for a decent, hot meal.

Brutal physical abuse was a common enough event in the Lucas home; more so was the psychological battering Henry received on an almost daily basis. On one occasion, Viola took him into town where she pointed out a strange man. 'That's your real pa,' she sneered. 'He's your natural pa.' The seven-year-old was devastated and, when he arrived home in floods of tears, he asked Anderson if this were true. It was.

The same year, Viola smashed Henry over the back of the head with a wooden board. He lay where he fell for three days before

Bernie, fearing that he would never get up again, took the lad to hospital. In the admission room, Bernie claimed that Henry had fallen from a pick-up truck. After his discharge, Henry suffered from dizzy spells and black-outs – and they continued until the day he died. He described the sensations as 'like floating on air'.

Those who have met Henry Lucas, or have seen his photograph, will also notice that his left eye is artificial and made of glass. This came about as he and his brother, Andrew, were attempting to make a swing in a maple tree. While Henry was holding a vine, Andrew slashed to cut it with a knife, but the blade slipped and slashed across the bridge of Henry's nose and into his eye. During the following six months of hospitalisation, his mother only visited him once. On the day he arrived home, she shot his pet mule in a fit of rage, then whipped him for costing her the few bucks to have the carcass hauled away.

Although the injury caused Henry great discomfort, gradually the wound began to heal. Nevertheless, for a long time afterwards, he tended to see only shadows and because his peripheral vision was damaged, he tended to walk sideways like a crab.

It seems that the only love and attention Henry received, during his formative years, came not from a rare, helping hand at home, but from his teachers at school. Due to his long periods of absence from class, he fell a grade behind his contemporaries. Annie Hall, in the true American school-ma'am tradition, not only kept him well fed, but she went to other lengths to help him overcome his new problems with reading. With a weak eye, he had trouble with small print, so she bought him books with large type so that he continued to learn. Then, ironically, it was at school that his problems surfaced again, when he walked into the hand of a teacher called Mrs Glover, who was about to strike another pupil. His eye injury opened up, and this time it was beyond repair. The glass eye was fitted a year later.

Sadly, Henry Lee Lucas had considerably less than an ideal childhood. Out of the 13 'family background characteristics' the FBI have found to adversely affect a child's later behaviour, amongst their study group of serial killers, Lucas experienced ten of them. A staggering 77 per cent, which, by FBI calculations, would have placed him at the top of their 'At High Risk Register'. Lucas would have tick-boxed alcohol abuse, psychiatric history, criminal history, sexual problems, physical abuse, psychological abuse, dominant mother parent, negative relationship with male caretaker figures, negative relationship with mother and he had been treated unfairly.

There is no way of knowing when Lucas's criminal career started, but he says it was when he stole a battery-powered television, because he liked to watch *The Lone Ranger*, and *Sky King*. He is quoted as saying, 'I just started stealing, I guess, as soon as I was old enough to run fast, 'cos I didn't want to stay at home, I figured if I could steal, I could get away from home.'

Henry's sexual history also goes way back through the calendar of time. He claims that he was encouraged into bestiality by his half-brother, cutting the throats of the animals and then having sex with them. He told a psychiatrist, that he had sex with his half-brother's wife when he was 13-years-old. 'I just went along with it … I didn't feel it was right,' he said. Then Henry graduated to attempted rape and murder, or so he claims in his unverified account of a crime he says he committed at the age of 15.

In March 1951, Henry spotted a 17-year-old girl at a bus stop. He cornered her on an embankment, where he attempted to rape her before strangling her. In his interview with me, he recalled the event:

'I had no intention of killing her. I don't know whether it was me or what. That was my first, my worst, and the hardest to get over. I just couldn't see what happened. I would go out sometimes for days, and I'd be looking behind me and watching for police and be afraid that they were going to stop me and pick me up. But they never did bother me.'

Years later, when Lucas was finally brought to justice for the last time, law enforcement officers from all over the United States descended upon him in their efforts to clear up unsolved murders. During these lengthy interviews, Henry never mentioned this first murder and, despite more recent, careful research into this case, police officers now believe that it never took place.

In March 1952, Henry's brother joined the US Navy, and then his father left home, in a simple wooden coffin. 'He went out and lay in the snow to get away from his wife having sex with another man,' Henry said. 'That's what made him die. He laid down in the snow and caught pneumonia and he was drunk and he just died.'

That very same month, the law caught up with Henry Lucas, who was now an accomplished thief. He was charged with petty larceny and sent to the Beaumont Training School for Boys. He claims to have liked the place because this was the first time he ate regularly, and he was able to enjoy hot water and electricity. But, this statement contradicts his behaviour, as school records show that he was continually trying to abscond. Henry was released from Beaumont, in September 1953, and he periodically worked as a general hand on a farm. In October, he raped his 12-year-old niece.

Nine months later, he was back in custody for the second time and the 18-year-old Lucas was sentenced to four years in the tough Virginia State Penitentiary, for burglary. He became an accomplished carpenter in the prison chair factory, learning skills that would serve him well when he was released. The tailor shop taught him a little about sewing, the chain gang showed him how to break sweat.

On 28 May 1956, with the very real chance of being brought down by dogs, or a bullet in the back, Lucas and a fellow convict escaped from an outside road repair detail. They stole a car and sped off for Ohio. When they ran out of gas, they stole another vehicle and crossed the state line into Michigan. Interstate flight and auto theft across a State line are federal offences, and State Troopers arrested them in Toledo in July, after which, Henry started a 13-month term at the Ohio Federal State Reformatory at Chillicothe. After his federal term had expired, he was returned in shackles to the Virginia State Penitentiary to complete his original sentence. He was back on the streets in September 1959.

After his release, he moved to Tecumseh, Michigan, to live with his half-sister Opal. While there, he met a woman called Stella, and after dating her for a short time, he asked her to marry him. She agreed and they announced their engagement. During the evening of 12 January 1960, he was boozing the evening away with Stella. 'She was my first true love,' he said. 'She just understood me, an' we had plans to marry, an' stuff.' However, there was another visitor in town that night in the form of his irate mother who had got wind of where he was staying. Viola tracked Henry down to the bar where he was drinking, and she demanded that he get rid of Stella, and that he return to Virginia forthwith. This outburst reduced Stella to tears.

It was an inappropriate moment for the 'Mother from Hell' to force her way back into Henry's life, for that night he and Stella were making plans for the wedding, and he was as drunk as a skunk. In a telephone conversation with me, Stella remembered, 'When Henry was drunk, he got as mean as mean can be. He drank Jack Daniel's like it was water in the desert. That night, the old girl really upset me. I threatened to break off the marriage and I walked out and went home. He truly hated his mom, and what she got, she deserved.'

Lucas now risked losing the only women he loved, and 20 minutes later he was hammering on Opal's apartment door where his mother was staying. Viola, who was also drunk, started cursing him, and wrongly accused him of being intimate with Opal. She berated him for leaving her all alone in Virginia, for by now Bernie had found pastures new. What happened next is best taken up by Lucas himself.

'I'd gone back to where she was staying to calm her down, and she done picked up a broom handle and smacked me with it. I guess it was about 12 o'clock that night when she finally made me so mad that I hit her. All I remember was slapping her alongside the neck, but after I did that, I saw her start to fall, and went to grab her. But she fell to the floor, and when I went to pick her up I done realised she was dead. Then I noticed I had my knife in my hand, and she had been cut.

'I got scared and turned out the lights and went outside and drove back to Virginia. I only stayed there one day, and I started to worry about my mother and wondering if she had been found. I left Virginia and started back to Tecumseh to give myself up. I was picked up by the police in Toledo, Ohio, and later returned to Tecumseh. It was a terrible thing to do, and I know that I have lost the respect of my family and people who know me, but it was one of those things. I think it had to happen.'

As it turned out, Viola hadn't died immediately after the attack. She was still alive 48 hours later, when Opal returned to the apartment and found her lying in a pool of blood. An ambulance was called but, because of the length of time she had been bleeding and the resulting shock, they were unable to save her and she died a short time later. The official police report stated that she had died of a heart-attack, precipitated by the assault.

Henry was picked up in Toledo, Ohio, and returned to Michigan where he was charged with second-degree murder.

Despite assuring police that he had acted in self-defence, he later pleaded guilty and was sentenced to 20–40 years in the State Prison of Southern Michigan. Far from losing the respect of members of his family – along with the multitudes of relations, distant or otherwise – the Lucas clan, and the citizens of Blacksburg, were overjoyed to hear of Viola's demise. She had been a nuisance for as long as they cared to remember, and everyone was delighted to see her disappear under 6ft of dirt.

When interviewed in Ellis Unit, Texas, Henry, a slightly-built man, with his weeping false eye, which he constantly wipes on the sleeve of his shirt, had changed his mind about the murder of his mother. After having first admitted to murdering his mother, he contradicted himself. 'My half-sister, Opal, done the killing, an' now she's dead,' he argued pathetically.

Understandably, Henry says that his incarceration in the State Prison of Southern Michigan was not a happy time in his already distorted life. He claims he was plagued by the voice of his dead mother, who haunted him in his cell. 'She kept tellin' me to do bad things,' he recalled. 'She told me I had a destiny with death behind them walls.' He slashed his wrist with a razor and slashed open his stomach with a knife in two suicide attempts, and none of this behaviour went unnoticed by the prison guards.

In his own interests, the doctors decided that he would be better off being admitted to the Ionia State Mental Hospital where he underwent electro-convulsive shock treatment and was placed under close observation. He stayed there for almost five years before being returned to prison, in 1966, after a psychiatrist concluded, 'Lucas is making good progress. I am impressed with his growth.' However, another psychiatrist disagreed. 'Lucas is totally lacking in self-confidence, self-reliance, willpower and general stamina,' he reported. 'He does not have the courage to take responsibility for his behaviour, but blames others for his mistakes and misfortunes, and he is inclined to engage in aggressive social behaviour, aimed at alleviating some of his discomfort.'

Lucas had been prescribed Prozac, an anti-psychotic with sedative side effects, and this more-or-less kept a lid on his boiling emotions, but it is known that he had warned the authorities not to release him from prison because he knew that his murderous tendencies would flare up again. He even told the doctors, 'Let me out, an' I'll leave a body on your doorstep. I guarantee you that.'

During that period of imprisonment, the Michigan Department of Corrections housed around 37,000 inmates and ran at 125.5 per cent of capacity; each facility was bursting at the seams with prisoners. For his part in the scheme of things, Lucas had simply been reduced to a prison number and, despite his protestations and murderous threats, anxious to make more cell space for the 9,000 new inmates that are admitted every year, on 3 June 1970, correctional staff literally dragged him to the gates and threw him out.

That afternoon, a young woman was murdered in Jackson, just a few miles from the grim prison walls. Another girl's body turned up, a few blocks away from where the first corpse was found, on the following day. Officially, neither of these murders has been attributed to Lucas, although the cases are still classed as 'open'.

For his part, Lucas claims responsibility, adding, 'They [the prison authorities] know I meant what I said. I hated everything. I was as bitter as bitter can be. I was madder than hell.'

Unofficially, the story is somewhat different. A senior law officer, who cannot be named, exclusively told the author, 'Sure, everyone knew it was Henry who killed those girls. The decision not to arrest him went right to the top, and I mean the top. But those assholes didn't want the shit that would come their way if the press knew that he had threatened to kill somebody on the day he was released. If they had, the rinky-dinks and the governor would have been thrown out of the gates with him.'

* * *

Many of the incidents in Henry's chequered history, sandwiched between his release from prison in Michigan to his final arrest in Montague County, Texas, 13 years later, are shrouded in mystery. Initially, he was paroled to live with Almeda, another half-sister, who lived in Maryland and, for almost a year, he kept out of trouble with the police. In August 1971, his supply of Prozac ran out, and he failed to renew the prescription. Lucas said that this lack of medication made him restless and very angry.

In October 1971, he approached a 15-year-old girl, walking to school. He ordered her to get into his car or he would shoot her. An approaching school bus came into view, and he raced off in a cloud of dust, leaving the terrified girl by the roadside. A few days later, he tried to abduct another schoolgirl and she escaped without harm. However, both potential victims had made a note of his licence plate number and they reported it to the police.

In March 1972, Lucas was back before the courts and sentenced to a further five years in prison, for attempted abduction and kidnapping. Following his release, on 22 August 1975, Lucas travelled to Port Deposit, Maryland, to visit his half-sister, Almeda Kiser, and her daughter, Aomia Pierce. Records show that he stayed there for three days, after which he moved to Chatham, Pennsylvania, with Aomia Pierce and her husband. He found menial work as a farm hand before being introduced to Betty Crawford, the widow of one of his nephews. Initially, they were just friends but the relationship developed steadily until they were finally married, on 5 December 1975.

After living with the Pierces for a short time, Lucas, Crawford and her three children moved back to Port Deposit to live in a trailer park. Henry drifted from job to job earning only small amounts of money. The bulk of the family's income was provided by Betty's social security payments. The family lived in this manner until June 1976, when, in company with another family from the trailer park, they moved to Hurst, Texas. The plan was for Betty to visit her mother while Henry looked for work. When this plan failed, they moved to Illinois, before returning to Maryland.

Shortly after returning, Betty Crawford accused Lucas of molesting her daughters. Lucas denied the charges but told her that he had decided to leave anyway. On 7 July, Lucas packed his few belongings and headed off towards Florida. On the way south, he stopped off to stay with Opal. Less than a month later, Henry and his brother-in-law, Wade Kiser, travelled to West Virginia for a family reunion. On the way, while caught in heavy traffic, Henry struck up a conversation with another man and, shortly after, he left Kiser, to team up with the stranger for a trip to Shreveport, Louisiana. After a brief stop-over in Virginia, to visit his half-brother, Harry Waugh, Lucas arrived at his destination.

While in Shreveport, Henry was offered the job of driving a car to Los Angeles but declined after he became convinced that he would be working for the Mafia. He left Louisiana and went back to Port Deposit. He didn't stay long and moved on to Wilmington, Delaware, where a relative, Leland Crawford, gave him work in a carpet store. This employment lasted for several months, then he returned again to Port Deposit to spend Christmas with another relative, Nora Crawford. The following January, he left Nora and moved to Hinton, West Virginia, and went to work for Joe Crawford, who was not only a relative, but also owned a carpet store. While in Hinton, he met a woman called Rhonda Knuckles and lived with her, until March 1978 when he tired of the relationship and returned yet again to Port

Deposit. Lucas stayed for a short time until his sister Almeda offered him lodgings and a job in her husband's wrecking yard. Henry seemed settled until Almeda accused him of sexually molesting her granddaughter. Again, he denied the accusation.

On or about 4 September 1977, Lucas says he was in California, where he claims to have murdered Elizabeth Wolf, in Davis, a medium-size city, some 25 miles west of Sacramento. Quite what he was doing, so far south, remains a mystery, although, his late mother had had a relationship with a man named Dixon, who hailed from a city of the same name, 15 miles from where he killed Elizabeth Wolf. Perhaps he was searching for his natural father?

After stabbing Mrs Wolf, Lucas hightailed it to Houston, Texas, where, on 7 September, he shot to death Glenda Beth Goff. On 17 September 1977, he was arrested for a misdemeanour in Jacksonville, Florida, and was jailed for 45 days. The morning after his release, he told the Kisers that he needed their truck and tools, to collect a couple of wrecked cars for the yard. When Lucas didn't return that night, or the following day, the Kisers reported the car as stolen. The vehicle was later recovered outside Jacksonville, Florida, in an undrivable condition. It was here that Lucas met his future sidekick, Ottis Toole.

* * *

Ottis Elwood Toole was born on 5 March 1947, in Florida. His background was similar to Henry's, and, aged four, Ottis was run over by a car. By the age of six, his alcoholic father had been sexually abusing him for several years and, when his genetic father left home, Robert, an equally perverted stepfather, moved in and took over where his predecessor had left off.

Aged eight, Ottis fell through a broken board on his front porch, impaling his forehead on a nail that went three inches into the frontal lobe of his brain. That injury, it is said, resulted in his suffering from *grand mal* epileptic seizures for the rest of his life.

The youngest of four children, Ottis had been born into a family that was totally inbred, schizophrenic and psychopathic. His mother, Sarah, a Bible-bashing Baptist who chanted verse at the drop of a hat, had grown accustomed to her second husband passing young Ottis around his drinking cronies for sex. And if that form of abuse was not bad enough, the lad was bullied, 24 hours a day, by his elder brothers and sexually abused by his sisters, Drusilla and Vonetta, who made him dress up as a girl and made him wait on them like a little Cinderella. Notwithstanding this torment, Ottis grew into a strapping, 6ft 2in hulk, with large hands and a powerful 200lb physique.

The Toole's run-down, clapboard house was set deep in alligator country, in Springfield, Florida, and it put a leaking roof over the heads of Ottis's family as they came and went in this explosive powder keg of overcrowding, poverty and sexual deviation. Perhaps no one can sum up Ottis Toole better than the American author, Sondra London. Sondra interviewed Toole at the Appalachee Correctional Institute, in July 1991, and she made this observation about this serial killer in her book, *Knockin' on Joe*:

> *To him, life itself is so unmeaning, and the distinction between living and dead people so blurred, that killing is no more than swatting a fly. Retarded and illiterate, he has been out of control since his early childhood. Born in the shadow of the "Gator Bowl", Ottis is a real live "gator' – a bottom feeder, more reptilian than human, scuttling through the swamps of society, ceaselessly scanning for helpless prey.*

Lucas met his future sidekick in a soup kitchen, not far from Jacksonville. At this time, Ottis was sharing a house with his mother, Sarah, and her husband, Robert, Ottis's wife, Novella, a nephew, Frank Powell Jr, and Frieda 'Becky' Powell, Ottis's 11-year-old niece. It seems that the Toole family was quite used to Ottis bringing home strange men from the mission. Sarah Pierce, a one-time house guest, later told police that Ottis, a known bisexual, often picked up men to bring home for sexual purposes. As well as his homosexual tendencies, Ottis also enjoyed watching his male guests have sex with his wife and the under-age Becky. Henry soon adapted to his new home, and soon he shared the main bedroom with Ottis, after Novella was sent to stay with neighbours.

Ottis got a job for Henry in the paint factory where he worked, but it was only a few days before he quit and headed south to his former hunting grounds in Texas, where, on 22 October 1977, he shot dead Lily Pearl Darty with two bullets to the back of her head. On 1 November, in Bellmead, near Waco, Texas, he shot Glen D Parks, twice, with a .38-calibre revolver, after first hog-tying his victim.

Lucas's next murder spree started in and around Jacksonville in late 1978, but not until he and Toole had, by his own claim, joined a satanic cult called The Hand of Death. In fact, Lucas attributed his most heinous crimes – 'The Crucifixion Killings' – to the Devil and 'his doings'. Later, he claimed that he underwent cult training in the Florida Everglades some time after he was released from prison. According to a 1985 book called, *The Hand of Death,* which was written by Lucas and co-authored by Max Call, there were some 200 inductees in his class, representing six different nations, and all ethnic groups and social classes. Henry further claims that during his first week of training, he began by teaching a class in the techniques of killing with a knife. They practised hand-to-hand combat, studied law enforcement manuals, and memorised radio communication codes. All of this must have been an uphill struggle for Henry with an extremely low IQ. After careful research by this author, it was realised that this large class of students, and the training they enjoyed, only existed in the fantasy-driven imaginings of Lucas's mind, and nowhere else. He also says that they read a satanic bible, and since the participants believed that acts of perversion would provoke the reincarnation of the Devil, and glorify Satan, the group leaders encouraged the practice of sodomy, sadomasochism, bestiality and necrophilia that followed each Black Mass, all of which were subjects that Lucas was already at home with.

During these alleged Devil-worshipping ceremonies, Henry told the author that they sacrificed kidnapped children, or traitorous members, on an altar within a sacred circle. Dancing worshippers carried the luckless victims on their shoulders while the remainder of the group chanted 'Ambe iske ho a secco', which remains a mystery! Nevertheless, Lucas has it that a high priest, called 'The Hand', wearing the obligatory cloak, walked, through rings of fire, to the altar where he slaughtered the victims, and everyone was required to drink the blood and eat the flesh. Henry says that he left the camp after seven weeks, to carry out the murderous orders of a superior called Don Meteric.

On his first mission, presumably with the Devil sitting on his shoulder, Lucas claims he kidnapped small children and dropped them off at a large sheep ranch, just across the Mexican border. When he returned to the cult, his superiors tattooed a scorpion on his hand. Metric then asked Lucas and Toole to kill a man. This victim was lured to a beach where Lucas cut his throat as the victim took a drink from a bottle of whisky. Lucas's reward, for committing this crime, was a second tattoo. Later, he was tattooed with a snake, then the Devil holding a cross, for abducting young prostitutes, who were forced to take part in pornographic snuff movies.

When I asked Lucas to reveal his tattoos, he blandly explained that they had vanished after he turned to Christianity. He apparently turned to God immediately after murdering 72-year-old Librada Apodaca in El Paso, Texas, on 27 May 1983.

If one were to believe a single word about the cult – and there isn't one iota of evidence to support even a hint that it ever existed – one is left wondering how Lucas and Toole found the time to drive to Kennewick, Nevada, where it is known that the duo raped and killed Lisa Martini, in her apartment, on 31 October 1978. By his own reckoning, Lucas was either in the Everglades learning radio procedures – obviously vital for Devil-worshipping – or in Mexico, trading in kidnapped children, of which law enforcement has no knowledge whatsoever. The killer then returned to Jacksonville and resumed his old job. Later, Ottis's mother bought a house and moved her extended family into it. Henry quit his job again and went into the scrap metal business, soon filling the backyard of the new house with wrecked vehicles and parts.

On 5 November 1978, police established that the two serial killers were driving along Interstate 35 in Texas, when they spotted a teenage couple walking along the side of the road after their car had run out of petrol. Toole shot Kevin Kay in the back and head with a .22-calibre pistol, while Lucas raped Rita Salazar, before firing six bullets into her. Kevin Kay, who had a minor criminal record, was identified through fingerprints, and the attractive Rita was his steady girlfriend.

Now, ever mobile, the two men drove to Michigan where, on 3 October 1979, they robbed, raped and murdered Sandra Mae Stubbs. Then, they turned around and headed south, to Austin, Texas, where Harry and Molly Schlesinger were shot to death in their liquor store ten days later. Throughout this short period, the killers financed their criminal activities through robbery, culminating in murder.

* * *

Arguably, the most infamous Lucas/Toole murder was the raping and shooting of a still-unidentified young woman in the case that has become dubbed 'The Orange Socks Murder'. Found in a culvert on Halloween, 31 October 1979, the victim wore no clothes except for a pair of orange socks. A motorist, who had been driving north on Interstate 35, stopped to relieve himself and, to his horror, he found himself peering down at a corpse, lying face down and hugging the dirty concrete. 'I had just taken ma pecker out,' he told a police officer, who arrived quickly on the scene, 'an' shit! Ya know, Jesus, fuckin' shit! It was there, ya know. Took a pee anyways, though.'

This murder fell under the jurisdiction of Williamson County Sheriff Jim Boutwell and, back at his jail in Denton, some ten miles north of Fort Worth, the veteran cop pored over the few clues available. He was hoping that they would reveal something positive. He was looking for anything that could lead to identifying 'Orange Socks' and her killer.

The attractive female was in her mid-twenties. She had reddish-brown hair, weighed between 125–130lb, and was 5ft 9in tall. Apart from the orange socks, she wore a silver, inlaid abalone ring. There was no purse, handbag or driver's licence. There was nothing else whatsoever.

At autopsy, the body gave up a few clues, one of which indicated that she had venereal disease. There were tiny insect bites on her ankles, probably flea bites. Her stomach contents contained traces of a partially digested meal – burger, fries and Coke. Her teeth were almost perfect, so dental records might not even exist, and an X-ray showed no broken bones. On more intimate examination, a makeshift tampon made from toilet tissue was removed from the vagina, and that was all Boutwell had to go on. There was nothing that could help identify her to family or friends, and circulating her photograph around the entire North American continent was out of the question.

After his arrest in Montague County, Texas, Lucas admitted that he had killed 'Orange Socks', but he refused to name Toole as an accomplice. Lucas says he picked her up while she was hitch-hiking out of Oklahoma City. He thought her name was either Joannie or Judy. They drove south down Interstate 35, and he said they had consensual sex before they ate a meal at a truck stop. He described the meal, which was consistent with the medical examiner's evidence.

After eating, they drove further south, and Henry said he asked her for more sex, but she refused. A struggle ensued with him nearly losing control of the car, which screeched to a standstill in a cloud of dust after almost leaving the road. 'After I pulled over,' he said, 'I done choked her until she died. I had sex with her again, then I pulled her out of the car and dropped her down the culvert.' He also mentioned that she wore some kind of sanitary towel, which he called a 'Kotex'.

Sheriff Boutwell would not leave this particular case alone; he was determined to solve it for he reasoned that this was just one of a string of sexually-related homicides committed along the Interstate 35 corridor. Bodies just kept turning up on the much-travelled highway between Laredo on the Mexican border, and Gainesville, Cooke County, in the north.

On 27 November 1979, Lucas and Toole were back in Jacksonville. In Cherokee County that night, during the course of robbing a motel, Lucas raped, then shot to death, 31-year-old Elizabeth Dianne Knotts. Two weeks later, an 18-year-old was raped and stabbed to death in her home. Debra Lynn O'Quinn's remains were later discovered in woods close by.

On 5 January 1980, the two men wheedled their way into the home of 76-year-old Jamie L Collins, whom the two men sexually assaulted and stabbed.

27 March brought the beating and hacking to death of 45-year-old Jo Scheffer. Her body was found, in a day-care centre, 12 hours later.

On 12 July, 24-year-old Regina Azell Campbell was found dead underneath a car. She had been raped by both men, then strangled.

20 July witnessed the brutal rape and murder of Tammy Keel Conners. Aged 19, this beautiful young woman, with aspirations of becoming a model and actress, had been dragged screaming from the roadside, and subjected to unspeakable acts of savagery before being tossed, half-alive, into a ravine, near Jacksonville.

There is no way of ascertaining the total victim count of Lucas and Toole. The eight murders may only be the tip of the iceberg. However, it is known that the two men struck again, on 22 December, when the 28-year-old mother of two children, Brenda Elaine Harden, was found raped and stabbed to death in her bedroom.

1981 brought no respite for the residents of the area as the festive season ended. Lucas says they killed again and again. Certainly they ended the life of down-and-out, 58-year-old Shirley Ogden, for her mortal remains were found near trash cans, on an alley, on 14 April.

Toole was also enjoying his criminal hobby of arson. He has claimed to have started '100 of 'em'. On 4 January 1982, the two men killed 65-year-old George Sonenberg, who died an agonising death a week after Toole poured petrol over him, while he lay in a drunken stupor, and set him alight. By all accounts, this offence started as a robbery which went wrong, and as was their usual practice when committing arson, the men watched from the brush as the flames shot into the night sky, laying low as the fire-fighters fought the inferno, rescuing a fatally burned Sonenberg during the process. With any evidence of the robbery and attempted murder reduced to cinders, the police believed that the victim had tragically set fire to himself after dropping a lit cigarette as he dozed off. That Sonenberg reeked of gasoline appears to have been overlooked by the police. Toole later confessed to this murder when law officers visited him, after his arrest, and while he was a resident at the Raiford Penitentiary. For this crime, Toole received the death sentence.

On 9 January 1982, and just five days after torching George Sonenberg, Lucas and Toole broke into the Jacksonville Home for Children and 'rescued', as they say, Becky and Frank. The foursome hit the road on a crime spree that would encompass many more States, including Nevada, New Mexico and Texas.

* * *

Back at the ranch, so to speak, the indefatigable Sheriff Boutwell had a list of 20 unsolved homicides cluttering his desk. It had not been an easy four months for him and, back in October 1981, he had been forced to take a bold initiative. With the assistance of Texas Rangers company 'F', based in Waco, and the Crime Analysis Section of the Department of Public Services, in Austin, Boutwell had organised a meeting to pool any information on the Interstate murders. From border to border, 29 officers and agents, from the 500-mile stretch of I-35, came together for the first time. Methodically, they sifted through photographs, witness reports and evidence, comparing *modus operandi* in an effort to disentangle the mystery surrounding the killings.

After Christmas, Sheriff Boutwell summed up the results: most of the victims had been dumped along I-35. They had been shot, beaten to death, strangled, set on fire, crucified, raped or sodomised and stabbed. There had also been a hit-and-run, which smacked of murder. The sheriff was up to his eyes in murder most foul, and up the creek without a paddle.

In Florida, the Jacksonville City Police and Sheriff's Department were experiencing similar difficulties, as were their colleagues in Michigan and elsewhere. But Lucas and Toole were ever-mobile interstate killers and, unless they made a mistake, they might carry on with their murderous spree for years to come. The two men also enjoyed another advantage; they were not committing federal crimes, so the FBI and US Marshal's Service had no interest or jurisdiction. In every respect, it was left to the relatively inexperienced local police agencies to solve their own crimes. State by state, city by city and town by town, these agencies had neither the budget and the time, nor the interest to liaise with each other.

* * *

Henry Lucas was 40 years old, and he had fallen in love with the 13-year-old Becky, who looked every bit of 19, when it was required of her. The two men often used her as jailbait to lure unsuspecting truckers into their murderous net. Hauling long distances, the bored and lonely drivers were unable to resist the temptation of a scantily-dressed girl, thumbing a ride. It became an all-too-familiar scenario; the hiss of air brakes, a cloud of dirt and dust, the throbbing engines of those big trucks. 'Hop up here, gal,' they'd shout. Then, as soon as the cab door was thrown open, the driver would find himself examining the dangerous end of a loaded pistol.

A similar technique would be used with Becky 'dressing down' for the killing to be done. On one occasion, their car overheated under the blistering Texas sun, so they stopped in Tyler County. Becky knocked on an elderly woman's door, asking for water to top up the radiator. The trusting lady cooked them all breakfast, and while Becky and Frank finished off their easy-over eggs, grits and ham, the two men finished off their host with a brutal rape and two well-placed shots to her head.

Eventually, though, Lucas claims that Toole began acting weird and doing things that he didn't approve of, such as mistreating Becky, mutilating bodies, even barbecuing and eating their victim's flesh. And, there was another problem. Ottis had fallen in love with Henry who, in turn, was in love with Becky. It seems that Ottis didn't want to share Lucas with Becky – or anyone else, dead or alive. That Lucas raped his victims didn't help the problem with the possessive Toole, and the rift was the starting point for the men parting company. They broke up in late January 1982, when Lucas raped and sodomised a young girl, while Becky and Frank watched and Ottis seethed with anger.

Now at the point of almost complete mental disintegration, Toole took out his hatred on this victim, beating her mercilessly and slashing her until she died. When he had finished, Toole headed home to Jacksonville, while Lucas, Becky and Frank made for California.

Fifty miles east of Los Angeles, they stopped at the unremarkable city of Hemet and, while searching for work as a carpenter, Lucas met Jack and Becky Smart, who owned an antique refurbishing business. Using his skills learned in prison, Lucas exchanged his labour in return for room and board. As time passed, Mrs Smart grew to like Henry and, at some sacrifice to her own business, she decided that he would make a much-needed handyman for her 80-year-old mother, Kate Rich, who lived in Ringgold, Clay County, Texas. The Smarts bought bus tickets for the trio and, pressing some much-needed cash into their hands, stood and waved their goodbyes.

* * *

Kate Rich was an energetic widow who had difficulty walking. She was well liked by her neighbours, sewed patchwork quilts, enjoyed fresh crayfish, and delighted in the frequent visits made by her many children, grandchildren and great-grandchildren, several of whom lived in the vicinity. When Henry knocked on her door with a message from her California daughter, Granny Rich ushered him in with open arms. Inadvertently, Mrs Smart had sent her mother the Angel of Death.

Before long, however, Henry's dingy clothes, backwoods talk, foul language and strange behaviour began to make Kate's family and friends feel uneasy; besides, he didn't seem to be so handy after all. It was either that, or he was just bone-idle. For the better part of each day, he chain-smoked cigarettes and drank coffee or beer. Then, making one mouth less to feed, Frank departed, to hit the road on his own. Shortly after this, Kate told Henry and Becky that they had to go. He was a waster, she wanted nothing more to do with him, and the following morning, they went in search of another place to live.

The sun had climbed high in the Texas sky, and the temperature was well over 100 degrees, when preacher, Rubin Moore, spotted Henry and Becky trying to thumb a lift near Ringgold's bus station. He picked them up and drove them to his House of Prayer, ten miles south, in Stoneburg, Montague County. In 1994, when the author visited the place, with Paul Smith, an investigator for the District Attorney, the place had changed little. It was, and still is, a converted chicken farm inhabited by a small group of religious fundamentalists, who keep the gates padlocked and do not entertain visitors.

Rubin Moore owned a roofing company, and the preacher and Lucas agreed that the couple could live in a shack and use the communal kitchen. In return, Henry would work for Rubin Moore, while Becky would stay behind to help out with the chores around the House of Prayer.

For a while, all seemed rosy in the garden. Becky was very happy, and she attended Sunday services, visiting Granny Rich who had a soft spot for the young girl, whenever she could. And, considering her close contact with the religious comings and goings, it was not long before she got caught up in the spirit of things.

In August 1982, she renounced her life of sin, and decided to leave Henry and return to Florida. Henry could, if he wished to mend his unrighteous ways, join her, she told him. On 24 August, they argued well into the late hours, with Henry finally caving in to her demands, but he would go with her when she left. Around midnight, they silently gathered together their belongings, slipped out of the property without telling a soul, and started to hitch a ride for Florida.

A typically hot and sticky Texas night found them under a flyover intersection in Denton. There, in an open field, they spread out a blanket and undressed. Henry set aside his heavy Bowie knife for protection and asked Becky for sex. She refused, and they started to argue again. Lucas had changed his mind; he didn't want to return to Florida after all, he wanted to remain at the House of Prayer. Becky was determined to go her own way, then she slapped him across the face. Without thinking, he heaved the knife into her chest. The blade sliced her heart, and she died minutes later. When he realised what he had done, Lucas cradled her in his arms and wept.

Before sunrise, Lucas decided that he should bury the body. He removed a ring from her finger, cut her into pieces, put all but the legs into pillowcases, and placed her in a shallow grave. Then he tied a belt around the legs, and dragged them into the brush where they would be eaten by wild animals. Henry returned to the House of Prayer with the story that Becky had hitched a ride from a truck driver. He appeared calm as he reiterated the phoney account to Rubin Moore, who apparently found it all quite plausible.

On 16 September, a Sunday evening, Lucas announced that he was taking Granny Rich to church. He went to her house, and, as it was too early for the service, they decided to drive across the State line, into Oklahoma, for several six-packs of beer. They drove and talked for almost two hours while the church service started and finished. Then murder took place.

Kate was a regular attender and she was furious at having missed church. As they turned in the direction of her home, Lucas suddenly veered off Route 81, drove along a track, crossed a railway line towards a disused oil well, and slammed on his brakes. Why Lucas killed Kate Rich is unknown and he won't discuss the matter, but it is known that the old lady was very fond of Becky, therefore it seems feasible that she had been asking Lucas a few, very awkward questions. He stabbed Kate and, as her last breath was leaving her lungs, he slashed an upside-down cross between her breasts and had sex with the dead body. Afterwards, he dragged the corpse over a nest of fire ants, and down into a reedy ditch, where he stuffed Kate Rich into a dried-out culvert. He lodged the corpse in place with a length of two-by-four timber, which he found by the railroad. He buried her clothes nearby and returned to the House of Prayer.

Known as 'Hound Dog', Sheriff Conway of Montague County, told me that Kate's relatives had grown anxious about her disappearance and had reported the matter to him. The sheriff soon learned that she had last been seen alive in the company of Lucas, so he hauled him in for questioning. But the ugly man just clammed up. 'There was not enough evidence for me to arrest that little sonofabitch,' Conway said. 'I checked his name through the National Crime Information Center's computer and, yes, Lucas had a criminal record. But, that wasn't enough and I had to set him free. We did keep an eye on him, believe me.'

The end for Lucas was not far off, for he had two serious problems. Kate Rich and Becky Powell were now reported as missing, both having last been seen alive with Lucas and, in that neck of the woods, news travels fast. Dozens of accusatory fingers were now pointing in his direction, so he left town, spinning the yarn that he was off to find Becky.

From Ringgold, he made his way to California, where he intended to lay a smokescreen by talking to the Smarts. But, while he was there, Mr Smart noticed blood on Henry's car seat and he contacted the local police, who, in turn, contacted Sheriff Conway.

Lucas spent the remainder of October bumming around the country before he foolishly returned to Montague County. There, 'Hound Dog' had found an old 1981 Maryland arrest warrant for Lucas, who had previously violated his parole conditions. Sheriff Conway arrested his man and hooked him up to a polygraph machine, and the print-out indicated that Lucas was not telling the truth about Kate Rich. This was not sufficient evidence with which to charge him with capital murder, so, in an attempt to detain him longer, Conway teletyped his colleagues in Maryland. The Maryland police curtly informed Sheriff Conway that they were no longer interested in Lucas, and they certainly would not pay the extradition costs to have him brought back to their jurisdiction. Lucas was set free again.

* * *

For several months, Lucas drove the interstate highways of America. He visited Mexico, California and Illinois, where he met Gloria Ann Stephens, whom he brought back to Texas with him. He killed her and dumped the body outside the town of Magnolia, near Huntsville. Then, brazen-faced, he returned like a bad penny to the House of Prayer. Fearing that someone might stumble across the corpse of Kate Rich, he drove out to the culvert and retrieved the remains, which he later cremated in a wood-burning stove at the House of Prayer. He dumped the ashes into the garbage for their regular collection.

On 9 October 1982, Wise County Sheriff, Phil Ryan, from Decatur, and Denton County Sheriff Weldon Lucas, interviewed Henry at the House of Prayer, but still no charges were pressed. Within an hour of the law leaving, he went to Kate Rich's home and set it ablaze, before travelling back to California. His car broke down in Tucumari, New Mexico, so he phoned Rubin Moore, asking him to collect him and take him back to Montague County.

'Hound Dog' Conway didn't earn his name from being anything less than a tenacious law enforcement officer, and it transpired that Rubin Moore had taken possession of a .22-calibre pistol, which Lucas had given to him for safekeeping. With the Maryland parole violation a dead duck, Conway now had a rock-solid reason to arrest Lucas. 'It is a felony for any ex-prisoner, convicted of a violent crime, to possess a firearm,' Conway explained, 'I was rubbing my hands with glee.'

'Hound Dog' arrested Lucas at the House of Prayer. He threw him into a cell where he complained about the cold – the sheriff had deliberately turned up the air-conditioning to freeze his suspect into talking. He also stopped Lucas's ration of cigarettes and coffee. For his part, Lucas bitterly complained, 'You sure know how to put a man down, sheriff.'

It was perhaps inevitable that a deal would be struck, as Lucas habitually smoked up to 80 cigarettes a day, drank coffee by the gallon, and hated the cold. He was soon confessing to a large number of murders, drawing pictures of his victims, and writing pages of notes, such as these:

one killed in new
york
light Brown hair
Blue eyes
New York
Buffalo
would Have Been Strangled
with white cord
gold ear
pins

had dress
inside apartment
Joanie
white pretty teeth
with gap in front
Top Teeth
Blue eyes small pin
Ear
Hair below shoulders
through over
Bridge
with head and fingers
missing

In Wichita Falls, on 1 October 1983, Lucas pleaded guilty to the murder of Kate Rich, and he was given a 75-year sentence. But he still had Becky's murder to account for, and he stood trial for this at Denton County Court. His defence was that it was an involuntary act, committed in the heat of the moment, during an argument. In addressing the jury, Henry's attorney, Tom Whitlock, threw in the only mitigation he had. 'I think it happened in such a way it was strictly an accident,' he said. However, what Tom Whitlock said, and what the jury of seven men and five women believed, were poles apart. On 10 November 1983, they deliberated for two hours before reaching a verdict of guilty. The judge gave Lucas a life sentence.

A Texas life sentence does not necessarily mean life, and there was every possibility that Lucas might be paroled in the future. However, Williamson County Sheriff, Jim Boutwell, had other ideas. If he had had his way, he would have seen to it that Lucas went to the electric chair, for the murder of 'Orange Socks'.

Boutwell had questioned Lucas while he was being arraigned for the murder of Kate Rich. He had shown him a photograph of the body of 'Orange Socks', being careful to cover the neck area so that Lucas wouldn't see the cause of death. The suspect could have come up with a number of causes; instead, he claimed, 'Yeah, that one was a hitch-hiker, and she would have been a strangle.' He went on to give other details about this murder, along with another 156 homicides across the country. But his confession to the 'Orange Socks' murder was all Sheriff Boutwell needed, and so that there would be no retraction, he filmed the confession on a video camera.

In the United States, the death penalty is usually sought when murder is accompanied by another serious offence, making the crime 'aggravated'. With his attorney strongly advising his client to shut up, Lucas rambled on and on, saying that he had raped 'Orange Socks' before and after her death. Death by execution is merely a legal formality after that type of admission. Lucas had bought a ticket to his own perdition.

* * *

Captain Bob Prince, of Texas rangers Company 'F', is a law officer who is larger than life. Weighing in at well over 200lb, he stands 6ft 4in, and he is a formidable cop in every sense of the word. As a sergeant who was placed in charge of co-ordinating the 875 police agencies, with more than 1,000 investigators who wanted to interview Lucas about unsolved murders committed in their respective jurisdictions, Bob Prince was kept so busy that he had to book the interviews six months in advance. So popular was Lucas, that Bob Prince kept written records of most telephone calls and written requests.

Lucas now held centre stage during the greatest crime show on Earth and he was revelling in every moment of it. Dressed in an expensive new suit, shirt and shoes, he visited the dentist for the first time in his life and had a set of dentures fitted. Police officers competed to be photographed with Henry Lucas, who was becoming known as the most prolific serial killer in American history. It seems that no expense was spared as the police were as anxious to clear up as many crimes as possible.

By April, police had cleared up 190 cases, although Bob Prince explained that if Henry had had it his way, the number would have totalled 3,000 and more. In their rush to clear up unsolved homicides, and wipe the red chalk from their incident boards, officers did not concern themselves that he often confessed to murders committed on the same day, some 600 miles apart, when his only form of transportation was his feet.

As the files built up, police assumed that common patterns between the murders might emerge, although very few did. Apart from the I-35 and Jacksonville murders, when there was a common MO, the murders had been committed using pistols, rifles, shotguns, table legs, telephone cords, vases, knives, hammers, tyre irons, four-by-two lengths of timber, axes, vacuum cleaner cable, nylon rope, fire, and even a car. Although Lucas has said, 'They was killed by every way known to man, except poison,' it is now commonly agreed that he may have only actually killed a fraction of the total he admitted to. Indeed, before Sheriff Boutwell passed away a few years ago – not getting his wish, to see Lucas executed – he was interviewed by a British television crew on this very subject.

Boutwell was adamant that Lucas had killed hundreds of people during his reign of terror, but when confronted with solid evidence that suggested otherwise, he refused to comment further, and threw the documentary-makers out of his jail. Bob Prince now agrees that Lucas may have murdered 30 people, if that, in his time.

* * *

As we are beginning to understand, the structure and quality of family interaction is an important factor in a child's development. Especially in the way the child perceives family members, and their interaction with the child, and with each other.

The FBI states, 'For children growing up, the quality of their attachments to parents and to other members of the family is most important as to how these children, as adults, relate to, and value other members of society. Essentially, these early life attachments (sometimes called bonding) translate into a map of how a child will perceive situations outside the family.'

Psychotherapist, neuropsychologist and neuroscientist, Dr R Joseph, is highly recognised as a creative, insightful and profound theorist and scientist. He is one of a handful of experts on both the brain *and* the mind, so what does Dr Joseph have to say on this subject? In his book *The Right Brain and the Unconscious*, he writes:

> *As a tree grows, the young tree that once was, never disappears; rather, layer by layer, comes to be superimposed on its core. Deep inside, the baby tree that it once was is still alive. The way in which the young tree took shape, the forces that acted on it, the twists, turns and bends and breaks that have been caused by wind and rain, humans, or disease, all determine the shape the tree assumes as it matures and ages. No matter how well it is cared for, it will never completely outgrow any neglect when it was just a sapling. If we were to cut down and examine the innermost portion of this tree, we would discover that the young tree that it once was continues to exist at its central core. It is alive and forever retains its original form. What the young tree was, it will always be. What it was becomes the foundation for what it will be.*

The adult tree retains this living core, having grown outward from it. If we were to root out this central core, the tree would die, as the integrity of the tree depends on it [for survival]. If the central core is weak and diseased, then no matter how expert the care, the adult tree will be as feeble as its foundation.

Just as the living tree retains its early core, within the core of each of us is the Child that we once were. This Child constitutes the foundation of what we have become, who we are, and what we will be.

Reflecting on Henry's childhood, there is no doubt that he was psychologically damaged during his formative years. However, as most authorities will agree, millions of people, from all walks of life and cultures, suffer similar abuse, and they don't turn into serial killers.

In his book called, *Serial Killers – the Growing Menace*, the late Joel Norris mentions Henry's diet as a child:

These years of malnutrition, especially during childhood, resulted in stunted development in the cerebral tissue as well as an impaired judgement and cognitive performance. It was only during his incarceration that his diet was stabilised to the point where he no longer suffered from elevated levels of blood sugar and severe vitamin deficiencies.

Yet, although this may have the ring of truth about Lucas's problems, I doubt, given the available case history, that this is the entire story.

We know that Lucas's behaviour, while in prison, was extremely psychotic and antisocial to say the least, and that is why he was prescribed Prozac, a drug that effectively controlled his emotions. It was this treatment, perhaps in concert with the balanced diet, that combined to settle Lucas down during his lengthy periods behind bars. However, inmates often calm down and act more responsibly within the structured penal system, so in this respect, Lucas was not unique.

Before his death, I interviewed Lucas a number of times. He comes across as something of a zombie, but an affable zombie. Without doubt, the cocktail of psychological and physical child abuse, use of drugs, accidents, four packs of cigarettes a day, large consumption of alcohol and a poor diet, caused a progressive degeneration of his neurological system. As Joel Norris points out, 'The physical connections between the different areas of the brain, the hundreds of millions of electromechanical switches that balance primeval feelings of violence with logical, socially disordered behaviour, simply didn't work properly.'

So, here is a man, therefore, who, like so many of his killer breed, died emotionally and socially before he was into his teens, and for whom life itself had just become a search to satisfy his dysfunctional urges from one day to the next. Of course, none of what has been suggested is intended to imply that Lucas was, by legal definition, insane. He knew the difference between right and wrong, good and evil. He knew he was taking long strides outside the social order, and he didn't care a jot about the consequences, the carnage and heartbreak that he caused during the years of his homicidal spree.

During the last interview with Lucas, he argued that he had never killed anyone. Becky Powell was still alive and well, he said, even though police have since recovered a set of bleached bones from a site in Denton County identified by Lucas. But there was no forensic evidence categorically stating that these were the remains of Becky Powell. Furthermore, it would be in Lucas's interest to report that, recently, a woman has come forward to claim that she is Becky Powell. She has even offered to take a polygraph test and give blood samples, which could be used for DNA analysis. The police will not entertain the idea, even if it was for a little fun, or an interesting exercise. But what if Becky was still alive? The Devil's work, with his 'Black Hand of Death' cult of followers? Real-life zombies returning from a Texas grave. This is the sort of stuff for which the Hammer House of Horror film production company would pay a handsome fee!

'I did not kill Kate Rich, either,' Henry protested. And it could be argued that only the widow's ashes were left blowing in the wind. No one could identify her from those grey traces. Nevertheless, parts of her spectacles *were* found near the wood-burning stove, the very same stove in which he originally claimed he had cremated the body.

As the last interview drew to a close, Henry was asked how it was that he had led so many law officers to shallow graves. How he had described details that could only have been known to the murderer. His convoluted answer was that he had been shown pictures of the bodies *in situ*, so he was able to repeat that information. This, of course, begged the question: 'How did you know where the bodies had been dumped?'

Once again, Lucas gave what he thought was a credible answer. 'They [the police] done took me there beforehand, and then they came back to me afterwards and asked me where the bodies were.'

The problem with this answer is that the police had no idea where these corpses were, until Henry told them.

In a last ditch effort to get Henry to tell the whole truth, he was asked about the murder of his mother. Wiping the dripping green gunge, from his false eye, with his shirt cuff, he replied, 'Nope. I just never killed no one. I just always thought I'd killed her dead. But my sister said on her deathbed that she'd killed my mom … I never knew that. There was a witness to that, but she's dead, too.'

Just two weeks previously, Lucas had been visited by police officers. During the interview, he confessed to another two murders, and gave them details of the burial sites. The bodies were subsequently recovered.

Henry Lee Lucas was like a rare, prehistoric specimen preserved in amber. He was insidious in a fascinating sort of way. Ugly, mentally flawed, he wore perfectly the persona of a serial killer in that human warehouse known as the Texas Department of Corrections.

* * *

Ottis Elwood Toole died in prison, of cirrhosis of the liver, in September 1996. Convicted killer Henry Lee Lucas was rescued from Death Row and almost certain execution by the then Governor of Texas, now President of the United States, George W Bush, on 25 June 1998.

Bush said, 'While Henry Lee Lucas is guilty of committing a number of horrible crimes, serious concerns have been raised about his guilt in this case [Orange Socks].'

Work records and a cashed pay cheque indicated that Lucas had been in Florida, where he worked as a roofer, and these records coincided exactly with the date of this murder. Clearly, Lucas could not have been in two places at once, and now there is good reason to believe that the late Sheriff Boutwell knew this, too.

In Texas, a governor has the legal authority to commute a death sentence, only on the recommendation of a majority of the 18-member Board of Pardons and Paroles. The same panel rejected a clemency plea from Karla Faye Tucker, a 38-year-old woman, who confessed to the pick-axe slayings of two people, but said she had become Christian in prison and asked for mercy. She was executed on 3 February 1998.

Since Governor Bush had been in office, a majority of the Board has voted to recommend commutation of a death sentence on only only one occasion. The only independent authority that a Texas governor has, in a death penalty case, is to grant a one-time, 30-day delay of execution. There had been 134 executions between the time Bush took office and the date of Lucas's commutation.

'There's an 80 per cent chance I will walk out of prison some day,' Lucas told Associated Press writer Michael Graczyk. 'He [Bush] stood up for what he believes in the law and law says no innocent person should be executed,' added Henry, who had been set for lethal injection on 30 June for the 1979 slaying, in Williamson County, of Orange Socks.

On 30 June, he was taken from Death Row to the Texas Department of Criminal Justice Diagnostic Centre in Huntsville, where he underwent medical and psychiatric tests to see if he was sane enough to be executed. His conversation with psychiatrists lasted about a minute. 'They changed my record,' he said afterwards. 'They said I was a nut. They sent it back over here; I went back down to these people. They said, "They changed you to a nut." These people changed my record back to the way it's supposed to be. I'm just a person trying to do their time, trying to clear these false cases and get back to my own life. That's all I am trying to do.'

Escaping execution by the skin of his teeth, Henry was returned a week later to Ellis Unit, about 15 miles north-east of the town. But instead of returning to Death Row at Ellis, he was placed amongst the general prison population.

His life in the general population was not without adjustments. He still walked the corridors with his hands behind his back, a routine procedure on Death Row, where inmates are handcuffed. He also had a new prison number, trading his three-digit Death Row ID for a six-digit regular number.

'Down there, it's something different completely,' he said of Death Row. 'It's a tight feeling. Once you get to population, it's not that way.' He explained that when he arrived at his new cell, his cellmate requested an immediate transfer when he learned Lucas would be his partner. Henry was given a cell of his own.

Bush, who had said that Lucas would never be released from prison, said questions raised by Lucas, and others, about the murder for which he was subsequently given the death sentence, convinced him to allow the commutation. 'It shocked me, to be honest,' Lucas said. 'I didn't think he was going to do it. Everybody was against it. He stood up for what he believed in. I gave up, yeah. Anybody would, with the kind of record I've got. But I only killed my mom, an' I served my time for that.'

Aged 64, Henry Lee Lucas died of a heart-attack during the late hours of Monday, 12 March 2001. He was removed from his cell and transported to the medical area at Ellis Unit after complaining of chest pains, and he was pronounced dead at 10.17pm. After an autopsy at the University of Texas Medical Branch, in Galveston, he was buried at Peckerwood Hill Cemetery, the final resting place of thousands of Texas Department of Criminal Justice inmates whose bodies have been unclaimed by friends and family, in Huntsville on Thursday 15 March.

Over 500 people attended the service: more than three times the number to attend any killer's funeral in history.

This chapter is based on exclusive Death Row interviews between Christopher Berry-Dee and Henry Lee Lucas within Ellis Unit, Huntsville, Texas in 1996, and additional correspondence and research.